Principalities and Powers

" . . . a heavyweight examination of almost everything you've always wanted to conjure, from Cabala to werewolves."

—*Christianity Today*

"In the proliferation of Christian-oriented books on the occult this is by far the most comprehensive, up-to-date treatment I have run across."

—H. Robert Cowles in *The Alliance Witness*

"The value of this study is . . . that it provides a strong historical introduction to the kinds of occult appeals from the past, and then considers a number of areas where there has been a recent upsurge of interest. The discussion is sane, well-documented, with clear conclusions as to where the Christian should recognize conflicts with the teachings of his faith."

—*The Church Herald*

"Worth reading. It will provide answers to many of your questions, especially relating to the more unusual occult phenomena."

—James Bjornstad in *Moody Monthly*

"A brilliant, fascinating and factual analysis of the occult and allied subjects."

—David Otis Fuller

"He has attempted to cover the full range of the occult in as objective a fashion as possible, neither falling victim to the naive fascination of the gullible nor repudiating everything as humbug or demonic."

—*The Paraclete*

Michael Angelo Onyule

John Warwick Montgomery

Principalities and Powers

BETHANY HOUSE PUBLISHERS
MINNEAPOLIS, MINNESOTA 55438
A Division of Bethany Fellowship, Inc.

Copyright © 1973
Bethany Fellowship, Inc.
All Rights Reserved

Published by Bethany House Publishers
A Division of Bethany Fellowship, Inc.
6820 Auto Club Road, Minneapolis, Minnesota 55438

Printed in the United States of America

Library of Congress Cataloging-in-Publication Data

Montgomery, John Warwick
    Principalities and powers

    1. Occult sciences. 2. Psychical research.
I. Title.
BF1411.M6   133   73-3206
ISBN 0-87123-470-X

For
my maternal grandmother
FLORA WELLMAN WATROUS
now among the "cloud of witnesses" (Heb. 12:1)

There are actions—justified only by faith—which can lift us into another sphere, where the battle is with "Principalities, Dominions and Powers." Actions upon which—out of mercy—*everything* is staked.

—Dag Hammarskjöld, *Markings*

Contents

Illustrations

Figure 1. Bartholomeus Sybilla's *Mirror of Questions concerning Wandering Souls,*

Prologue

TO THE READER FASCINATED
BY THE OCCULT

Not long ago a good friend of mine who is a high school teacher prevailed upon me to descend from the Olympian heights of graduate school teaching and address one of his assemblies. I agreed—with misgivings—on condition that he would first survey the students to determine what subjects "turned them on." He dutifully collected from the student body the questions that "grabbed" them, organized them by general subject, and presented me with the results. An entire category related to the occult. Here is the list, just as he gave it to me:

> I'm very interested in witchcraft but I'd like to know if while practicing it, one has to contact the devil and do it through him? Can it be done through God? Why or why not?

> Could you speak on what you know about the occult sciences?

> Would you know the real differences between white and black magic and explain them?

> Do dreams signify insight? Can they ever foretell the future or are such dreams merely coincidence?

How can one tell if he has ESP?

Is ESP just a gift to some people or do all people have it, like a sixth sense, but just aren't capable of using it? If so, can you learn to use these powers?

Do you have any way of proving that witchcraft works?

What are the practices of the present day witches? Are their practices effective?

Can Tarot cards actually tell the future? Does one have to have a special talent to read meaning into them?

Do you believe that spirits (ghosts) could exist?

Are there such things as ghosts?

Is reincarnation compatible with the teachings of the Christian church?

Do you believe in reincarnation?

From what I've experienced about the occult I don't believe there is a place called Hell, but more like free spirits wandering around. What do you think?

Do you "believe" in witches? devil worshipers? witchcraft? psychological weapons such as voodoo, curses, etc.? How do you feel about ESP? reincarnation?

I have extra-sensory powers; should I develop them? Can they help me? Do you have any particular advice as to which books on the subject I should read?

Do you believe in communication with the world beyond?

Two things about this list of questions particularly struck me: the range of theoretical or book knowledge of the occult it reflects (from

ESP to black magic, from prophecy to reincarnation, from the Tarot cards to spiritualism),
and the degree of personal or experiential
activity in this realm that it presupposes ("I
have extra-sensory powers"; "from what I've
experienced about the occult . . ."). If this
suburban, north-shore, Chicago public high
school is in any way representative of the
country as a whole (and one would be hard put
to deny it), then the occult is "where it's at."

Can't today's occult revolution be dismissed
as "un-Christian"—as the by-product of
increasing unbelief and limited to those who
have given up traditional Christianity? By no
means. Christian young people are as fascinated
with occult possibilities as their unchurched
friends, and their prior belief in the supernatural
seems to give added incentive to these interests.
It is common knowledge that at Christian camps,
conferences, and retreats occult experimentation
by participants is by no means an isolated
phenomenon. Moreover, specific efforts are
being made to coordinate the occult with the
religious. I was recently given a direct-mail
advertisement from "Astro-Analytics
Corporation" (inevitably a California-based
firm!) offering a "personal computerized
horoscope from a Christian point of view." This
advertisement informs us that "the man of faith
sees Astrology as a God-given scientific
revelation—a way of revealing each person's
unique character and potential destiny—so that
each of us can better develop our talents to do
God's will in the world." (Parenthetically,
readers interested in this author's horoscope will
find it minutely and agonizingly discussed in
Chapter Four.) Who's interested in the occult?
We all are, the religious and the non-religious
alike.

*   *   *   *   *

Indeed—and this is by no means always the case with those who write on a subject—*I* am interested in the occult. The present volume is not the laborious effort of a rationalistic academician who has always known that the occult was humbug, nor the pious product of a stuffy theologian who knew before he took up his pen that all occult phenomena were non-existent or demonic. This writer has been hooked on the occult for a very long time, and writes out of a genuine and positive concern for the subject. Perhaps in this connection a sprinkling of autobiography will not be out of place.

As a World War II teenager growing up in a small town in upstate New York, I poured continually over the pages of the mail order catalogs of the (now defunct) Johnson Smith Novelty Company of Detroit, Michigan. More fascinating by far than their dribble glasses and disguise kits were their booklets, available for 10 to 25 cents: *The Book of Forbidden Knowledge: Black Magic, Superstitions, Charms, Divination, Signs, Omens, Etc.; The Sixth and Seventh Books of Moses: Hermann's Wizards' Manual; Secrets of Black Arts: Witchcraft, Demonology, Omens.* I collected these faithfully, and suffered the agonies of suspended animation when the mail deliveries from Detroit were slow. Now the pages of these cheaply printed pamphlets are yellow and cracking, but somehow, as I copy their titles now (I have retained them all), they serve as a crystal ball to conjure up a *jeunesse perdue*. Perhaps I was born out of due time: my individual interests then were precisely the widespread occult interests of today.

Over the years I have collected a very large personal library, and the occult section is, by any standard, very considerable. It contains not only the important secondary literature on all

branches of the occult sciences, but numerous
16th, 17th, and 18th primary texts: the Latin,
French, and German grimoires or manuals
of occult practice which are rarely ever seen.
These works have been obtained primarily in
Europe, through my personal contacts with
specialized antiquarian and occult book dealers.
All bibliographical materials cited in the present
volume are in my personal possession. Indeed,
as former Head Librarian of the Swift Library
of Divinity and Philosophy at the University of
Chicago, I made certain that current works
reflecting the occult revolution were obtained
for that collection; I recall with delight the
uproar in central University Library cataloguing
when Loehr's *The Power of Prayer on Plants*
arrived (was it to be classified in botany??).

While Chairman of the History Department
of a Canadian university, I was invited to
deliver a paper before the Royal Society of
Canada. I took as my subject, "Astrology and
Alchemy in the Age of the Reformation," and
this essay was subsequently published in English
in the *Transactions* of the Royal Society and
in *Ambix: The Journal of the Society for the
Study of Alchemy and Early Chemistry*
(Cambridge, England), and in French in the
Revue d'Histoire et de Philosophie Religieuses.
On receiving a Canada Council Senior Research
Fellowship, I took a second doctorate at the
Faculty of Protestant Theology of the University
of Strasbourg, France, expanding on my Royal
Society essay to satisfy the dissertation require-
ment. The result was *Cross and Crucible*, a study
of the life, alchemical labors, and alleged
Rosicrucian connections of 17th century Lutheran
theologian J. V. Andreae, whose career was
spent in the still mysterious Black Forest, across
the Rhine from Strasbourg; this work is scheduled for publication in 1973 in the "International

Archives of the History of Ideas" (Nijhoff,
The Hague). During my period of European
research on this topic, which we shall discuss
in Chapter Four, I came into contact with the
great collections of occult literature on the
continent, and met many contemporary
practitioners of the hermetic arts and members
of secret societies. Since that time, as Director
of my institution's European Program, I have
spent almost half of each year abroad, and have
continued my contacts with sources of occult
literature, particularly in Paris, that center of
occult activity in Europe. What other major
city in the world has its own guidebook to
spiritualists, arranged geographically[1]—and
with the perfectly correct editorial comment
that there are *arrondissements* (quarters)
without notaries or surgeons, but none without
occultists?

Being half-European has also facilitated
genealogical research on my family. It has been
possible to trace the related Montgomerys and
Warwicks almost to the Scottish plantation of
Ulster at the beginning of the 17th century. This
research has yielded some interesting sidelights
that play upon the subject matter of this book.
I have found that those of Scottish lineage often
possess a strange quality known as "second
sight," and this is said to explain that they are
able to see the "Wee People" while others are
not. (The fact that I have not seen them may
be attributed to a combination of the following
factors: the Montgomerys were a more civilized
lowland clan, while second sight is especially a
characteristic of primitive highland Scots; and
I have yet to be in the Highlands on Midsummer
Eve! But more on second sight in Chapter Five.)
My son David and I have driven the road to
Loch Ness and seen the fog-bound lake surrounded by craggy hills and concealing what

turns out to be very real monsters.[2] And in strife-torn Ulster as we researched the family history of our County Antrim forebears, we discovered that a 19th century Montgomery had been involved in the last witchcraft trial in Ireland. Here is the story:

> The backward state of education in the parish in the early years of the last century may be illustrated by the last trial for witchcraft in Ireland, which was held in Carrickfergus in March, 1808.
>
> The Carnmoney tailor, Alexander Montgomery, had a cow from whose milk no butter could be extracted. The women of Ballyduff agreed that the cow was bewitched and it was decided to send to Carrick for Mary Butters, an old woman thought to be skilled in magical arts. Mary Butters arranged that Montgomery and his young friend Carnaghan, should spend the night in the cow shed with their waistcoats turned inside out. She herself remained in Montgomery's house with his wife and son and an old woman named Margaret Lee.
>
> At dawn Montgomery and his friend left the cow shed but were unable to gain admission to the house. They peered through the window and saw four figures stretched on the floor apparently dead. When the door was burst open it was found that Mrs. Montgomery and her son had died and Margaret Lee died a few minutes later. Mary Butters was carried outside and after being severely handled she regained consciousness. The house smelt strongly of sulpher and a large pot on the fire contained milk, pins, needles and crooked nails. Mary Butters declared

that a black man armed with a huge
club had entered the house, killed the
three persons and stunned her.

The coroner's jury brought in a verdict
of death from suffocation owing to Mary
Butters having made use of some noxious
ingredients, after the manner of a charm
to recover a sick cow. She was brought
to trial at the Assizer, but was discharged
by proclamation.[3]

Hopefully, present-day Montgomerys, while retaining their forebears' openmindedness to occult possibility, have lost a bit of their naïveté and will bring no others to harm through their investigations!

* * * * *

Amid the plethora of books on the occult available today, what has this volume to offer? How can another work on this subject be justified?

In the first place, as careful students of occult literature are aware, the quantity of current publishing in this field is no indicator of quality: the vast majority of today's paperback and hardcover occult literature being sold in bookstores, drugstores, supermarkets, and airline terminals consists of journalistic rehashings of yesterday's unscholarly popular treatments. My childhood *Book of Forbidden Knowledge* and *Secrets of Black Arts* have turned up again with slick covers and a deceptive air of modernity. The worthless character of this material can be detected by a very simple test: note the absence of documentation (specific footnote references and specific citation of bibliographical sources) in connection with the accounts of marvels and the recording of occult rituals. Most such undocumented material is, at best, culled from equally worthless popular books or,

at worst, simply invented by the writer who
wishes to capitalize on the gullibility of readers
caught up in a current fad. The present book,
however, is grounded in the serious literature
of the subject and offers a reliable map through
a largely uncharted and treacherous domain.

Secondly, this work does not focus on only
certain aspects of the world of the occult—the
realm of extra-sensory perception (because it
offers fewer scientific problems) or the area
of folklore (because it restricts itself to "motifs"
rather than occult realities) or the area of witchcraft and sorcery (because these subjects
maximally titilate the reader). An effort is made
here to touch all sides of the occult issue, for
it is clear (from the highschoolers' questions
above) that those concerned with occultism will
not be satisfied to see the subject arbitrarily
delimited. Thus we provide a general historical
overview of occult phenomena; a discussion of
prophecy and divination; an analysis of parapsychological evidence (poltergeists, fairies,
ghosts, haunted houses, spiritualism, communication with the dead); a treatment of alchemy,
astrology, and secret societies; a survey of the
occult side of mysticism, drugs, charismatic
gifts, miraculous healing, and the theosophical
religions; and a tour of the dark land of devil
worship, sorcery, witchcraft, demon possession,
necromancy, vampirism, and lycanthropy. This
study is not limited to a recounting of phenomena,
and indeed places relatively little stress at this
point, since reputable collections of parapsychological and occult accounts are easy to come by.
The accent is placed, rather, on the more difficult
and interesting problem of accounting for such
phenomena. It is the *interpretative* issue which
serves as our focus of attention, and here we
bring to bear the resources of psychology,
psychiatry (particularly the work of Carl Gustav

Jung), literature, and theology. Even the non-factual ghost story will serve our purpose, and the reader who accompanies us to the end of our journey will find that the last chapter of this book consists of a parabolic ghost story by its author.

Finally, this work pioneers by way of its perspective. It is, "evangelical." But those who do not share that viewpoint or who are put off by the connotations they attach to this term should not be too quick to cease reading at this point. As evangelicals we present an eternally true gospel embedded in a permanently veracious Scripture, but we refuse to baptize or damn any contemporary cultural expression simply because this is "how we've always felt." Here we have taken no a priori stand on the occult—and readers will find that, in the complexity of the subject, positive or negative judgment must always be applied to particular phenomena, never to the entire field as if it were a monolithic entity. The conclusions we have reached (and they are highly specific and definite) are the product of investigation, not of prejudice.

In a word, this is not a book for the doctrinaire—whether of the occult left or of the religious right. If you are (as the felicitous phrase puts it) so narrow-minded that you can see through a keyhole with both eyes simultaneously, this book is not for you, for in the world of the occult you need stereoscopic vision to avoid being a blind man leading the blind. The closeminded occultist will boggle at the theology of this volume (though, ironically, it is the path that fulfills the occult quest) and the close-minded religionist will be offended by its recognition of legitimate and positive occult domains (though, with parallel irony, the religionist himself has doubtless entertained

angels unawares). We take the conjoint path
marked out by the daimon-led Platonic Socrates,
who reminds us that the unexamined life is
not worth living, and Plato's noble student,
Aristotle, the founder of all scientific orthodoxy,
who wrote at the beginning of his *Metaphysics*
that all knowledge commences in wonder.

JOHN WARWICK MONTGOMERY

23 June 1972
Midsummer Eve
The Eve of the Nativity of John the Baptist

Acknowledgments

"We are as dwarfs sitting on the shoulders of giants" sagely observed Bernard of Chartres in the 12th century. He was referring, by a most effective bit of occult imagery, to the universal truth that the present generation relies upon the wisdom of those who have gone before. And so the present writer wishes to register his indebtedness to the giants whose labors have preceded his own, and he directs readers to the bibliographical notes at the end of the book for their names.

I also take this opportunity to thank contemporary institutions and individuals for the aid they have rendered. Elizabeth Kirchner, Librarian of the Mercantile Library Association of St. Louis, Missouri, put at my complete disposal during the summer of 1966 the 266 volume occult book collection of Lincoln's military advisor General Ethan Allen Hitchcock—an unparalleled source of early English and French printed works on alchemy, secret societies, and related subjects, the printed catalog of which (in R. Swinburne Clymer's *Book of Rosicruciae*, III [Quakertown, Pa.: Philosophical Publishing Co., 1949], 289-304) is incomplete and often inaccurate. The occult booksellers Editions Traditionnelles (successors to the great Maison Chacornac) on the quai St-Michel and Omnium Littéraire on the Champs-Elysées, Paris, were invariably helpful during my many bibliomaniacal visits. W. N. Schors at Reguliersgracht 52, Amsterdam, performed similar service on my trips to that city whose concentric canals made it Kafka's inferno. My good friend Dr. Arnold D. Ehlert, erudite librarian of Biola College, La Mirada, California, who has somehow managed to retain his sanity amid West Coast cultists, unselfishly provided me with valuable bibliographical leads and collateral materials.

The students who during the last several years have braved my thrice-repeated Seminar in the History of Christian Thought when its topic was "The Theology of Occult and Demonic Phenomena" are to be commended for their stimulating papers and electric discussion, all of which goaded this writer to new insights. Even their wives, the Seminettes, received a dose on January 18, 1971, in an invitational presentation to them; particularly commendable was their restraint as I drove another nail into the coffin of female ordination by emphasizing that the word witchcraft (rather than "wizardcraft" or "warlockcraft") is a continual reminder that the phenomenon has usually centered on the distaff side of the species!

Finally, author and publisher thank the editors of *Christianity Today* for permission to reprint as an appendix to this book the Current Religious Thought article, "The Gospel according to LSD," which first appeared in its July 8, 1966 issue.

1
But Is It Real?

The point, however, is: Is there anything out there?
And why? And must they be so noisy?
— Woody Allen, "My Philosophy"

Before embarking on a voyage, one should know something about the destination. Foolish indeed were A. H. Clough's mariners:

Where lies the land to which the ship would go?
Far, far ahead, is all her seamen know.

In a study of the occult, some working definition of the term is essential—and, even more important, some indication that the subject matter corresponds to reality and not to the "cloud-cuckoo land" of which Aristophanes spoke.

BY WAY OF DEFINITION

Mention of the word "occult" conjures up a bewildering variety of images: telepathy, ghosts, mediums, secret societies, witches, fairies, mystics and fakirs, werewolves and vampires, astrologers and alchemists, magicians and miracle workers. Can any single definition embrace these—and many other—areas which associate with the idea of the occult?

Three elements seem to be present in most phenomena regarded as occult, though not to an equal degree. Taken together, they characterize fairly well this difficult and amorphous subject. Occult matters generally relate (1)

25

to the paranormal, (2) to the supernatural, and (3) to things secret or hidden (Latin, *occultus*, "concealed").

By the "paranormal" we mean the extra-sensory; operations or events which seem to depend upon human powers that go beyond the traditional "five senses." Prophets who appear to see the future, parents who feel the pain of a loved one involved in a distant accident, mediums and mystics who levitate: these are only a sampling of many phenomena which seem to depend upon special human powers. Here no appeal has to be made to religious or metaphysical considerations; gods or devils need not be invoked. The powers in question are not necessarily "transcendent"; nothing more is claimed than that some people actually (perhaps all human beings potentially?) have powers that vastly exceed normal expectations.

But occult activity does not stop with the paranormal minimum. The transition from a "sixth sense" to the presence of angelic or demonic forces is a short step, and most mediums and spiritists easily take it. The very term "spiritualism" is appropriately ambiguous: it can refer to the powers resident in the human spirit, but more usually has reference to communication with or by means of "spirits" in a realm beyond our own. Thus a supernatural element invariably enters into occult discussion, and in the case of certain occult practices it is the most predominent characteristic. Both the poltergeist activity so carefully studied by parapsychologists and the "second sight" in Highland Scot and other folklore traditions relate directly to a presumed realm of intermediate, semi-transcendent nature spirits who occasionally impinge on (or more usually are impinged on by) human life. All "black magic" concerns itself with pacts with evil spirits and direct contact with negative supernatural realms. By the same token, exorcism and the combatting of sorcery, necromancy, and witchcraft assumes the existence of the transcendent: the transcendentally negative (the Devil) to be combatted, and the transcendentally positive (God) by whom the victory is to be won.

If the occult were limited to the paranormal, it would

be embraced fully by parapsychology or studies in extra-sensory perception (ESP). And if it were limited to the supernatural, it would easily become a species of theology, related to angelology and demonology in traditional dogmatics. Perhaps the uniqueness of the occult lies, then, in combining these two realms, the paranormal and the supernatural? Perhaps the difficulties arise when parapsychologist or theologian tries to reduce all occult phenomena to his own particular categories? These are fruitful insights, but to obtain a full picture of the nature of the occult, a third element must be introduced: the element of hiddenness or secrecy.

Secret societies loom large in any discussion of the occult, but they are only the most obvious reflection of the "concealed" character of occult activity in general. Prophecy and divination reveal (generally in veiled terms) the hidden secrets of the future; the Wee Folk no longer engage in open communication with men and only the few (those with "second sight") see them; spirit communication is open through the rare agency of a medium with special powers; ghosts are associated with particular (generally ancient and out-of-the-way) places and appear on limited occasions and often can be seen only by certain individuals; the wonders of the alchemical Great Work are available only to the initiate and must be transmitted by symbols and images and hermetic language which will be understood only by the true adept; occult theosophy and the Eastern faiths from which it derives intentionally state their teachings in language which will convey truth solely to the faithful believer and close the door to the profane; witches' covens meet in secret and satanic rites are carried out in wild and uninhabited places.

Thus the etymology of "occult" as "hidden" is by no means antiquarian trivia. It is the element of concealment which most clearly distinguishes the occult from parapsychology or religion. In parapsychology, as in all attempts at scientific investigation, the aim is to engage in open study of phenomena and to formulate interpretations that will adequately account for the data. While recognizing that ESP ability need not be universal to be valid (musical talent is not universal either), the parapsychologist nonetheless must carry out controlled experiments and objective observations in order to arrive at meaningful conclusions. Science is a public, not an esoteric pursuit.

And so (this will come as a surprise to many readers) is religion. Religions are distinguished from cults or sects not so much by size as by the public character of their proclamations. The cult, which maintains its "truth" *sub rosa*, approaches very closely, and often actually blends with, the occult secret society. In both cases only the initiate discovers the inner meaning of the teaching. Religions, in contrast, offer what at least appears on the surface to be a public message. Often, it is true, what seemed to be open religious teaching turns out to be little more than cult (or occult) hiddenness. Thus the ostensively objective Buddhist doctrines of karma and transmigration of souls and nirvana are found to be without any public testibility, and one is left with the mystic and occult inwardness characteristic of the oldest Zen koans: "How is my hand like the Buddha's hand? Answer: Playing the lute under the moon." [1] In the case of one religion, historic Christianity, the public character of the affirmation ("God was in Christ, reconciling the world unto himself") is backed up by concrete, objective events: the documentary evidence of Christian origins informs us that Jesus "showed himself alive after his death by many infallible proofs over a forty day period" (Acts 1:3) and the early preachers of the Christian gospel were able to assert in the very presence of hostile audiences that "none of the these things are hidden; this was not done in a corner" (Acts 26:26).[2]

This open, public nature of the Christian religion is not widely recognized today, and many consider Christianity to be essentially a cult, though a more successful cult than others. The reason is very largely the character of modern theology, which serves as the interpreter of Christianity to the modern intelligensis.[3] Karl Barth's unverifiable resurrection of Jesus in the realm of supra-

or metahistory; Rudolf Bultmann's reduction of the resurrection to existential myth, whose meaning is apparent only in the moment of personal "self-authentication": such positions have given many the impression that Christianity differs little from Eastern mysteries or occult hiddenness. A case could be made for treating many varieties of modern theology under the rubric of the occult, but historic Christianity cannot be so treated! There are indeed mysteries in biblical Christianity, but they are approached through the sunlight of public revelatory event. Christianity, as a "revealed religion," focuses on revelation—and revelation, by definition, makes manifest rather than concealing. The hidden is embedded in and justified by the revealed; one does not face a riddle wrapped in an enigma.

But if the occult is indeed a realm of the hidden, what can be said about it? Have we not painted ourselves into a corner, justifying a very short book on the occult (indeed, a book which could stop right here!)? If we proceed, will we not make the fundamental mistake of the mystics who insist on discussing the ineffable?

The answer lies in the important distinction between occult *facts* and occult *interpretations*. The interpretations which occultists place upon their data are generally of such an in-group character that it becomes impossible, even in principle, to prove or disprove them. But the occult experiences to which these interpretations refer are very frequently subject to evidential test and are capable of verification in the same manner as non-occult events. Thus, as we shall see, though one cannot demonstrate the spiritualists' claim that only one realm of the dead exists (in contradistinction to the biblical heaven and hell), the ghostly phenomena to which the spiritualist appeals are real enough to warrant the closest investigation. The problem becomes one of reaching more adequate interpretations of occult data—of providing theories and explanations which better fit the facts of occult experience.[4]

Here, however, the skeptical reader begins to pack his intellectual luggage for a quick departure. What gives us the idea that even the alleged facts of the occult realm are genuine? Hasn't modern science cleared the air of such hoary superstition?

DON'T KNOCK SPIRIT RAPPING

Almost everyone has heard of the clever techniques of fraudulent mediums—such as inflatable rubber gloves that leave the impression of spirit hands in paraffin and then, deflated, are able to be drawn out of the hardened wax through a small hole, leaving nothing but ghostly imprints.[5] Houdini claimed that he could duplicate by natural means any spiritistic phenomenon shown to him. And recent visitors to Disneyland have invariably been impressed by the computerized effectiveness of the "spirits" in the Haunted Mansion. Are not all occult phenomena capable of similar explanations?

Doubtless the world would be a more comfortable and secure place if the answer were yes; unfortunately, however, such an answer is not possible. Innumerable instances of occult phenomena resist categorization as "humbug" or natural occurrences in disguise. We noted above that the occult embraces out-of-the-way phenomena of a paranormal (ESP) and supernatural kind. Consider first some evidence of the reality of parapsychological experience.

My first contact with ESP came as a freshman at Cornell University when I found myself in a required elementary psychology course conducted by (1) a behavioristic lecturer, and (2) a sex-crazed laboratory assistant whose behavior was not above reproach. So much time and effort were spent in this course ridiculing ESP phenomena that I (who had no axe to grind one way or the other) was forced to think that where there was parapsychological smoke there was probably occult fire. It seemed less incredible to admit the reality of ESP data than to express wholesale doubt concerning the integrity of Dr. J. B. Rhine's entire career as director of Duke University's Parapsychology Laboratory! Dr. Rhine had shown, by impeccable experiments subjected to strict statistical control, that telepathy and clairvoyance indeed exist as properties of some minds. That is to say, some persons can communicate directly with others without sensory aid, and can perceive external physical objects at distances in space and time which preclude a sensory explanation and establish the reality of precognition; moreover, the mind can produce direct physical effects on objects (psychokinesis).[6]

Subsequent reading only served to confirm these conclusions. As early as the end of the 19th century, William James, the careful compiler of *Varieties of Religious Experience*, had become convinced of the empirical reality of parapsychological phenomena. His writings in the field span his entire career and offer a formidable block to any attempt at explaining away the paranormal.[7] In 1926, Clark University held a symposium on the subject to which were invited major protagonists, and the resulting publication is of more than routine interest even today.[8] Except for Harry Houdini and Professor Joseph Jastrow of the University of Wisconsin, those presenting papers were either "convinced of the multiplicity of psychical phenomena" (Sir Oliver Lodge, Sir Arthur Conan Doyle), "convinced of the rarity of genuine psychical phenomena" (Harvard psychology professor William McDougall, Leipzig professor of philosophy Hans Driesch, F. C. S. Schiller, fellow and tutor of Corpus Christi College, Oxford, and psychical researcher Walter Franklin Prince), or open-minded on the issue (Stanford University psychologist John E. Coover and Columbia psychologist Gardner Murphy). The strong view of Lodge and Doyle (that ESP ability is virtually universal) has declined since their time, in part because of the naïveté with which these men accepted inadequate evidence to support what they passionately wanted to believe (how unlike Sherlock Holmes his creator became in later life!).[9] But the view that psychical phenomena, though uncommon, are genuine has gained ground, as is illustrated by an important book which Walter Franklin Prince published two years after the Clark symposium, *Noted Witnesses for Psychic Occurrences*,[10] and by the fact that Gardner Murphy moved from an uncommitted position to Prince's view and has since written the most important "primer of parapsychology" under the title, *Challenge of Psychical Research*.[11] A word about these two volumes is in order, for they collect some of the most useful evidence in support of the genuineness of paranormal occurrences.

Prince employs the literary case method. He brings together the accounts of supranormal experiences as they occurred in the lives of some 170 famous persons in all fields of endeavor. The narratives, taken in almost every case either from autobiographical material or from eyewitness reporting, cover "men of science; lawyers and physicians; men of the army and navy; statesmen, diplomats and publicists; poets and playwrights; novelists; miscellaneous writers; artists, sculptors, actors, composers and musicians; clergymen, theologians and evangelists; persons of title, financiers, teachers, travelers and magicians." The persons so classified who had paranormal experiences constitute a veritable Who's Who of history: Susan B. Anthony, Arthur Balfour, Robert Browning, Luther Burbank, Horace Bushnell, John Calvin, Mark Twain, Charles Dickens, General Fremont, Goethe, Rider Haggard, Nathaniel Hawthorne's wife; Oliver Wendell Holmes, Henry Holt, Victor Hugo, Ben Jonson, John Knox, Andrew Lang, Martin Luther, William Lyon Phelps, Anton Rubinstein, John Ruskin, Shelley, Tennyson—to name only a few. The following account of an experience that occurred to evangelist Dwight L. Moody, as is recounted by his son and biographer Dr. William R. Moody, should be of more than routine interest, particularly to readers of evangelical persuasion:

> On his first evangelistic misson to Great Britain in the early seventies, he was invited to the city of Liverpool. You will remember that the prejudice against Americans, especially Yankees, was strong in the city of Liverpool, and even when Beecher made his famous trip to England in the interests of the North during the War he had his greatest difficulty in pleading the cause of the North in the city of Liverpool. How far this feeling influenced the press against my father I do not know, but during the earlier part of the meetings the opposition on the part of the secular press was very strong, and Mr. Moody was

made the object of numerous bitter attacks, his motives being impugned, and he himself being made the object of all sorts of ridicule. To this he paid no attention. My mother was not with him at the time, being with friends for a few days, when suddenly he had come over him a peculiar sense of fear or nervousness. My father was one of the most fearless men that I have ever known, and the experience was so new to him that he began to feel anxiety about his own condition, questioning whether he might have been overworking, with the result that his mind was affected. He would frequently cross the street if he heard anyone coming up behind him, and at night was careful to look under his bed, examine the closet, and always see that his door was locked. This experience lasted for several days and left him as suddenly as it had come, one day while going to the hall where he was preaching. At the close of his service he was surrounded by the gentlemen who constituted the committee who had invited him to Liverpool, and on one pretext or another they detained him for a few minutes until a police officer came to them and explained that everything was now satisfactory. The chairman of the committee then explained to my father that they had learned that day that for a week there had been at large in the city of Liverpool an escaped lunatic from a neighboring asylum, who was obsessed with the idea that he was commissioned to assassinate my father. For days he had been trying to get an opportunity to stab him and he had only just been caught and placed under arrest.[12]

Gardner Murphy collects and summarizes the experimental evidence for the paranormal from Rhine's work at Duke through the 1950s. Chapters are devoted to telepathy, clairvoyance, precognition, and psychokinesis, with extensive references to the journal articles in which the research results were first published. Here one finds instance after instance of statistically significant psi-experiments. To take but a single example: in several series of tests, it has been shown that certain persons can, by concentrating the mind, influence the fall of dice. This PK (psychokinetic) conclusion is drawn only after all alternative hypotheses are eliminated: chance (ruled out by the statistical level of significance attained in the experiments), faulty dice, "skilled throwing" (after shaking the dice in a dice cup, the subjects threw them down a chute over three feet long), recording or computing errors, and bad faith or collusion. "The original data

are open to the inspection of any interested person." [13]
The fact that such PK ability is not universally present—
equally characteristic of all persons—no more rules it
out than do tin-eared persons put in question the musical
inheritance of the Bach family. The importance of such
data as Murphy puts forward led, in 1959-60, to distinguished philosopher C. D. Broad's Perrott lecture series
at Cambridge University on psychical research. The published work[14] analyzes further experimental material
(particularly that originated in England) and subjects
the entire area to acute philosophical analysis. The result
is a clear admission of the legitimacy of the field as
a domain of empirical inquiry.[15]

The last decade has elicited even more striking evidences of the reality of parapsychological phenomena.
In 1965, J. H. Pollack published the first lengthy account
in the English language of "Croiset the clairvoyant":
Gerard Croiset, a Dutchman whose ESP faculties were
the subject of eighteen years of scrupulously documented
study by Prof. Dr. Willem H. C. Tenhaeff, Director of
the Parapsychologisch Instituut of the Rijksuniversiteit
of Utrecht (the European counterpart of Dr. Rhine's Laboratory at Duke University).[16] Croiset's paranormal
faculties are so pronounced that on numerous occasions
he has been called upon by the police to locate missing
persons and to solve crimes. For example: when a gas
company employee failed to return home in late 1947,
one of his friends brought Croiset his cap as an "in-
ductor"; he told Croiset only that "this case is about
a loss." Croiset asserted that the man had probably been
swindling, had ridden off on his bicycle to a particular
town (he named it) through pine woods, was dressed
in work trousers and a blue jacket, and had hanged
himself from a tree. When the police were notified, their
search produced the body and confirmed every detail
of Croiset's statement—including details of the man's
fraudulent activity (in the gas company's office). The
autopsy showed that he had been dead at the time his
friend had consulted Croiset.

A similar and perhaps even more remarkable case

was the subject of a 1967 book by psychiatrist and psychical researcher Jule Eisenbud: Ted Scrios, an American who possesses the faculty of directly projecting mental images onto Polaroid film.[17] Dr. Eisenbud, who began his investigation skeptically, conducted controlled experiments over a two-year period; these were witnessed by more than twenty-five doctors and research scientists. Some 150 photographic reproductions in the published work offer overwhelming evidence of the genuineness of Scrios' extrasensory powers.

Even the "materialistic" Marxists have gotten into the act. Extensive research into the paranormal is presently being conducted in Russia, and the results have just recently become available to English readers. Oddly, I was apprised of this through a French television program! On July 7, 1971, I was watching channel 2 in my Strasbourg, France, apartment, and found myself engrossed in a replay of an old fantasy film. As is common on French television, the film was followed by a most interesting discussion-debate among several authorities with differing views on the subject. In this instance, the subject was the reality of paranormal phenomena, and the featured guest was Prof. Dr. Hans Bender, who directs parapsychological study at the University of Freiburg (the German Freiburg in Breisgau, at the southern tip of the Black Forest, not the French Swiss city of Fribourg). His chief opponent was a rationalistic, orthodox Freudian psychologist (Louis Bellanger), whose thorn-in-the-flesh was the British writer George Langelaan. The discussion was electric and delightful. Bellanger maintained with absolute dogmatism that energy is always physical, never psychic, and that the unconscious is a realm not of paranormal power but of natural energies. (Was he unaware that Freud himself had all kinds of ESP interests toward the end of his life? Bender perversely inquired.) Langelaan hit Bellanger with the illustration that I have myself often used with those who refuse to face the eyewitness testimony to the resurrection of Christ: the old farmer who had developed a completely closed view of zoological possibility by his years with domestic animals and who, therefore, on being shown a giraffe at the zoo, declared: "There haint no such animal." Professor Bender won the field hands down by citing example after example from recent Russian experiments showing the de facto character of paranormal experience. I was so impressed that I immediately contacted him for specific references to the published materials. He provided me with an important offprint from the journal which he edits, among whose contributing editors Prof. Tenhaeff's name prominently and significantly figures.[18]

Not until 1970 was any full account available in English of the extensive Russian work in this field. In that year Ostrander and Schroeder's *Psychic Discoveries behind the Iron Curtain* was published.[19] Though this book suffers from journalese and an excessive effort to popularize, it contains a wealth of valuable information—rendered twice as valuable by the fact that its data can hardly be regarded as the product of mystical or religious wish-fulfillment. Here one encounters numerous instances of experimental confirmation of psi-phenomena already met with in the west. Psychologist Pavel Naumov made studies of ESP linkage between mothers and their children in the Moscow gynecological clinic, and found that in 65 percent of the cases studied, mothers are aware when their babies are in pain, and vice versa, even when the two are in distant wards of the hospital.[20] A parallel phenomenon to Ted Serios' ability to impress his mental pictures on photographic film has been evidenced in Russian research on "seeing with one's fingers"—a faculty of transmitting colors and shapes to the mind through the fingers. Irrefutable experimental results have shown that some blind or even non-blind persons can actually read by passing their fingers over ordinary print. But examples need not be multiplied ad infinitum: paranormal phenomena, whether in the capitalist west or the communist east, are a reality.

Does the same evaluation apply to the supernatural dimension of the occult? One of the discussants on the above-mentioned French television production followed the standard Russian line and asserted that he can accept the paranormal though he doesn't believe in the super-natural—for, he declared, the occult is entirely the product of undiscovered human capacities. William James was always haunted by the question as to whether Frederic W. H. Myers' studies of man's "subliminal consciousness" offered a sufficient explanation not only for the paranormal but also for religious experience such that one would not have to predicate a supernatural realm to account for the data.[21]

Poltergeist phenomena offer a suitable introduction to the difficulties attendant on a naturalistic interpretation of all occult experiences. What is one to do with those innumerable cases[22] recorded across the centuries and clinically observed in modern times wherein heavy objects are hurled across rooms and various other forms of mischief occur without visible human agency? Instances abound paralleling the case of 17th century Huguenot pastor Perrault, whose house in Mâcon was subject to poltergeist disturbances for two months beginning on September 14, 1612. Stones were hurled, bedclothes were pulled off, fireirons and stools and metal dishes set up an unearthly clatter, and an invisible spirit carried on audible conversation with the occupants of the house as well as with their friends and neighbors—revealing details of their private affairs and speaking accurately of occurrences at a distance.[23] Robert Boyle, for whom Boyle's Law is named, a founder of the Royal Society, checked this story out with Perrault and others and sponsored the translation of his account into English, declaring that the evidence "did at length overcome in me (as to this narrative) all my settled indisposedness to believe strange things." [24] Herbert Thurston, one of the most careful 20th century students of poltergeistic phenomena, has emphasized that such early accounts precede modern stereotyping and thus offer particularly good ground for credence, since those who recorded them had no "model" into which to squeeze their data, and since elements

present in the stories so well parallel narratives uncon-
nected with them. On the supernatural character of poltergeistic activity, Thurston cogently argues:

> The phenomena seem to me to have their value as a proof
> of the existence of a world of spiritual agencies, not
> cognoscible directly by our sense perceptions. For the crude
> materialist such incidents must surely be very difficult to
> explain away. The stones have fallen, for they are solid
> and still to be seen; but who has thrown them? Crockery,
> chimney ornaments and glasses have been smashed, heavy
> pieces of furniture have been moved, pictures have jumped
> from the walls, but witnesses declare that they stood by
> and saw that no human hand came near them. Now it would
> be a very violent supposition to maintain that any human
> being is so psychically endowed that by taking thought he
> can make material objects external to himself fly about
> in eccentric paths, that he can move furniture, spirit away
> the contents of receptacles closed and locked, or set a curtain
> on fire by merely looking at it. . . . We may reasonably
> call upon materialists who deny the possibility of miracles
> either to provide a physical explanation of these extraordinary
> poltergeist disturbances, or to submit some reasonable
> ground for rejecting the mass of evidence by which their
> reality has been established.[25]

As for the supernatural reality of demonic phenomena,
sufficient data have been amassed by researchers such
as Montague Summers[26] to show the inadequacy of
explanations limited to human abnormality or para-
normality. It has become more and more difficult to
sustain the confidence expressed by psychologist-
clergyman George Barton Cutten at the beginning of
this century: "Since we are able both to produce and
cure demoniacal possession in our laboratories, it hardly
seems necessary to invoke the aid of demons to furnish
an explanation, especially when we can give a better
one without it."[27] What, for example, does one do
with the case of the great fin-de-siècle novelist Joris-Karl
Huysmans? This author of *Là-Bas* and *A Rebours* who
introduced flashback technique into modern French literature dabbled extensively in the occult during the years
of malaise that afflicted France after the German victory
in the Franco-Prussian War. The semi-autobiographical

character of *Là-Bas*, alternating between a historical reconstruction of the career of medieval satanist Gilles de Rais and a contemporary portrait of the occult circles of Huysmans' Paris, shows that he drank the cup of the black arts to the dregs. Ultimately he became a Christian, for, he wrote to Baron Firmin Van den Bosch, "it was through a glimpse of the supernatural of evil that I first obtained insight into the supernatural of good. The one derived from the other. With his hooked paw, the Devil drew me towards God." [28] Even after his conversion—indeed, to the time of his death—Huysmans was troubled by demonic attacks. At first he attributed these to the onset of some nervous disease, but then he discovered (these are his words) that "my cat, which is scarcely likely to be suffering from hallucinations, feels the same kind of shock as I do—and at the same time." [29] He attributed these attacks to the malice of old occult enemies, such as Stanislas de Guaita, and resorted to defensive weapons such as exorcistic paste and magic circles. The reality and supernatural nature of these attacks seems incontrovertible.[30]

Two recent examples of supernatural operation in this domain may be in order—particularly since they involve persons of my own acquaintance. The first has to do with C. S. Lewis, with whom I maintained correspondence and who, shortly before his death, wrote a commendation of one of my writings.[31] J. B. Phillips, the author of the superlative paraphrase, *The New Testament in Modern English*, records post-mortem appearances of Lewis to him; these accounts appear in Phillips' book, *Ring of Truth*, and do indeed have truth's ring about them:

> Many of us who believe in what is technically known as
> the Communion of Saints must have experienced the sense
> of nearness, for a fairly short time, of those whom we love
> soon after they have died. This has certainly happened to me
> several times. But the late C. S. Lewis, whom I did not
> know very well and had only seen in the flesh once, but
> with whom I had corresponded a fair amount, gave me
> an unusual experience. A few days after his death, while
> I was watching television, he "appeared" sitting in a chair
> within a few feet of me, and spoke a few words which

were particularly relevant to the difficult circumstances
through which I was passing. He was ruddier in complexion
than ever, grinning all over his face and, as the old-
fashioned saying has it, positively glowing with health. The
interesting thing to me was that I had not been thinking
about him at all. I was neither alarmed nor surprised nor,
to satisfy the Bishop of Woolwich, did I look up to see the
hole in the ceiling that he might have made on arrival!
He was just *there*—"large as life and twice as natural."
A week later, this time when I was in bed, reading before
going to sleep, he appeared again, even more rosily radiant
than before, and repeated to me the same message, which
was very important to me at the time. I was a little
puzzled by this, and I mentioned it to a certain saintly
bishop who was then living in retirement here in Dorset.
His reply was, "My dear J——, this sort of thing is happening
all the time." [32]

My second example was narrated to me by Omar Gjerness,
a clergyman and professor of systematic theology whose
reliability is above reproach. After listening to this account, I asked Professor Gjerness to give it to me in
writing.

You asked me to write about that incident on demonism.
Here it is:

I was speaking at a Bible Conference during the summer
of 1970. The evening evangelistic services were being
addressed by a layman who was a gifted evangelist. An
awakening was in progress,with several people seeking to
find peace with God.

One morning I was approached by a friend of many years
standing. She was obviously distraught, and wanted to talk.
She related to me a very strange story.

She had brought her neighbor with her to the conference.
Her neighbor had recently immigrated from Europe. She
had lived in the United States less than a year. To protect
identities, we will refer to her as "Mrs. Neighbor."

Mrs. Neighbor had gone forward at the evening service
to find peace with God. When she returned to her room that
evening, she had a frightening experience. Throughout the
night she states that she met the devil in her room. The
devil said "You have such admiration and respect for that
evangelist. You don't know what kind of a man he is."
The devil then proceeded to accuse the evangelist of having
been an ordained pastor, who had experienced a spiritual
fall, and had been involved in adulterous relationships with

women. Mrs. Neighbor was aghast. On the one hand she
was convinced that she had actually conversed with Satan.
On the other hand she was afraid she was losing her mind,
and that the accusing ideas she had of the evangelist were
the product of her own depraved imagination. She was
horrified that she could in her wildest imagination think such
evil thoughts of so fine a man. On the other hand, she
was certain she had talked with the devil. She shared her
problem with my friend, who related the problem to me.

Ordinarily I would have considered the problem a
psychotic problem. That which made this circumstance
different was that the story, envisioned by Mrs. Neighbor
in her encounter with the devil, was absolutely true! From
every angle that I investigated, there was no rational way
to account for her knowledge of the facts in the story.

The story, of course, was piecemeal. The evangelist had
been defrocked for his fall, and for a time excommunicated.
The event had taken place about 20 years in the past. He
had evidenced a genuine repentance, and had been offered
an opportunity by his own church body to return to the
ministry. Mrs. Neighbor knew of a fall, but nothing of a
restoration and repentance.

I counselled with Mrs. Neighbor the next evening. I did
not deal with her as a psychotic, but assumed that her
demonism was real. I took the approach of the Scriptures:
"He that is in you is greater than he that is in the world."
She returned to her room that evening with my friend.
Again she claimed that she sensed the presence of the devil
in that room. My friend says that she sensed the same.
She spoke of "noises" in the room, and tried later to find
a rational explanation outside of the supernatural. (Rats?
bats? birds?) Meanwhile Mrs. Neighbor said, "Devil, come
here. I have got something to say to you. I have given
my heart to Christ, and you no longer have any claim over
me. Now get out, and never come back." To be brief, this
seems to have conquered her problem. My friend did not
sleep after this final unusual prayer meeting. I have never
shared the experience with the evangelist, lest it so dishearten
him that he fear to share his testimony in public again.[33]

   To avoid a supernatural interpretation of such phenomena as these requires their reduction to the level
of the paranormal, i.e., to the explanation that latent
ESP powers on the human level account for what occurs.
But such a reduction from supernatural to paranormal
faces two grave objections: First, controlled parapsycho-

logical research, though successful in demonstrating limited telepathic, clairvoyant, precognitive, and even psychokinetic faculties in some subjects, has never yielded evidence of powers as extensive as would be necessary to account for the full range of attested poltergeistic, demonic, and spiritual phenomena. Second, occult events of the sort we have just been discussing are invariably attributed to supernatural agencies by those experiencing them; the old philosophical adage would seem to apply that if something looks, smells, and tastes like an onion, and you wish to maintain that it is in reality a turnip, the burden of proof rests on *you* to prove your case—not on the people who accept it as an onion.

Along the same line, it becomes evident on reflection that to reduce the supernatural to the paranormal necessitates the predication of all demonic, spiritual, and poltergeistic attributes to man—which leaves us with the same burden of phenomena under a different name. Nothing has really been accomplished. The situation parallels that of the Christian Scientist matron who kept pressuring her friends with her belief that "pain is but an illusion" until in frustration, they stuck her with a hat pin; after she calmed down, she said: "I will admit this: the illusion of pain is as bad as I imagine pain would have been"! Clearly if the illusion is as bad as the pain, nothing is gained by calling pain an illusion; and if the paranormal must be considered by the reductionist to be as remarkable as the supernatural, he accomplishes nothing in labeling the supernatural as the paranormal. Indeed, as we examine the whole problem of occult phenomena at depth level, we see that the materialist's reduction of supernatural to paranormal exactly parallels the rationalist's reduction of paranormal to normal:

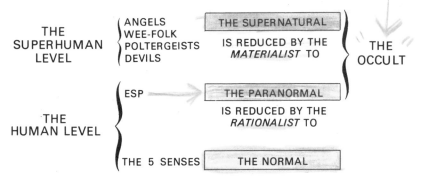

But is reductionism any more warranted in the one case than in the other? The data seem to require that all levels of explanation be sustained, whether one likes it or not. The ultimate reason behind materialistic or rationalistic reductionism appears to be the same: an anti-miraculous bias which would limit explanatory constructs to familiar terms (whether human or material). Let us therefore conclude our discussion of the reality of occult events with a brief word concerning the problem of "miracles" and scientific explanation.

SCIENCE AND THE MIRACULOUS

Since the rise of modern secularism in the 18th century "Enlightenment," arguments have been put forward to limit the range of happenings to the "natural" (as opposed to the supernatural or miraculous). Commonly these arguments are based upon an assumption as to the character of the natural or physical laws that everywhere apply. Thus the Scottish empirical philosopher David Hume (who evidently was not afflicted with Highland second sight!) gave classic formulation to this position when he wrote: "A miracle is a violation of the laws of nature; and as a firm and unalterable experience has established these laws, the proof against a miracle, from the very nature of the fact, is as entire as any argument from experience can possibly be imagined." [34] Hume's elimination of the miraculous has been considered definitive by a host of writers from his day to ours; introductory philosophy texts for college students today generally dispense with the supernatural and with arguments for the truth of the Christian revelation-claim (based chiefly on the resurrection and other miraculous acts of Jesus) simply by citing Hume's discussion. Even more sophisticated discussions of "historical religious claims," such as William T. Blackstone's *Problem of Religious Knowledge,* often do not move beyond Hume when the miracle question is raised.[35]

However, the Humean refutation of supernatural events cannot be sustained. It is indeed a classic argument, but not for the reason many suppose; in point of fact, as has been demonstrated by such critics as C. S. Lewis,[36] the argument is a classic example of *circular reasoning.* The only way to know whether "a firm and unalterable experience" opposes supernatural events would be to know *ahead of time* that no such events are experienced; but that is exactly the question! If evidence exists in behalf of supernatural occurrences, it must be taken seriously, and then there is no longer "firm and unalterable experience" to the contrary. Hume went against his own laudable empiricism in setting forth this argument which in reality short-circuits experience and declares, even before evidence of the supernatural is investigated, that "the laws of nature" rule out certain events.[37]

One of the most penetrating opponents of the supernatural in both the occult and the religious realms, Antony Flew, has attempted a more convincing formulation of Hume's argument. Any investigator of past or present events must assume "the same fundamental regularities" apply in the new situation, or he would be in no position to deal with it; but the uniqueness and non-natural character of the alleged miraculous event contradict such

a perspective and rule it out as a subject of inquiry.[38]
To answer this line of reasoning one need only reflect
upon its implications for all investigative inquiry. If
Flew's understanding of scientific activity were correct,
the scientist could only arrive at results which paralleled
what he *already* knew, for his prior experience would
necessarily determine what he could subsequently discover! An investigator could never, in principle, uncover
anything uniquely new!

In actuality, no one has a sufficiently comprehensive
knowledge of the universe to formulate in advance "firm
and unalterable" laws of nature. We use our past experience as a working hypothesis—not as a Procrustean bed—
in investigating new or strange phenomena. It is by the
very discovery of the new that our past experience under-
goes modification and our understanding of the universe
enlarges. Whenever science has become mesmerized by
its past formulations or hypnotized by the "absolute truth"
of its current conceptions, this has served to block avenues
to new truth. Thus chemists could have combined the
so-called "inert gases" with other elements decades before this was accomplished had they not been convinced
by their own classification of the inert gases in the periodic
table (with already completed outer electron rings) that
such combination was "impossible."

Such examples are (or should be) a reminder that
facts must always take precedence over explanations
in investigating the world. We must not allow already
established explanatory constructs (theories, "laws") to
blunt the edge of new investigations; nor can we rule
out factual occurrences because we cannot explain them.
Physicists have arrived experimentally at the conclusion
that light is both particulate and undulatory—but particles
are not waves and waves are not particles, and the theoretical model, the photon, rather than "explaining"
light, simply gives full weight to the experimental facts,
however paradoxical they may be. Thus, as I have pointed
out in detail elsewhere,[39] Christianity has formulated
its doctrine of the Trinity, not to "explain" God, but
to take fully into account the historical evidence that

Jesus was both man and God (by virtue of His miraculous acts and divine character) and to incorporate the truth which Jesus thereby validated as to His eternal relation with God the Father and with God the Holy Spirit. The evidence is seldom as good for psychical and for occult happenings as for the resurrection of Jesus Christ from the dead,[40] but it is sufficiently good in many instances to warrant our closest attention.

We must "suspend disbelief," check out the evidence with the care demanded for events in general,[41] attempt to formulate explanatory constructs that best "fit the facts," and at the same time be willing always to accept facts even if our best attempts to explain them prove inadequate. If we are religionists, we must avoid the orthodox presupposition that supernatural events "must" be limited to biblical times,[42] and the even less satisfactory presupposition of liberal theology that all supernatural occurrences, including biblical miracles, are the product of the naïve world-view of pre-modern man.[43] If we are members of the secular scientific community, we should do all that we can to counter the mind-set of scientistic prejudice[44] and strive for greater openness in an Einsteinian universe where no possibility can be ruled out *a priori*. With Gardner Murphy we should recognize that "in science we are not unused to discoveries of considerable magnitude; and if, after due scrutiny facts become compulsory, men of science must be ready to enlarge their scheme of the universe so as to admit them." [45] In the aphoristic words of Charles Robert Richet, recipient of the Nobel prize in psychology and medicine (1913): "Je ne dirai pas que cela est possible; je dis seulement que c'est vrai." [46]

2
A Bit of Hidden History

Her eyes lingered on the cromlech, the gate to the underworld: "At least I'm not sure that I like it. Things can fascinate and frighten at the same time."
—Godfrey Turton, *The Devil's Churchyard*

Histories of the occult, like demons, are legion.[1] No attempt will be made here to provide an exhaustive historical description of occult phenomena, but we shall try to offer a orientation sufficient to achieve perspective on a subject that touches all peoples throughout recorded history. In our rapid journey, we will seek insights capable of aiding in the interpretation of more complex occult issues to be discussed in subsequent chapters.

PRIMITIVE PEOPLES

Magic seems to be as old as man. Primitive peoples everywhere have attempted to gain control over nature by occult means. Some of these attempts can properly be regarded as "white magic" in that they do not depend upon compacts with evil powers; and such occult efforts are occasionally of a pre-scientific kind, leading to the practical control of nature even as alchemy was a precursor of chemistry. But in a vast number of instances, primitive magic is either "gray" or "black," in that it ties itself to or relies directly upon the conscious evocation of dark powers. Here we find poor and pitiful Fausts, selling their souls not for cosmic wisdom but for talismans that will make their hunt successful or keep their rival's from being so.[2] The motive seems always to be the same, however unworthy the object: to become like gods, to gain the kingdoms of this world. Lucifer's appeal to Eve and Satan's to Christ appear to be universalized across the landscape of fallen human nature. Mircea Eliade's studies of the magical rites of primitive peoples have attested to the universality of their symbolic patterns, attesting to the solidarity of the race in its schizophrenic desire both to become god and to find the true God who alone can save.[3]

Even today in parts of the world relatively untouched by what we call civilization primitive magic still goes on, and numerous attested cases of supernatural manifestations, particularly of a negative or demonic sort, have been recorded.[4] The following account of lycanthropy is of more than routine interest, since it is based upon eyewitness testimony:

> Now from the distance, out of the bush, came jackal cries, nearer and nearer. The deep growl of the male being answered by the shriller cries of the female.
>
> Suddenly a powerful young man and a splendid young girl, completely naked, leapt over the heads of the onlookers and fell sprawling in the clearing.
>
> They sprang up again instantly and started to dance. My God, how they danced! If the dance of the nyanga [the witch doctor] was horrible, this was revolting. They danced the dance of the rutting jackals. As the dance progressed, their imitations became more and more animal, till the horror of it brought the acid of vomit to the throat. Then, in a twinkling, with loathing unbounded, and incredulous amazement, I saw these two *turn into jackals before my eyes*. The rest of their "act" must be rather imagined than described. Suffice it to say, and I say it with all the authority of long practice of my profession [medicine], no human beings, despite any extensive and potent preparation, could have sustained the continued and repeated sexuality of that horrid mating.[5]

In a Foreword to the volume from which this passage is quoted (and it represents but one of numerous such events witnessed by its author), Montague Summers, whom we mentioned in the first chapter as a foremost specialist in this field,[6] stresses the parallelisms between these primitive incidents and "civilized" cases of sorcery and witchcraft as recorded by the western demonologists from the 15th to the 19th century: Kramer, Sprenger, Cardan, Weyer, Bodin, de Loyer, Delrio, Glanvil, Sinistrari, Von Gorres.[7] Concludes Summers: "These men were not fools. They were neither deceivers nor deceived." The devil, we may conclude, is equally at home in the jungle and in the metropolis.

CHINA, INDIA, AND TIBET

In the high civilization of dynastic China, occultism was conducted on a comparably high level. Alchemy and astrology, whose complex theories give them the status of "occult sciences," flourished,[8] as did that unique variety of mystical divination expressed in the pages of the *I Ching or Book of Changes*. Its most authoritative recent translator[9] sees this work as the common source of Confucianism and Taoism, the two branches of Chinese philosophy, and finds there the metaphysical concept of the Tao (immutable, eternal law in the midst of change), the numinal-phenomenal distinction, and a kind of existential call for decision in the face of the judgments of events. Be that as it may, the original use of the sixty-four hexagrams comprising the *I Ching* was divinatory. James Legge, who translated the work for Max Müller's great edition of the Sacred Books of the East, noted that one finds divination being practiced in China "as soon as we tread the borders of something like credible history."[10] The stalks of plants were early used for oracles, and in the 19th century Legge saw the Ptarmica Sibirica still cultivated on Confucius' grave. By manipulating the yarrow stalks, one obtained lineal figures, and the "key" to these figures was resident in the *I Ching*. The stalks were believed to be spirit-possessed, so that by means of their interpretation one could determine whether one's plans would turn out positively or negatively.

Carl Gustav Jung provided an interesting Foreword

to the Wilhelm edition of the *I Ching*, endeavoring to plumb its significance for his own psychoanalytical labors. He asked it for some word concerning his intention to write the Foreword! "The *I Ching* replied by comparing itself to a caldron, a ritual vessel in need of renovation." Jung's general conclusion is that the method, insisting as it does on "self-knowledge," is "open to every kind of misuse" by the immature but is appropriate for "thoughtful and reflective people." [11] This is doubtless correct, but it suggests that the "power" of the *I Ching* lies not in any objective message it has to convey (its content is as ambiguous as a Zen koan) but in the introspection it elicits.

Because the *I Ching*, like most divinatory techniques of a much less sophisticated kind (palmistry, tea-leaf reading, etc.), says virtually anything to anyone, its recent popularity in American occult circles has given rise to inevitable parody. An article titled, "I Thing," warns:

> It is not uncommon for a wrong answer to be given.
> This may come from imperfect concentration, either on
> your own part or on the part of the oracle, which has
> been listening to cases for seven thousand years and
> may confuse you with someone else. But bearing in
> mind that yang is always on the point of changing
> into yin,[12] or vice versa ("She loves me" can easily
> become "She loves me not," as the oracle knows only
> too well), it may be enough to know that since any
> pattern can change into any other, one cannot go wrong—
> at least, not forever. But since only the oracle lives
> forever, it *is* possible to go wrong throughout one's
> entire life. Therefore great care should be exercised.[13]

This warning goes beyond the facetious. Perhaps by opening up the vacumm of an empty soul to ambiguous oracles, one can invite seven devils to take up residence? Then the *I Ching* would indeed serve as a vehicle for change— a negative means of grace—whereby one could in fact "go wrong throughout one's entire life."

Occultism in India and Tibet has from time immemorial centered on the paranormal and supernatural acts of holy men: yogis, fakirs, and other initiates into the mysteries who have been able to increase bodily heat so as to melt the snow around them, create hypnotic illusions, levitate, etc. Though such practices are not placed on the highest plane by Tantristic (Hindu and Buddhist) religion, they definitely relate to the Tantristic religious atmosphere of asceticism and to its fundamental conviction that the phenomenal world is an illusion (maya). In his standard edition of *The Tibetan Book of the Dead, or the After-Death Experiences on the "Bardo" Plane*, Evans-Wentz (who is a Tantrist) emphasizes that classic Buddhism is incompatible with orthodox Christianity on at least three counts: whereas Christianity "teaches dependence upon an outside power or Saviour, Buddhism teaches dependence on self-exertion alone if one is to gain salvation"; Buddhism holds to reincarnation whereby one's sin (karma) is expiated by oneself through a series of existences leading ultimately to separation from the world of illusion in the nirvana state; and Buddhism neither denies nor affirms the existence of God, for "neither believing nor not believing in a Supreme God, but self-exertion in right-doing, is essential to comprehending the true nature of life." [14]

Two questions quite naturally arise in the face of Indian and Tibetan occult phenomena. First, are these occurrences "real"—do they attain the paranormal and supernatural levels? Secondly, if they are real, do they attest the truth of Tantristic beliefs? Though (to practice punning in its worst form) some fakirs have undoubtedly been fakes, it seems impossible in general to deny the reality of Indian and Tibetan phenomena as genuinely occult. Too many skeptical investigators have had their doubts removed—investigations such as French judge Louis Jacolliot who himself observed, inter alia, a fakir (or the ancestral spirits he evoked?) cause a gigantic bronze vase full of water to rise into the air and descend without perceptible shock.[15] Such phenomena are certainly paranormal, and, since they go well beyond the apparent limits of testible ESP, we may not reject the possibility that "spirits" or some form of supernatural agency is indeed involved. Are the religious beliefs of the Tantrists therefore validated? Hardly, for a miracle will only serve to attest a belief if two conditions are fulfilled: the miracle must be integrally bound up with the content of the belief itself, and the miracle must be "existentially significant," i.e., it must deal with a crisis issue of human existence. The elevation of a bronze pot from the ground (or the Indian rope trick, or melting snow by increased body heat) has no inherent connection with karma, transmigration, or any other fundamental doctrine of Tantristic belief; nor does it exactly touch the mainsprings of human need! Indeed, Jacolliot concludes his lengthy treatment of Tantristic miracles with the significant evaluation: "Decrepitude and imbecility appear to be the final end of all Hindu transformed Fakirs." [16] In contrast, Christ's resurrection from the dead both attested His claim to be the Lord of life and provided mankind with the answer to its most fundamental need, the need to overcome the decrepitude of death.

THE ANCIENT NEAR EAST AND THE BIBLE

The loftiest religion, aside from that of the Bible itself, to develop in the ancient Levant was the Parsi faith or Zoroastrianism. It appears that this dualistic religion of eternally existent Good and Evil had a direct influence on the Greek philosophical tradition.[17] Certainly it influenced subsequent western occultism by means of its developed hierarchy of good and evil spirits. Since the two fundamental cosmic powers, Ahura Mazda (God) and Angra Mainyu or Ahriman (the Devil), were regarded as coequal from the beginning of all things,[18] there was a natural tendency to elevate the status of the Evil One and his minions. This in turn led to debased religious practice and varieties of occult activity which, because they are so inconsistent with the high evaluation regularly placed upon Zoroastrianism, are seldom mentioned in works on comparative religion. For example, Zoroaster believed that the hair and nails could produce "Daevas on the earth which we call lice," and that one must therefore bury them, drawing "three furrows with a knife of metal around the hole, or six, or nine, and thou shalt chant the Ahuna Vairya three times, or six, or nine." [19] Otherwise, one's hair and nails could fall into the hands of sorcerers who were in league with Ahriman and his evil spirits. On a higher plane was the activity of Zoroastrian astrologers; undoubtedly the Magi of the Christmas story were of this company, and we shall have more to say on this subject in a later chapter.[20]

Egyptian magical practices, especially in conjunction with their elaborate pyramid rites, are probably too well known to deserve comment here.[21] But we must say a word concerning the belief of many present-day occultists that the rites ostensibly to guide the dead through the underworld were actually initiatory vehicles into a secret pyramid wisdom—particularly since not a few Christian writers have attempted to correlate the measurements of the Great Pyramid with the apocalyptic dating in the biblical books of Daniel and Revelation. Even such a stalwart modern saint as Joseph A. Seiss, the translator of the hymn "Beautiful Saviour" into English, wrote a book seriously arguing that the dimensions of the Great Pyramid constitute a valid secular prophecy.[22] Perhaps the most devastating analysis of this issue comes from French scholar Bouisson, who notes that "by a similar method applied to the Eiffel Tower, if we subtract from the number 1,927 (that of the steps and landings from the base to the summit) the number of those who partook of the Last Supper, we get 1914, the date of the beginning of the First World War." [23]

When we compare the occult activities of the Babylonians, Hittites, and Canaanites with the position taken on these matters in the Bible of their Israelite neighbors, the contrast is literally staggering. The Canaanites practiced sympathetic magic and gross divination; the remains of Asshurbanipal's great library at Nineveh feature magical and divinatory tablets; charms and incantations were regularly employed to invoke and palliate a host of demons.[24] Here particularly contemporary biblical scholarship finds "the Old Testament against its environment." After noting the wholesale prohibitions relative to sorcerers, diviners, and necromancers (Ex. 22:18; Lev. 20; Deut. 18:9-15; Is. 47:12-15), G. Ernest Wright declares: "The whole pagan world of magic and divination is simply incompatible with the worship of Yahweh." [25]

While thoroughly condemning pagan occultism, the Bible clearly recognizes the reality of the occult world.[26] In antediluvian times "the sons of God took wives of the daughters of men" and "there were giants in the earth in those days" (Gen. 6). Moses and the Egyptian magicians competed with each other, and God's power was such that Moses triumphed (Ex. 7-8). The witch of Endor actually conjured up the ghost of Samuel, but Saul's reliance on this forbidden practice is associated with his spiritual degeneration and madness, and the text expressly says that his departure from the God-appointed means of guidance (dreams, true prophecy) had brought him to this pass (I Sam. 28).[27] As Moses won over the pagan magicians, so the true prophet of God routed the false prophets of Baal by calling upon the supernatural resources of the Most High (I Kings 18).[28] Is. 34:14 asserts: "Demons (*siyim*) of the desert shall meet with goblins (*'iyim*); the satyr (*sa'ir*) shall call to his fellow; yea, there the fiend of the storm (*lilith*: the female night-demon) shall house, and find a secure retreat." [29] Though the elaborate angelology and demonology of later Hellenistic and Cabalistic Judaism cannot be found in the canonical Scriptures,[30] the Bible unequivocally declares that seraphim, cherubim, archangels (Michael is named), and angels (such as Gabriel) exist, and that Satan and his demonic forces are no less a reality.[31]

Even the casual reader of the New Testament is aware of the pervasive recognition given to demonic powers. Again and again Jesus casts out demons, even engaging in dialogues with them (cf. the Gadarene demoniac incident, Lk. 8); and his followers cast out demons in His name (Acts 19, etc.). Jesus' public ministry commences after He is "driven by the Spirit into the wilderness to be tempted of the devil" (Mt. 4; Mk. 1; Lk. 4).[32]

Central to the entire New Testament teaching concerning the end of the world is Christ's return "with all his mighty angels," God's triumph over the evil powers, and the casting of Satan into the lake of fire forever (Mt. 25; Mk. 13; II Thess. 1; Rev. 19-20).[33]

What is to be done with such material? One of my theological professors used to state flatly that the demonic in the New Testament was to be regarded as symbolic (of evil, psychosis, disease, etc.), and he became quite agitated when I asked him whether we should also regard Jesus as symbolic (of the good, of mental and physical health, etc.) since in the narrative of Jesus' temptation in the wilderness a dialogue takes place between Jesus and the devil—both evidently regarded as having comparable reality or unreality! This points up the difficulty with demythologizings of the satanic in the New Testament: they are integrally bound up with the reality of Jesus and His entire message.

But can we not suppose that in this regard Jesus either consciously or unconsciously limited Himself to the thought-forms of His own day? I have dealt with this variety of kenotic ("limitation") theory elsewhere;[34] suffice it to point out that if Jesus is to be limited whenever we think that our knowledge exceeds His, we reverse roles with Him and become Lord ourselves! Moreover, He plainly indicated that He possessed self-knowledge of His incarnational limits when He declared His one noetic limitation (the hour of His coming—Mt. 24:36); He would hardly have had other limitations of which He was unaware when He demonstrated His understanding of His incarnational limits in the particular instance cited. Finally, in the words of Archbishop Whately, one of the greatest apologists of the Christian faith against an early 19th century rationalism not materially different from our 20th century rationalistic theologies:

> These two things are what any man of honesty, and condour, and common sense, is competent clearly to perceive:
>
> 1st. That Jesus did *not* accommodate Himself to the religious prejudices of His time and country; else, He would not have been rejected and crucified by His countrymen;

who would have received Him gladly if He would have consented to fall in with their notions, and to become such a King as their expectations were fixed on.

And 2ndly, That His followers would never have knowingly exposed themselves, as they did, to scorn, and persecution, and violent death, but in the cause of a religion which they believed true, and in attestation of what they had plainly seen and heard: and that consequently we must, if we would be Christians indeed, and fellow-disciples with them,—receive their words (in all that relates to religion) as true, and true in the sense in which they themselves knew that they were understood.

What is revealed to us, therefore, in Scripture on various points,—and, among the rest, concerning Evil-spirits,—is to be received, (however different it may be from what we might have conjectured,) with humble faith and reverend docility.[35]

THE GRECO-ROMAN WORLD

Transmigration of souls, the mysticism of numbers, and the belief in a mathematical-musical "harmony of the spheres" characterized the philosophy of the pre-Socratic thinker Pythagoras. These ideas certainly betray Tantristic influence,[36] and Pythagoras' notion of cosmic harmony plays a considerable role in later occultism, especially in the emphasis on macrocosmic-microcosmic union at the time of the western European Renaissance.

Another potent occult heritage from Greek times is the legend of Atlantis—the lost continent—which is recorded for us by Plato in His *Timaeus* and *Critias*.[37] Was this tale of a golden-age civilization destroyed in full flower by volcanic eruption a mythologization of "the end of Minoan dominance in the Aegean world," as argued by a recent specialist?[38] Numerous efforts have been made to discover or identify this lost continent and the literature on the subject is immense.[39]

Certainly no proof exists that a secret tradition of occult truth passed from "Atlantis" to surviving initiates.[40] It seems reasonable to suppose that like the classical myth of the Golden Age, Atlantis expresses mankind's deepest longing for the lost Eden.[41] Perhaps medieval man was exhibiting laudable sensitivity when

he saw in Vergil's Fourth Eclogue (on the return of
the Golden Age) a direct parallel with Isaiah's prophecies
concerning the reign of Messiah.[42] The modern occultist
who searches for Atlantis and its alleged secret knowledge would do well to meditate on Thomas Wolfe's theme
that fallen man cannot "go home again"; the cherubim
still stand at Eden's gate with "a flaming sword which
turns every way, to keep the way of the tree of life"
(Gen. 3:24). All of us—occultist and non-occultist alike—
are caught, as Steinbeck well puts it, "east of Eden."
The only way back (Jn. 14:6) is a route that passes
by a Cross set high on a hill, outside a city wall. Only
the sword of the spirit (Eph. 6:17), which is the Word
of God—Christ Himself—can overcome the obstacle that
keeps us from Paradise, for that obstacle is the result
of our own sin and self-centeredness, and only Christ
Himself can remove it by His atoning death.

One often gets the impression that our notions of ghosts,
haunted houses, and spectral phenomena come from medieval Christian superstition. This idea is occasionally
fostered by critics of Christianity who evidently believe
that ghost lore arose in a Christian setting. This is by
no means the case. The Greeks and the Romans were
not only strong on prophetic augeries and divination,[43]
but they had developed a full-scale spectral lore before
Christianity even came on the scene. Ovid's *Metamor-
phoses* draw heavily on Greek sources for their tales
of magical and miraculous shape-shiftings,[44] and
Apuleius' *Golden Asse* is replete with stories of witch-
induced transformations, some of which have affinities
with the literature of lycanthropy and vampirism. The
very fact that these treatments are poetic (Rabelaisian,
in the case of Apuleius!) only makes clearer the extent
to which the occult was in common parlance. The Younger
Pliny, whose correspondence with the Emperor Trajan
is so important as an insight into primitive Christian
worship, enjoyed a good ghost story, and tells two excellent
ones in a surviving letter to a friend.[45] Here we read
what have come to be standard fare: a haunted house,
clanking chains, and the laying of the ghost after proper

funeral rites are performed. Pliny's stories are also alluded to by Lucian (*Philopseudes*, 35) and Tacitus (*Annales*, XI, 21), showing the degree of interest the ancients attached to such narratives. A distinguished classicist notes that Pliny "evidently believes in ghosts or at least fears very much that they are real. Such belief was quite universal among his contemporaries." [46]

Early Christianity soon found itself at war with classical occultism. Apollonius of Tyana, a 1st century Neo-Pythagorean, was turned into an occult Christ—a veritable counter-Christ or Antichrist—by his 3d century biographer Philostratus.[47] This biography "bears every evidence of being a historical novel, and its miraculous details are not deserving of analysis, but non-Christians ever since have pretended to find in Apollonius a pagan Christ, and in the stories told about him, counterparts to those related of Christ and his apostles." [48] It is most instructive to contrast the historical worthlessness of this portrait with the primary-source historical character of the New Testament documents, written by eyewitnesses and by associates of eyewitnesses between the 40s and the 80s of the 1st century.[49]

A more serious threat to Christianity came from Gnostic occultism. Gnosticism had several varieties, but the common element was the dualistic conviction that man was originally spiritual but has fallen into the sensible, bodily world, from which, by self-knowledge alone, one can reenter the spiritual domain. R. M. Grant sees Gnosticism as "passionate subjectivity" and finds a close resemblance between it and modern existentialism.[50] Christians radically differed from Gnostics on at least three counts: (1) They placed a high value on the body and on the physical world as the product of God's creativity, whereas the Gnostics generally attributed the world of matter to the work of a lesser deity. In consequence, the entire Old Testament, with its stress on God as creator, as well as the central New Testament theme of Incarnation—God becoming flesh to serve man—were anathema to Gnosticism. (2) Christians believed in salvation by grace through faith in Christ's incarnate work and atoning death, not by some form of knowledge (*gnosis*). Gnostics tried to save themselves through self-knowledge; Christian salvation was never "by works, lest any man should boast" (Eph. 2:8-9). (3) As emphasized in Chapter One, Christianity based its case on the public, objective evidence of Christ's work and proclaimed a truth accessible to all men; Gnosticism maintained a secret wisdom of existential subjectivity. Not surprisingly, present-day critical theology, so thoroughly permeated with existential categories, joins esoteric occultists[51] in identifying Gnostic elements in the Christianity of the Bible. Rudolf Bultmann, whose theology is so heavily dependent on the existentialism of atheist philosopher Martin Heidegger, finds Gnostic influence throughout the New Testament, and especially in the Gospel of John. Such an argument, however, is impossible to sustain; it is modern existentialistic commitments, and not the historical data, which lead to a conclusion that contradicts both the Gnostic texts and the clear teaching of the New Testament itself.[52]

FROM THE AGE OF FAITH TO
THE AGE OF REFORM

The growing corruption of life in the latter days of the western Roman Empire drove sensitive believers to Christian monasticism, first on an individual (anchorite) basis and then according to communal rules. Monastic isolation was a precursor of the general societal isolation which inevitably followed the collapse of Rome. The disappearance of central government, the loss of effective communications, and the threat of barbarian attack everywhere led naturally to the decentralized, self-sufficient life of the feudal manor. Such conditions fostered the acceptance of travellers' tales of strange and remarkable phenomena in parts of the world to which the listener had virtually no access.[53] Thus arose the fascinating bestiaries—with their accounts of monsters, accompanied by edifying morals[54]—and mysterious legends such as that of the Wandering Jew, who insulted our Lord on His way to Calvary and was condemned to wander the earth until the Last Trump sounded.[55] It is easy to dismiss the entire corpus of this literature as mythology, but some of it doubtless relates to factual occurrences (for example, accounts of monsters which may really have existed or, like the Loch Ness monster, may still exist).[56]

The isolated life-style of medieval man provided the ideal garden in which hidden arts could grow and flourish. Theologians such as pseudo-Dionysius the Areopagite peopled the celestial and infernal regions with hierarchies of angelic and demonic ranks, and correlated the ecclesiastical hierarchy with heavenly counterparts. Alchemists strove to transmute the dross of earth and of their own being into the gold of perfection. Monks and mystics acquired paranormal and supernatural powers to reproduce the stigmata (wounds) of Christ in their own bodies and to levitate. This latter phenomenon was so important in medieval piety and is so well attested that it warrants our attention.

Among verified instances of medieval levitations are the following:

> St. Peter of Alcantara was unable to hear the lofty words of St. John, *Verbum caro factum est*, pronounced without falling into ecstasy and being raised above the earth. The Franciscan, Biagio of Caltanisetta, went into esctasy simply at the names of Jesus and Mary, and enraptured with their beauty, sprang into the air. Blessed Giles, of the Order of St. Dominic, remained suspended in the air in ecstasy for whole nights without it being possible to bring him back to earth, or even to give the least inclination to his body. After her communions, Mary of Agreda became slightly raised from the ground, like a dead body, and seemed to be so light that those who stood by were able to rock her with the slightest breath. King Philip II experienced the same phenomenon with Fr. Dominic of Jesus-Mary, who also performed the same ecstatic flight in the monastery of Valencia. St. Thomas of Villanova, whilst preaching one day in his cathedral, suddenly went into ecstasy and remained suspended in the air for twelve hours, and so on.[57]

How are cases of this kind to be explained, a number of which occurred in broad daylight and extended over a considerable time interval? Görres suggested a "psychical force"; de Rochas appealed to "forces non définies" (undefined physical forces: animal magnetism, odic current, vital effluvia, etc.); others have argued for the intervention of spirits of the dead; the Roman Church has declared that these levitations are evidence of God's miraculous power in the lives of true ecstatics.

The official Catholic explanation seems doubtful—or at least insufficient—in light both of the success of Tantristic mystics in bringing about not dissimilar phenomena,[58] and of the admission of Pope Benedict XIV that "non enim id ejus daemonis efficaciam et potestatem excedit" (the phenomenon does not go beyond the power and ability of a demon himself).[59] Even if we admit that God might give such a power to one of his saints for a special purpose, the fact that the power could also have a demonic source requires a criterion of discrimination. It is precisely the lack of recognition of the necessity of such a criterion that leads to so much confused thinking on the matter of post-biblical "Christian miracles." Once the truth of the Christian faith is established by way of the resurrection of Jesus Christ (whose existential significance over against other miracle claims has already been discussed),[60] lesser miracles do *not* become the arbiter in denominational battles. How could they? As Boston University philosopher Edgar Sheffield Brightman used to say: "Christian Science and Roman Catholicism are both systems of belief that have led to practical results; yet both cannot be true at the same time unless the universe is a mad house." [61]

The criterion for arbitrating among competing Christian or allegedly Christian positions is expressly stated in the New Testament Scriptures: "Though an angel from heaven preach any other gospel unto you than that which we have preached unto you, let him be anathema" (Gal. 1:8). Conformity of teaching and belief with the primitive Christian message is the sole criterion for properly evaluating denominational claims. If levitations, healings, or other "lesser miracles" appear to attest beliefs that run counter to biblical truth, Benedict XIV's admission of the extent of demonic power may serve as a two-edged sword! In any case, the non-duplication of medieval levitations in ESP experimentation or in controlled spiritist settings[62] seems to rule out explanations restricted to the paranormal level or to the "intervention of the dead." Medieval man saw life as a battleground between God and the devil; perhaps his miracles serve to support this contention.

Though heresy is hardly the product of orthodoxy, it cannot exist without it. The reason why the modern church finds it virtually impossible to rid itself of heretical beliefs (such as the beliefs of the late spiritualistic Bishop Pike in the Episcopal Church) is simply that it has ceased to hold any definable standards of orthodoxy. This was not the problem in the medieval church—quite the opposite. True, Roman Catholicism was not defined in rigid propositions until the Counter-Reformation's Council of Trent,[63] but the Church of Rome so fully embraced the life of medieval man that heresy seemed often to be the only way to cast off the smothering embrace of spiritual totalitarianism. It is not accidental that the revival of Gnostic occultism should have taken place among the Albigensians or Cathari at the very time the medieval papacy reached its authoritative height. One extreme bred another, and it was characteristic of Innocent III (his papal name remains perhaps the most singular and ironical misnomer in the history of that office) to solve the problem by fomenting a crusade which succeeded in totally exterminating those poor folk seeking greater innocence and light than the established church could provide. A sad instance wherein the blood of the martyrs became, not the seed of anything—but simply the blood of martyrs! [64]

More pitiful and horrible yet was the Satanism which came to the fore as the towering edifice of medieval society began to crumble in the 14th and 15th centuries. Everyone has heard of the trial of Joan of Arc and her condemnation to the stake for having listened to "heavenly voices" that told her to drive the invading English out of France; her subsequent rehabilitation and sainthood do not disguise the fact that this peasant girl, representing the common people of her day, was beginning to hear voices other than official ones. Joan's Satanic counterpart—virtually forgotten today, though his trial was as much a cause célèbre as hers in 15th century France—was Gilles de Rais, a nobleman who sought occult powers by demonic infanticide and child murder. So extensive were his killings that as late as the 19th century in his château at Tiffauges a physician happened on an oubliette (a secret dungeon) containing piles of skulls and bones. De Rais' trial was significant in many ways, not least of which was the defendant's genuine confession of guilt and restoration to the church before his execution.[65] As we shall see, modern occultists have often trod Gilles' path but unlike him have gloried in their folly to the very end.

The black magic, Satanism, and witches' sabbaths of the time are a direct reflection of what the great cultural historian Johan Huizinga has called "the waning of the middle ages." [66] The Church embraced all aspects of life and not infrequently placed its imprimatur on social evils. The peasantry and the disenfranchized lower classes had no recourse against such practices—no socially acceptable means of protest. So they expressed themselves in blind, hopeless peasant revolts[67] and in the black arts, whose prime characteristic was the inversion and perversion of orthodox Church practices (the Cross upside down, the black mass employing a Satanic wafer or a stolen and desecrated Host). Thus did a corrupt Church cast men into the very arms of its age-old Adversary. The surrealistic horrors of Jerome Bosch's paintings well display this breakup of society and the demonization of its values.

Another reaction to the medieval synthesis occurred simultaneously in Italy. This was the Renaissance movement which, though generally maintaining Christian connections, dug back into the pagan past and out into the new world for a more adequate perspective on the universe. Cornelius Agrippa, Giordano Bruno and many others sought to become adepts in ancient magic; [68]

Figure 2. "The Last Judgment," by Hieronymus Bosch

Paracelsus and his followers,[69] while laying the foundations of modern pharmaceutical chemistry, developed a "nature mysticism" (*Naturphilosophie*) which located salvation in the Book of Nature, and contributed, through Protestant mystics, enthusiasts (*Schwärmer*), and pietists, to the deistic-rationalistic opposition to orthodox Christianity in the 18th century and the romantic distaste for biblical revelation in the Goethe-Schiller "Sturm und Drang" movement of the early 19th century.[70]

Renaissance explorers brought back tales of strange wonders and hidden mysteries—from Ponce de Leon's Cindad de Oro and Fountain of Youth to the story of the Christian Kingdom of Prester John, an ideal Priest-King whose land of plenty stood impregnable though surrounded by Muslim infidels.[71] These tales, like the Atlantis legend, bespeak the longings of man for a New Age that would restore the lost Eden; in times of fearful change, such hopes become particularly acute.[72] In one respect, the Renaissance was anti-occult: strong opposition to astrology was expressed, though not on scientific ground. Renaissance man wished especially, in his focus on man's power and potential, to free himself from the trammels of destiny, fate, or cultural patterns; thus Freewill became a cardinal watchword of the Renaissance, and astrology was rejected as a limitation upon it.[73]

The Protestant Reformers had less negatively to say about astrology, for they denied absolute human freewill on the basis of God's predestination of the elect to eternal life. Many theologians of the Reformation period, such as Melanchthon, engaged in astrological activity. Luther, however, was not as strongly pulled in this direction; he remarked on one occasion that his friend Melanchthon pursued astrology "as I take a drink of strong beer when I am troubled with grievous thoughts." [74] The activities of Lutheran astrologers (Brahe, Kepler) and alchemists (Libavius) were of first importance for the development of modern astronomy and chemistry in the 17th century,[75] and the work of Lutheran pastor and littérateur Johann Valentin Andreae was instrumental in providing a Christian counterweight to Parscelsian, esoteric, self-realization alchemy and the new Rosicrucian mysticism so fully bound up with it.[76]

To attribute the witchcraft mania of the 17th century to Protestant causes is as unjust as to explain the Thirty Years' War as a consequence of the Reformation. The tensions productive of the Thirty Years' War were at root political (as is evidenced by the fact that religious alignments were unceremoniously scrapped when the interests of Realpolitik dictated); witchcraft during this same period was also a social manifestation whose linkage with a particular theological position was often only accidental.[77] The classic treatments of witchcraft upon which the judges in the 17th century trials chiefly relied were an inheritance of the late Middle Ages (e.g., the *Malleus maleficarum*), not a product of the Reformation. Even the New England witch burners were by no means innovators; their methods were acquired from long-dead predecessors in this grisly art. The root cause of the witch mania of the 17th century can also be found at work at the end of the Middle Ages: again a society had reached full term; again old rigidities held men in cultural straightjackets; again the birthpangs of a new age unsettled the timeworn order of things. Under such conditions, witchcraft served as a vehicle of radical social protest, and its ruthless repression—by excessive cruelty —attests to the neurotic fear of radicalism on the part of those who were unsuccessfully trying to hold on to the fading ghost of a dying era.

"ENLIGHTENMENT" AND MODERNITY

The 18th century ushered in the modern secular age, with its depreciation of "religious superstition," particularly as exemplified in miracle-ridden Christian revelation. Deists in England and *philosophes* in France were caustic in their criticism of the very idea of the miraculous. Now Reason and Natural Law would become the arbiters of truth, and mankind would enter a new epoch of enlightened progress.

This ideal, however, had almost nothing to do with the actual state of things. "Enlightened" 18th century

man was more racially prejudiced than his Christian predecessor,[78] and "the much glorified eighteenth century,
the 'gallant Age,' and 'era of enlightenment' was also
a period in which much nonsense flourished, and in which
every kind of tomfoolery immediately found enthusiastic
admirers." [79] What tomfoolery? The Freemasons, a
Deistic religion of ritualistic works-righteousness, though
claiming mystical origins in the building of Solomon's
Temple, became a force to be reckoned with only in the
18th century; the Masonic rites, incorporating questionable elements from Rosicrucianism and other earlier
occult rituals, gave men of the epoch a theatrical worship
experience while affording them the opportunity to criticize
the "superstition" of the infinitely richer historic Christian liturgies.[80] Also, the age abounded in mystagogues,
occult charismatics, and quacks.

At the least reprehensible end of the spectrum were
the occult romance writers Jacques Cazotte (*Le Diable
amoureux*) [81] and the Abbé de Montfaucon de Villars,
whose *Comte de Gabalis*, though published in 1670, was
to electrify the 18th century and create the model for
Bulwer-Lytton's 19th century Rosicrucian novel, *Zanoni*.
Next came the mystics—blind leading the blind—the most
influential of whom was the "unknown philosopher," Louis
Claude de St. Martin, who was influenced by Freemasonry, the 17th century German mystic Jakob Boehme, and
his own contemporary Emanuel Swedenborg (a scientific
genius turned religionist, whose *Heaven and Its Wonders
and Hell* offered technicolor visions of the next world—
in stupifying detail). St. Martin held the belief, so hospit-
able to his anthropocentric century, that "man is divine
despite the fall recounted in the Scriptures, and dormant
within him lies a lofty quality of which he is too often
scarcely conscious, and it is incumbent on him to develop
this quality, striving thereafter without ceasing"; [82] St.
Martin's philosophy of human self-perfectibility led to the
founding of the Martinist Order, which exists to this day.[83]

The clearest evidence of how irrational were the advocates of the Age of Reason comes by way of the alchemical charlatans who hoodwinked an entire century.

De Lisle, after murdering his master and appropriating his alchemical equipment and "transmuting powder," took up with a married woman; the two of them fooled royalty into believing that they possessed the secret of the Great Work, and their bastard son became rich by carrying on this tradition, even convincing the Duc de Richelieu of his ability at gold production.[84]

Better known than de Lisle is Cagliostro, whose checkered career focused on my European home-city, Strasbourg. There he bamboozled the "enlightened" (and therefore hopelessly naïve) Cardinal-archbishop and Prince de Rohan; the Prince believed in Cagliostro's transmutations and even in his supposed "elixir of life" (he built him a home where he could undergo physical regeneration).[85] Cagliostro was initiated into Masonry by a no less bizarre character, the Comte de St. Germain, who said that he had lived for centuries and been acquainted with Solomon, the Queen of Sheba, etc. He unabashedly posed as a "deity," and the Landgrave of Hesse actually gave him a residence so that he could pursue the occult sciences in style. Lewis Spence says of him and his age:

> It would be a matter of real difficulty to say whether
> he possessed any genuine occult power whatsoever, and
> in all likelihood he was merely one of those charlatans
> in whom his age abounded. Against this view might
> be set the circumstance that a great many really clever
> and able people of his own time thoroughly believed
> in him; but we must remember the credulous nature
> of the age in which he flourished. It has been said that
> XVIII century Europe was sceptical regarding everything
> save occultism and its professors, and it would appear
> to unbiassed minds that this circumstance could have
> no better illustration than the career of the Comte de
> Saint Germain.[86]

Why was Enlightenment man skeptical of everything but occultism and therefore subject to such incredibly bad judgment? Bila concludes his study of "The Belief in Magic in 18th Century France" with the damning critique that the *philosophes* were incapable of discrediting magic because they themselves believed in it.[87] The

MÉMOIRE

POUR

LE COMTE DE CAGLIOSTRO,

DEMANDEUR:

CONTRE

M. CHESNON, LE FILS,

COMMISSAIRE AU CHÂTELET DE PARIS;

ET LE SIEUR DE LAUNAY,

Chevalier de l'Ordre Royal & Militaire de S.-Louis,
Gouverneur de la Bastille, Défendeurs.

Il est parti, accoutumé à se soumettre, sans murmure,
aux volontés des Rois. *Page* 37.

A PARIS,

De l'Imprimerie de LOTTIN, *l'aîné*, & de LOTTIN *de S.-Germain,*
Imprimeurs Ordinaires de la VILLE, rue S.-André-des-Arcs, Nᵒ 27.

M. DCC. LXXXVI.

Figure 3. Cagliostro's Defense against his Accusers, 1786
(Title page of original edition, in the author's collection)

reason was simply that, in rejecting the authority of Holy Scripture—the one sure guide in matters supernatural (because it alone is *God's* word on the subject)—the men of the 18th century lost all moorings and sailed onto the occult sea with neither compass nor chart. Moreover, having substituted a credulous faith in Science for an informed faith in God's revelation, they became sitting ducks for even the wildest chicanery as long as it appeared in pseudo-scientific garb. The so-called Age of Reason offers us our first laboratory example of the unrecognized truth that rationalism and superstition are two sides of the same coin. This example will not be the last.

Two opposing ideologies dominate the 19th century: the growing scientific and technological advance (an inheritance of the Age of Reason) and the Romantic reaction. Both of these movements contributed to occult interests. Romanticism idealized the strange, the irrational, the hidden: the secret lost in the byways of history, *la recherche d'un monde perdu.* Thus Goethe extensively employed occult imagery, and it was no accident that his best-known work was a development of the theme of the Faustian pact with the devil (albeit reworked largely in humanistic terms).[88] The beginnings of monster literature stem from the summer of 1816 when Mary Shelley conceived of *Frankenstein* during a writing contest among her lover and future husband Percy Bysshe Shelley, Lord Byron, and his paranoic physician Polidori, who was to write (and try to palm off on Byron) the first literary vampire tale of modern times.[89] The greatest ghost stories and supernatural fiction in the English language were produced by the now sadly neglected 19th century Irish novelist, Sheridan Le Fanu.[90] Strindberg's literary activities, particularly during his last years at the close of the 19th century, were deeply bound up with occult involvements.[91]

On the "scientific" side, the last century witnessed the rise of mediumistic spiritualism and the organization of Societies of Psychical Research on both sides of the Atlantic to investigate alleged occult happenings and communication with the next world.[92] Spiritualism, in turn, had a profound influence on the development of Theosophy in the English-speaking world and Rudolf Steiner's Anthroposophy on the European continent; both movements blended Tantristic occultism with 19th century western salvation-through-self-effort.[93] French occultism—always strong due to the impetus given to it by the Enlightenment and the cultural shock of the French Revolution—became even more powerful through the voluminous writings of such pagan occultists as Eliphas Lévi (who, it will be remembered, Huysmans, after becoming a Christian, blamed for supernatural attacks on him), Stanislas de Guaita, alchemist Jollivet-Castelot, and "Papus" (Dr. Gérard Encausse) who founded the journal *L' Initiation*, continued today by his son.[94] Following the 19th century trend toward the systematization of knowledge and specialized instruction, the French occultists organized "The Free University of Higher Studies," comprising a "Faculty of Magnetic Sciences," a "Faculty of Hermetic Sciences," and a "Faculty of Spirit Sciences." These activities seemed to fill a societal vacuum in the closing years of the 19th century after France lost the Franco-Prussian War, and with it her place as the most powerful European state. Here again—as in the decline of the medieval age and in the 17th century—we see a positive correlation between the rending of the cultural fabric and heightened involvement in occult practices.[95]

Is this the sobering tocsin which should be sounded concerning the present-day mania for the occult in America?[96] The current "occult explosion" has certainly come as a rude shock to many—who thought that our scientific age, with its impressive conquest of space through incredible technological refinements, was incapable of such interests. But the veneer of Christianity has largely rubbed off our materialistic society, revealing the pagan value system of the "American way of life." What Bellah calls our "civil religion" of national piety[97] has worn pitifully thin in the credibility gaps of the Vietnam war. Into our national vacuum rush the seven devils of Christ's parable. Science, technology, and American-

L'INITIATION

Revue philosophique des Hautes Etudes, publiée sous la direction de

PAPUS ✷ ○. ⌖

Docteur en médecine, de la Faculté de Paris,
Docteur en Kabbale

MENSUELLE — 100 PAGES — 11ᵉ ANNÉE
60 RÉDACTEURS

L'*Initiation* est justement considérée comme la plus sérieuse et la plus scientifique des Revues étudiant le vaste domaine des phénomènes psychiques, des Sciences et des Arts occultes : Kabbale, Orientalisme, Sociétés secrètes, Théosophie, Mystique, Magie pratique, Hermétisme, Phénoménologie générale, tels sont les principaux titres sous lesquels se rangent les questions traitées par une pléiade de savants et de littérateurs dont la compétence n'est plus à prouver. Le nombre de ses rédacteurs, l'entière liberté d'appréciation qui leur est laissée, à quelque école qu'ils appartiennent, et la diversité de leurs travaux, justifient le succès de l'*Initiation* qui compte aujourd'hui plus de 1.600 lecteurs.

ABONNEMENTS :

Un an (France) 10 fr. | Union postale. . 12 fr.
Le Numéro 1 fr.
Envoi d'un numéro spécimen sur demande affranchie.
ADMINISTRATION, 5, RUE DE SAVOIE

DIRECTION

Faculté des Sciences Hermétiques

Année Scolaires 1897-1898

CONSEIL D'ADMINISTRATION

Dʳ PAPUS, *Directeur*.
Administrateurs. — LUCIEN MAUCHEL, licencié
en droit M∴ S∴ C∴

SISERA M∴ S∴ C∴

CONSEIL DE PERFECTIONNEMENT

F. CH. BARLET, licencié en Droit D∴ S∴ C∴

STANISLAS DE GUAITA. — Président du Suprême
Conseil de l'ordre Kabb. de la Rose-Croix. Docteur en Kabbale.

DOCTEUR MARC HAVEN, docteur en médecine, docteur en Kabbale.

SÉDIR, Docteur en Kabbale S∴ S∴ C∴

Tête Buste artistique en plâtre, représentant les centres nerveux moteurs et sensitifs et le siège de quelques facultés mentales et intellectuelles, du professeur H. Durville, exécuté par M.M. Queste, sculpteur, premier prix des arts décoratifs, médaillé de la Ville de Paris.

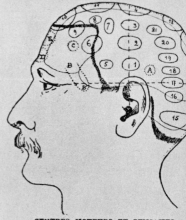

CENTRES MOTEURS ET SENSITIFS

1. Centre sensitif du bras. — 2. Centre sensitif de la jambe — 3. Centre moteur de la rate. — 4. Centre des nerfs spinaux. — 5. C moteur de l'oreille. — 6. Centre moteur de la tête, de la langue e yeux (à gauche, langage articulé de Broca). — 7. Centre moteur du c — 8. Centre sensitif des seins — 9. Centre sensitif des poumons 10. Centre du foie. — 11. impression, croyance. — 12. Centre du ne 13. Centre moteur de l'estomac. — 14. Centre génésique. — 15. Coordination des mouvements, tact. — 16. Centre du larynx. — 17. C sensitif de la bouche et des dents. — 18. Centre de l'audition 19. Reins, organes génito-urinaires. — 20. Centre de la vision 21. Centre moteur de l'intestin.

FACULTÉS MORALES ET INTELLECTUELLES

A. douceur à gauche, colère à droite. — B. Formes de la mémoire B' à gauche, souvenirs gais; envie de rire et de se moquer, prendre en riant; satisfaction. — B' à droite, souvenirs tristes; rend sombre, rêveur; mélancolie, mécontentement. — C. Gaîté à gauche, tristesse à droite. — D. Attention. — E. Volonté.

Figure 4. Pages from the Catalog of Papus' "Free University of Higher [Occult] Studies" (From the author's library)

ism have betrayed us, so perhaps the answer lies in the Dark Powers. Irrationality, drugs, the Sharon Tate murders, LaVey's Church of Satan: such horrendous non-solutions appear as meaningful options when nothingness seems the only alternative. In like manner did Hitler and his minions turn to astrology.[98]

Unless this disease is seen for what it really is, it cannot be cured. "We wrestle not against flesh and blood, but against principalities and powers"; and only Christ the Word of the living God has the resources to overcome the Foe and fill the vacuum in our societal and personal lives.

> *Though devils all the world should fill,*
> *All watching to devour us,*
> *We tremble not, we fear no ill,*
> *They cannot overpower us.*
> *This world's prince may still*
> *Scowl fierce as he will;*
> *He can harm us none:*
> *He's judged, the deed is done,*
> *One little word o'erthrows him.*
>
> *The Word they still shall let remain,*
> *Nor any thanks have for it;*
> *He's by our side upon the plain*
> *With His good gifts and Spirit.*
> *Take they then our life,*
> *Goods, fame, child, and wife,*
> *When their worst is done,*
> *They yet have nothing won:*
> *The Kingdom ours remaineth.*[99]

3

Cabala and Christ

*Do they think, the fools, that their powers of ob-
servation are clearer than the devices of a god?*
—Thornton Wilder, *The Cabala*

Our historical voyage through the realms of the occult
has provided a bird's-eye view of a most extensive landscape. Now we need to turn in depth to certain of the
more sophisticated occult subjects in an effort to understand them in detail. Only in this way will their attraction
become clear; and only thus will we be in a position
to pass accurate judgment upon them. We begin with
a variety of the secret tradition that has had tremendous
influence over the centuries—from the days of medieval
Jewish mysticism through the revival of learning in the
Italian Renaissance to the occultism of the present day.
Our study of the Cabala will focus particularly on its
introduction into the Christian sphere by way of that
Renaissance "Phoenix of the wits," Giovanni Pico della
Mirandola.[1]

WHAT IS THE CABALA?

Readers of Thornton Wilder's novel, *The Cabala*, will
think of hidden, recondite wisdom when the term is mentioned. They are not far off. The word is Hebrew and
means "tradition"—an oral tradition present among the
Jewish people, the origin of which has been lost in time.
In very early Jewish history, Cabala was, as one specialist
nicely puts it, "the traditional framework into which were

God's attributes equal = emanations (Beings)

placed all the laws and new ideas that in the course of the centuries associated themselves with the Bible, particularly the Pentateuch ... a kind of very flexible chain capable of receiving as many links as one wished, providing that the links did not, at least in outward appearance, seem too out of proportion with those already in place." [2] As diametrically opposed groups as the Talmudists and the Karaites applied the term Cabala to their beliefs in order to give them greater authority.

Later, Cabala became more specific in meaning: "a type of mysticism which strikes one from the outset by its abstract metaphysic infinitely removed from Jewish doctrinal orthodoxy as well as from earlier Jewish mysticism, yet reconcilable with both if one is aware of the astonishing elasticity of Jewish thought and the flexible interpretive method the Jews applied to their sacred texts." [3] In the form which it achieved at its maturity, and the one which influenced Christian scholars in the Renaissance, Cabala can be divided into three aspects: the emanation (*sephiroth*) doctrine, the methods for interpreting the Scriptures, and the Redeemer doctrine. More commonly Cabala is divided into a "theoretical" and "practical" aspect. Karppe's definition of the latter will make clear their relationship to the three divisions just given. Karppe speaks of "the theory focusing on God and His attributes, and a practice occupied with theurgic and magical techniques." [4] In the following discussion I shall employ the threefold rather than the twofold division for the sake of greater precision.

The Emanation (Sephiroth) Doctrine. The Cabalists conceived of God's attributes being actual emanations from Him. These emanations were, in a sense, beings *per se*. They were produced by a voluntary retraction or self-limitation of God; this retraction was the birth-pain of creation. To the Cabalists, God was the infinite, the boundless, the limitless, the En or Aïn Soph. The following diagram represents the *sephiroth* as they were most generally conceived. The lower particular emanation, the more removed it is from God's sublimity and transcendence and therefore the less perfect it is. [5]

Key

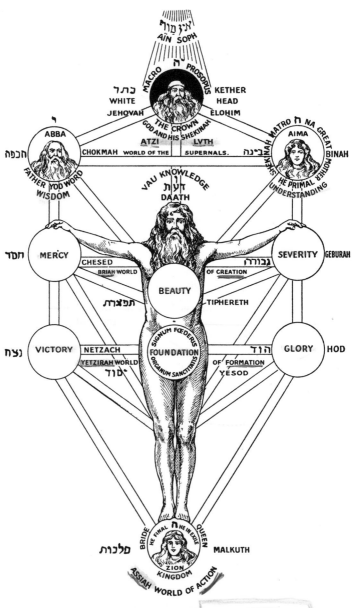

THE SACRED TREE OF THE SEPHIROTH

The entire ten emanations were repeated on four levels so that there were forty regressions from God to our world. These four realms were termed, in order of descent, *atziluth* (the world of supernals), *briah* (the world of creation), *yetzirah* (the world of formation), and *assiah* (the world of material action). "A variant scheme, which seems to be more closely related to non-Jewish thought, limits the number of worlds to three, the worlds of angels, celestial bodies, and elements. This is the presentation of this subject given by Menahem Recanati." [6]

What led to development of such a complex (and apparently bizarre) understanding of God's creative activity? At least two factors were at work. First was the problem of God's attributes as formulated at Alexandria. In that rationalistic environment, Jews came to conceive of their God as utterly transcendent; they went beyond the traditional, Old Testament notion of an imminent-eminent God.[7]

> Not until the Jew was placed in a philosophically keener environment, in Alexandria, did the concept of transcendence, toward which the Jewish view of the nature of God had been unconsciously moving, enter openly into the theological picture. Not until then was the reconciliation of the two aspects of God by reason rather than by faith necessary.[8]

It is well to note that the term transcendent can have a number of meanings; the following series will assist in clarifying terminology:

Imminence—
   God is very close to man.

Eminence—
   God is much more lofty than man (but this in no way limits His contact with man).

Transcendence—
   God very seldom has contact with man, *or*
   God never has had contact with man, *or*
   God cannot logically have contact with man.

It was the third of the above definitions of transcendence which the Jews embraced at Alexandria, and Jewish belief has been plagued by it ever since.[9] The Old Testament does not present such a conception of deity. Clearly God must in some sense descend to man to reveal His will, but a doctrine of extreme transcendence keeps God from descending, at least in the sense of entering into time, for if He were to do so, He would cease to be God.[10] The conflict between an imminent and transcendent God demanded a resolution. This need for resolution undoubtedly had a strong emotional element in it, for God had become as far away at Alexandria as He could logically be. However, because of the rational environment of Alexandria, and because of the flat logical contradiction which had entered the Jewish notion of deity (imminence-eminence vs. extreme transcendence), we are safe in assuming that the question of resolution was more an intellectual than an emotional one. An emanation doctrine seemed to provide a way to escape the horns of the dilemma. Philo of Alexandria was the well-known exponent of one emanation doctrine.[11] The *sephiroth* provided another. "The *sephiroth* combined both aspects of previous emanation theories; they reveal God to the earnest seeker through gradually more exalted attributes and thus provide a way from man to God; they are also the intermediaries by means of which God's intervention in human affairs takes place, and thus they provide a way for God to man." [12]

The second, and immediate, cause of the growth of *sephiroth* teaching was Talmudic legalism, ritualism, and intellectual slavery, which reached a peak about 1200—at the very time the *sephiroth* and systematic Cabalism rose to clearest prominence. The *sephiroth* doctrine was a revolt against the Talmudists; it was "modern" in approach and purpose, in the sense that it emphasized faith and love against law, and freedom of spirit.[13] Karppe effectively argues that "the Cabala is above all an opposition to Talmudic casuistry—or, if you prefer, a kind of revolt of faith against law. . . . Since the school of Rashi and the Tosaphists had created a scaffolding of interpretations on interpretations, commentaries, supercommentaries, and hypercommentaries, and Maimonides' Mishna had catalogued and labeled everything,

Talmudic scholasticism had become walled in, suffocating, deadly. The Cabalists broke down that wall behind which one could no longer breathe." [14] It is apparent, therefore, that the Cabala was both rationally and emotionally motivated. Further evidence in support of this assertion is the fact that the cabalists had within their ranks both the unsystematic-mystic (e.g., the author or authors of the *Zohar*)[15] and the systematic-rational (e.g., Moses Cordovero).[16]

To recapitulate: at Alexandria, the Jews made their God utterly transcendent, and then felt the necessity of explaining rationally His transcendent, yet imminent, nature. Then, at a time when Jewish legalism, ritualism, and intellectual slavery was at a peak, the *sephiroth* notion appeared. The *sephiroth* satisfied many Jews by seeming to provide the most satisfactory solution possible for the imminence-transcendence problem, and gave a more immediate and pleasurable approach to God which by-passed the legalistic methods and intellectual confinements of the Talmudists.

The Methods of Interpreting Scripture. This aspect of the Cabala is the most well-known, even though one probably has not heard the name Cabala applied to it. As a matter of fact, the symbolism of numbers made up such an important part of the Cabala that at least one scholar has considered it to be equivalent to the Cabala itself.[17] The basic presupposition for the validity of the methods to follow is the verbal inspiration of the Torah. The Jewish belief in this fact was so strong that the *Sefer Yetsirah*, one of the most important cabalistic texts, presents at its very beginning a theory of creation in which the letters play an active part: "By means of thirty-two mysterious paths of wisdom [the twenty-two letters, plus ten sefirot, or vowels] did the Lord of hosts ... ordain to create His Universe." "The twenty-two fundamental letters God appointed, established, combined, weighed, and changed, and through them he formed all things existent and destined to exist."[18]

Three primary Cabalistic methods of interpreting the

Bible were employed. We shall examine each in turn.[19]
(1) Gematria. Trachtenberg defines gematria thus: "A process of creating equivalences from the numerical values of words."[20] Gematria involved the fact that in ancient languages such as Hebrew, Latin, and Greek, the letters of the alphabet also represented numbers. An example of this method is the proof that *God* is solely *good* and the *first* of all beings, for *Yahveh*$=1+5+6+5=17$; *tov* ("good")$=9+6+2=17$; *rishon* ("first")$=2+1+3+6+5=17$. The seven most common ways of employing gematria were the following: (a) Simple addition (as in the example just given). (b) The sum of the letters plus 1 for the word. (c) The sum of the letters plus the number of letters in the word. Sometimes (b) and (c) were joined. (d) Addition of the values of the *names* of the letters (the first letter of the Hebrew alphabet, *aleph* = 111). (e) Addition of the cardinal numbers. By a combination of (d) and (e) one can "prove" that the letter *yod* mathematically represents the "crown" of glory. (f) Adding the values of all the letters in the alphabet which proceed each letter of the word. (g) Adding the squares of the numerical values.

(2) Notarikon. Notarikon is an acrostic system. "The initial or final letters of the words of a phrase might be joined to form a word which was then given occult significance. The significance of another word might be explained by expanding it into a phrase, using each letter of the original word as initial letter of one word of the phrase."[21]

(3) Themurah ("Transposition"). Themurah consists of "transposing the letters of a word . . . or more frequently, replacing them with artificial equivalents obtained from one or another of a group of formal anagrams."[22] The six most popular types of replacement were the following: (a) By folding the alphabet in the center and placing one-half below the other, we obtain a "code" in which corresponding letters on the upper and lower lines could be substituted for each other in interpreting a Scripture passage. (b) The lower line could be reversed and similar substitutions made. (c) The alphabet was divided into *three* equal parts, the last letter

not being used. Any one of the three letters in each unit might be substituted for another. (d) An arrangement based on the same principle as (c), but with the final letter included. (e) Each letter in a word could be replaced by the letter immediately succeeding it in the alphabet.

These five replacements were by no means the only ones employed. Some Cabalists even made replacements based on the *shape* of letters. Moreover, in analyzing a given passage a Cabalist did not necessarily confine himself to only one of the above methods; a combination of techniques could be used in interpreting the same verse.

In order to understand why gematria, notarikon, and themurah came to be employed, we must know precisely to what use they were put. These methods were used for two prime purposes: first and foremost, to derive from the Scriptures a hidden, occult meaning; second, to validate the Scriptures as literally inspired of God by showing the remarkable numerical relationships which presumably existed in them. More specifically, the very reverence held by the Jews for the Torah explains why they should have invented such methods. The nature of their belief in the Bible made them desire to get every possible meaning from it and to demonstrate its divine origin in every possible way. Scholem says:

> All Jewish mystics, from the Therapeutae, whose doctrine was described by Philo of Alexandria to the latest Hasid, are at one in giving a mystical interpretation to the Torah; the Torah is to them a living organism animated by a secret life which streams and pulsates below the crust of its literal meaning; every one of the innumerable strata of this hidden region corresponds to a new and profound meaning of the Torah. The Torah, in other words, does not consist merely of chapters, phrases and words; rather it is to be regarded as the living incarnation of the Divine wisdom which eternally sends out new rays of light. It is not merely the historical law of the Chosen People, although it is that too; it is rather the cosmic law of the Universe, as God's wisdom conceived it. Each configuration of letters in it, whether it makes sense in human speech or not, symbolizes some aspect of God's creative power which is active in the universe.[23]

We have seen that the immediate cause of the rise of the Cabala was a reaction against Talmudic casuistry and intellectual calcification; thus, about 1200, these two approaches to Biblical interpretation vied with each other in Jewish circles, both of them attempting to discover a maximum amount of data and proof of the authenticity of the Scriptures. The Cabala, in reaction to the Talmudic approach, emphasized the text itself (the letters, words, their numerical equivalents, etc.) instead of making attempts at allegorical interpretation and extension of the text to cover specific problems.

Although the Cabalists were more concerned with the letters of the text than were the Talmudists, they were certainly not literal interpreters of it. The Karaites— another movement reacting against Talmudic casuistry— were the extreme literalists of the Jewish tradition; their concern was limited to the surface meaning of the text. For example, the Karaites would light no fires on the Sabbath, even in the coldest climate, because the Torah states that fires should not be lit on that day. The Talmudists, in their characteristic way, asserted that it was all right to light fires the day before the Sabbath, and let them burn on the Sabbath. A Cabalist, faced with the passage in question, would have worked the gematrias of the Hebrew words for "fire," "light," etc., and would then have derived a "hidden" meaning from them. Why did not the Cabalists take the simple, straightforward, literal approach of the Karaites? Why did they maintain a mid-position between the Karaites and Talmudists? Just as the casuistry of the Talmudists drove the Cabalists to their right, the rationalistic and scholarly attitude of mind which the Cabalists inherited from Alexandria and employed in formulating the *sephiroth* doctrine would not permit them to be satisfied with the simple and unsophisticated approach of the Karaites.

The Doctrine of Redemption. This Cabalistic doctrine does not require special treatment here, since it is already familiar through the Old Testament expectation of a coming Redeemer. The Cabala "in its original form" [24] did not alter the Old Testament conception; it simply placed new emphasis on the expectation, and devoted its exegetical techniques to gain greater knowledge of the Saviour who would come.[25] The reason that a doctrine of redemption loomed large in Cabalism is undoubtedly connected with the fact that Cabala arose in a time of excessive legalism, ritualism, and intellectual rigidity. In times of dissatisfaction, Jews have looked forward with greatest expectation to One who would usher in a new era.

THE BAPTISM OF THE CABALA BY PICO OF MIRANDOLA

The Cabala entered the Christian tradition through the work of one of the most remarkable figures of the Italian High Renaissance. Giovanni Pico della Mirandola lived only thirty-one years (1463-1494) but he typified in every way the ideal Renaissance man. All knowledge was his province—and esoteric knowledge in particular; he published no fewer than nine hundred theses on all manner of topics and was even willing to pay the travel expenses of those who wished to debate with him. His Oration on the Dignity of Man was a classic defense of man's free-will, and has been taken by many to be the Renaissance declaration of man's independence from the stifling medieval synthesis. He wrote a major work against astrology in the same vein: man was free even of stellar and cosmic control. He was a close friend of Ficino, the leading light in the Platonic Academy at Florence who did so much to revive Neo-Platonic mysticism during the Renaissance. Three years before his death, Pico underwent experiential conversion which put Christ rather than man at the center of his life. His confessor in his last illness was the great revival preacher of Florence, Savonarola. So impressed by his career was Sir Thomas More that he translated G. F. Pico's biography of him, thereby making him a model for the English Renaissance.[26]

Pico's importance for the history of the Cabala has been well summarized by Blau:

> Whatever had been done before his time, it was Pico who first attracted his fellow humanists in any con-

siderable number to the cabala. His contemporaries and immediate followers with one accord agree with his statement that he was the first of the Latins to have mentioned cabala. It is particularly noteworthy that Pico's interpretation of the cabala gained so firm a hold on the minds of his period that Ricci, writing about 1510, had to defend his far more competent work in the cabala against the accusation that it was not cabalistic, because he had included material which Pico did not mention.[27]

Where did Pico acquire his knowledge of the Cabala? To answer this question we need to say a word about the fortunes of the Cabalistic tradition from its emergence as a developed and mature philosophy about 1200 until Pico's own day. At the outset we have the three famous Cabalistic schools—that of Isaac the Blind (fl. 1190-1210) with his disciples Ezra and Asariel, that of Eleazar of Worms (fl. ca. 1220), and that of Abraham ben Samuel Abulafia (1240-ca. 1292). "To this school belonged Joseph ben Abraham Gikatilia (ca. 1247-1305), whose works formed the major background of John Reuchlin's studies in the cabala." [28] Karppe says:

> In the interval separating the confusion of Jewish mysticism before the Cabala from the even greater confusion of the *Zohar*, we glimpse a certain attempt at system and classification which allows three schools to be distinguished: (1) the school of Isaac the Blind— one could call it the metaphysical school, not in that metaphysics was its exclusive focus but because metaphysics predominated there; (2) the school of Eleazar of Worms, which devoted itself particularly to the mysticism of letters and numbers; and (3) the school of Abulafia which combined both of these interests and developed them in the direction of pure contemplation.[29]

The writing of the *Sefer ha-Zohar* (the "Book of Splendor" or "Book of Light"), the most important single Cabalistic work, marks the next point in the history of the Cabala. It was presented to the world about the end of the 13th century. "The Zohar is not a single book; it does not develop a consistent system, but behind its repetitive and discursive comment there lies a theosophical doctrine which is a riot of lush esotericism." [30]

Around this work there arose "the school of the Zohar," which combined and absorbed all the features and doctrines of the Cabalistic schools which had preceded it. Menahem ben Benjamin of Recanati (ca. 1290-ca. 1350), who wrote a Bible commentary based on the *Zohar*, was the most illustrious member of this school.

It is generally conceded that Menahem was Pico's chief source for the Cabala. Blau says:

> The point is made by Gaffarel in the seventeenth century
> and by Anagnine in the twentieth that the major source
> in Hebrew cabalistic literature for the conclusions of
> Pico was the Bible commentary by Menahem Recanati.
> It is important to mention this only because Menahem's
> commentary is not an original work by a simplification of
> the Zohar. Pico's source may be said, therefore, to be
> a watered-down version of the cardinal document of the
> cabala. The Zohar, however, is thoroughly unsystematic;
> it is a lush and luxuriant jungle of mystical ideas, often
> brilliant, often mutually inconsistent. The same comment
> would apply, to a lesser degree, to Pico's conclusions . . .
> Although this work is broadly symbolic, it is cabalistic
> only with respect to the doctrine of the worlds therein
> presented.[31]

In her work, *The Library of Pico della Mirandola*, Pearl Kibre writes:

> There were . . . writings on cabala by Abraham
> Abulafia ben Samuel, thirteenth-century grammarian and
> philosopher as well as cabalist; by Nathan, probably
> Abigdor ben Nathan of Avignon who compiled mystical
> notes on the Commandments; and Recanati, identified
> by Dukas as Rabbi Menahem, a native of Recanate
> (d. 1290). He was the author of a commentary on the
> Pentateuch in mystical vein and is named by Pico among
> the writers on cabala.[32]

At this point Cabala enters into Christian thinking, since Pico was "mediator and introducer of cabalism to the Christian world." [33]

How extensive a knowledge of the Cabala did Pico have? Let us look at the Cabalistic content of three of his most important works: the *Heptaplus* (a "rhapsodic treatment of the Biblical account of creation" [34]), his 900 Theses, and his *Apology* in behalf of his Theses.

Cabalism in the Heptaplus. The *Heptaplus* manifests

the smallest amount of Cabalistic knowledge as compared with the Theses and *Apologia*. Here a "doctrine of the worlds" is presented, following Menahem of Recanati and classical sources. Although the ten *sephiroth* which provide the Cabalistic inner structure of each world, are not mentioned, the three worlds themselves are clearly delineated. Pico states that the "angelic" (or "intellectual") world, the "celestial" world, and the "sublunary" world arise from the same source, and consist of the same material; they differ in the degree of purity of this material.[35] The connection between this fact and the creation of worlds by emanation in Cabalism is obviously very strong.

Cabalism in the Theses. In the "Conclusions" or Theses, Pico demonstrates that he knows not only the outlines of doctrine of the worlds, but also the *sephiroth* conception; he shows us that he is acquainted with the approach of number exegesis (although he does not distinguish the three major techniques); and he goes to great length to prove that the Messiahship of Jesus and the other cardinal points of Christian doctrine are supported by the Cabala. It is highly significant that no less than 47 of the 900 Theses are directly and explicitly drawn from Cabalistic sources, and 72 others involve Pico's own deductions from these sources.[36]

Cabalism in the Apologia. Owing to the inclusion of one Cabalistic thesis among the thirteen which were at first condemned as heretical (exoneration came eventually), we are fortunate to have in Pico's *Apology* his defense of Cabalism. Here he demonstrates most clearly his command of Cabalistic learning. Blau notwithstanding, Pico presents a beautifully systematic discussion, which may be outlined as follows: [37]

1 Lack of knowledge of the Cabala on the part of those who criticize Pico.
2 Brief historical definition of the Cabala.
3 Testimonies of authorities to the validity and orthodoxy of the Cabala (Esdras, Paul, Origen, Hilary, Matthew).
4 Expanded historical definition of the Cabala.
5 Cabalistic interpretation parallels the accepted anagogical method.[38]

6 Answering two objections:
 a If Cabala attests the Christiain faith, why aren't
   all Jewish Cabalists Christians?
 b Why don't Augustine, Jerome, and other doctors
   of the Church mention the Cabala?
7 Final clarification: the various meanings of the term
 Cabala, its two valid senses, and its false appropriation
 by necromancers.

At the very conclusion of his discussion of Cabalism
in the *Apologia*, Pico shows that he is acquainted with
not merely the traditional, but also the actual history
of the Cabala in Judaism. He says that the term Cabala
was usurped by many who are not Cabalists at all, and
that it came to refer to any form of Jewish occultism.
He affirms that the true Cabala has two divisions—
divisions corresponding to what is today called the "theoretical" and "practical" Cabala. Thus Pico understands
fully both Cabalistic history, and the inner structure of
Cabala in its more mature form.

WHAT IS THE CABALA WORTH?

Now that we have some idea both of Cabalistic teachings and of their entrance into Christian context through
Pico's work, we must face the hard question of evaluating
this important occult subject. How many Jews and Christians and esoteric searchers for truth have wandered
in Cabalistic labyrinths! Can such wanderings be justified? If not, can historical understanding at least be
brought to bear on the motivations involved?

*The Truth-Value of the Emanation (Sephiroth) Doc-
trine.* This Cabalistic doctrine must be rejected on two
counts. First, its truth is not sufficiently attested by Scriptural revelation, the only means by which such a metaphysical concept could in principle be verified.[39] The
Bible does not mention the *sephiroth* anywhere within
it, and, more important, the tenor of some passages of
Scripture seems definitely to contradict such a notion.
Observe the following:

> There is one God, and one mediator between God and men,
> the man Christ Jesus. (I Tim. 2:5)

> Let no man beguile you of your reward in a voluntary
> humility and worshipping of angels, intruding into those
> things which he hath not seen, vainly puffed up by his fleshly
> mind, and not holding the Head, from which all the body
> by joints and bands having nourishment ministered, and
> knit together, increaseth with the increase of God. (Col.
> 2:18-19)

One might argue that the Bible does not expressly declare that the *sephiroth* doctrine is false; but the danger of believing unfounded religious doctrines must be emphasized. Religious doctrines are concerned with the most important matters in the universe, and we should "believe not every spirit, but try the spirits whether they are of God: because many false prophets are gone out into the world" (I John 4:1). When the statements of tradition are concerned with the most lofty of religious issues (e.g., God's nature, creation, revelation) we should be particularly careful not to believe what is unverified. If such traditions were true, they would undoubtedly appear in or be attested by the infallible authority, since they deal with such high matters. The more lofty the religious statements which tradition makes, the more mistrustful we should be of them, for the more harm can be done if we accept them and they are false. We may come to have the wrong emphasis on the most important matters in the universe.

Secondly, the *sephiroth* doctrine is not logically necessitated by the nature of the Jewish or Christian faiths. The *sephiroth* are a "construct"—an attempt to solve a problem which their creators believed insoluable without their aid. Constructs, even if they have no direct empirical support, are not to be rejected *per se*. If a construct succeeds in explaining something inexplicable without it, it certainly deserves credence.[40] But if a construct does not succeed in doing the job for which it was invented, or if the job itself is an unnecessary one, we should certainly reject the construct. The *sephiroth* doctrine falls into this category. We saw earlier that the Old Testament concept of God never extends beyond eminence, and the New Testament sets forth no more than an incarnationally qualified transcendence.

The *sephiroth* doctrine is an attempt to explain the nature of a God who is both imminent and *transcendent to the degree that he cannot have contact with man and remain God.* This latter view of God is not justified by either the Jewish or Christian Scriptures; it was the product of rationalism at Alexandria. Since an imminent-eminent conception of God does not require logical resolution, and since Christ "shows us the Father" in the New Testament (John 14:8-11, etc.), the *sephiroth* doctrine is unnecessary. It attempts to explain a problem which need not be a problem for either the Jew or the Christian. Furthermore, even if the problem of an imminent-extremely transcendent God were a real one, the *sephiroth* would not solve it. Imminence and extreme transcendence are logically contradictory concepts,[41] and to say that God retracted himself in the beginning, producing *sephiroth* of varying degrees of perfection extending down to the material universe, is merely to beg the question.

The Truth-Value of the Cabalistic Exegetical Techniques. Gematria, notarikon, and themurah must also be rejected, and for three reasons. First, there is no Scriptural justification[42] for Hebrew being the "sacred language."[43] The Tower of Babel incident resulted in the "confounding" of the original language, which implies certainly that no tongue existent after that time would show forth the original language with any degree of purity. And if a post-Babel language did show forth the original tongue more than others, there would be no way to prove it, because the record implies that no speakers of the pure original language were left for comparison.[44] But even if Hebrew were a "sacred language," the written form of it would not necessarily have the identical sacral qualities of the spoken language; and even if written Hebrew were more sacred than other languages, its sacredness would not have to extend past perfect clarity of expression: "sacred" would not have to mean "capable of being interpreted by the Cabalistic exegetical techniques."

Secondly, just because the Scriptures claim that they are the only infallible revelation of God, does not mean that they should be interpreted by Cabalistic techniques. Infallibility certainly does not *logically necessitate* that there be numerical symbolism and numerical relationships in the words of the text, or that by arranging the letters in its words one will discover hidden meanings. Infallibility refers to *accuracy*. Because Scripture is unique—God's only written revelation—it is only reasonable not to apply to it methods of interpretation which are not justified or advocated by the Book itself, and Scripture does not advocate or even mention Cabalistic exegetical techniques. The Cabalists imposed these methods on the text from without. Hopper's argument can be applied to the Old Testament as well as to the New:

> Later New Testament exegeticists were able to discover numerical secrets everywhere in the life and preachings of Jesus, but it is obvious to the most casual reader that such scholarly interpretation is utterly at variance with the spirit of naïveté and directness which distinguishes the scriptural accounts. The Pauline epistles, earliest and most certainly authentic of the original records, are completely innocent of number theory. The synoptical Gospels, together with . . . John and the Acts, all first-century compositions, do contain numbers, but these are "symbolic" numbers only in the most elementary sense.[45]

Ironically, the Cabalists felt justified in applying their methods to the Bible because it claimed to be a unique Book, God's sole written revelation, whereas the very fact that the Bible is a divine product is one of the strongest warnings against such approaches to its contents.

Thirdly, one gets from the use of Cabalistic techniques just what he puts into them through his presuppositions; thus the exegetical methods of Cabalism are not capable of yielding truth. Trachtenberg says: "The possible number of permutations and substitutions is endless, and when we realize that all of these methods, Notarikon, Gematria, and Temurah (the three were usually lumped together as Gematria during the Middle Ages), may be used together, the possibilities are breathtaking.[46] The innumerable different and indeed contradictory interpretations which could be derived through the use of the Cabalistic exegetical techniques—and which had indeed been derived by Jews and Christians—should have suggested to scholars like Pico the fallacy of the procedure.

But lest we become too smug in our judgment upon him, we would do well to note that his successors have benefitted even less than he from past experience. Though it may seem incredible, the very Cabalist numerical devices Pico employed in biblical interpretation have reappeared at intervals not only in esoteric and occult contexts[47] but also in evangelical Christian circles right to the present time.

On the eve of the 20th century, E. W. Bullinger, an Anglican clergyman and direct descendent of the great Bullinger of the Swiss Reformation, produced his book, *Number in Scripture* (1894), in which, along with valid remarks concerning the symbolic character of certain numbers in the Bible (3, 7, 40 etc.), Cabalistic operations are carried out which might even have made Pico blush. Pico would have been quite satisfied with Bullinger's employment of gematria (the number of Nimrod's name is "294, or 42 x 7; it will be often found as a factor in the Anti-christian names"; "it is remarkable that the numerical value of the 'Song of Moses.' (Exod. xv. 1-18) is 41626, which is the product of the significant factors 13 x 42 x 70"; etc., etc.). But would Pico, as representative of the Renaissance era when the search for ancient manuscripts was the means by which the first printed edition of the Greek text of the New Testament was produced (Erasmus' *Novum Instrumentum* of 1516)—would even Pico have tried to establish biblical authorship by numerics? Bullinger can seriously argue: "Of the 21 Epistles of the New Testament 14 (2 x 7) are by Paul, and *seven* by other writers. In this we have an argument for the Pauline authorship of the Epistle to the Hebrews."[48] What is perhaps even more remarkable, Bullinger's *Number in Scripture* was photolithographically reprinted—with no revisions or even a new preface to warn readers of its questionable arguments—by a reputable American evangelical publisher in 1967! And interest in the work has been sufficient to warrant a second printing in 1969.

Evangelical Protestant periodicals occasionally publish articles dealing with the "remarkable attestations" of the truth of the Bible provided by the lifelong labors of the Russian mathematician Ivan Panin. Panin, after his conversion, worked out a system of "Bible Numerics" which differs in no essentials from the Cabalism we have been discussing. He produced numerous publications on this subject in the early decades of this century (most of which were ignored by serious scholarship) and even went to the length of establishing a final critical text of the New Testament on the basis of numerical considerations. For example, Panin argued that since the Westcott and Hort revision of the Greek text [49] includes 897 words in chapters one and two of St. Matthew's Gospel, and since

$$897 = 23 \times 3 \times 13 = 13 \times 69 = (7 \times 8 \times 8 \times 2)^{+1} =$$
$$(8 \times 8 \times 2 \times 7)^{+1},$$

"distinct schemes of twenty-threes, thirteens, eights, and sevens run through these 897 words"; thus the exact number of words in such text sections can be established on the basis of the fact that "a single change in any one of the numbers vitiates" the numerical results.[50]

Such operations are truly pitiful in our day when the problems of Cabalistic number interpretation have been so well known for so long. It does the legitimate arguments for the inerrancy of Holy Writ [51] no service to associate them with bizarre techniques that could as well "prove" the inerrancy of the daily newspaper. Pico's Cabalism is perhaps comprehensible and forgivable in terms of his epoch; modern repetitions or even extensions of it warrant no parallel consideration. To make certain mistakes graciously, you must live in the right historical period.

Why Pico Believed in the Cabala. At the beginning of his work Blau states: "Like astrology, alchemy, and other pseudo-sciences, cabala fell a legitimate victim to the development of scientific thinking." [52] Yet Cabalist Pico's longest work was written against the astrologers.[53]

In the face of this paradox, we must certainly accept Greswell's evaluation of Pico's intellectual honesty:

> For the aversion which Picus manifested to the science
> of astrology, several futile reasons have been assigned by
> writers, who ignorant of his true character, knew not that
> he was incapable of yielding to any other motives than his
> love of truth. Some pretend that the astrologers having
> adduced certain of his Theses published at Rome, in favour
> of their superstition, he thought himself obliged thus
> publicly to disavow the imputation. Others allege that he
> had himself discovered by the science in question, that he
> was destined to die young; and took up his pen against it
> out of pure resentment. Others, not aware of these motives,
> pretend that the astrologers, alarmed by his meditated
> attack upon them, and consulting together upon the most
> effectual means of repelling it, resolved upon calculating
> his nativity; and sent him the result by one of their order,
> Lucius Bellantius of Sienna: and subsequent events, it is
> added, justified their prediction. These contradictions
> sufficiently refute themselves.[54]

As we observed earlier, it was Pico's recognition, as a child of the Renaissance, that astrology could be employed to dehumanize man that caused him to reject it. In our day he would have been an equal opponent of Skinner's behaviorism! But why was not Pico aware of the apparently no less obvious failings of the Cabala? It is important to note, in the first place, that Pico did not exercise belief in the Cabala without what he believed to be excellent historical justification. Passages in the (to him infallible) Apocrypha made him feel that God had given an oral law to Moses, which Esdras finally wrote down; [55] and since he believed that this law was neither the Talmud nor the approach of the Jewish philosophers, by process of elimination the Cabala obtained divine attestation in his eyes. The force of this evidence apparently prevented Pico from recognizing the truth of the objections leveled at Cabalism above, and from seeing that before accepting as God's revelation the whole of Jewish Cabalism as it was in his day, he should have determined accurately the age and source of its several doctrines. Even though Pico understood well that during Jewish history the term Cabala had been appropriated by those who were clearly not Cabalists, he did not attempt to analyze the Cabalism of his day to see what elements in it were the result of human accretion rather than divine revelation. Thus he gave himself over to error. In fairness to the Phoenix, we must admit, however, that his mistake was that of an age—an age whose passing virtually coincided with Pico's own demise. Walter Pater rightly says: "The scholars of the fifteenth century . . . lacked the very rudiments of the historic sense, which by an imaginative act throws itself back into a world unlike one's own, and judges each intellectual product in connection with the age which produced it; they had no idea of development, of the differences of ages, of the gradual education of the human race.[56]

Other factors contributed as well to Pico's interest in the Cabala. During his time the church placed particularly great emphasis upon the validity of tradition—tradition which was hardly if at all justified by the Bible. This was one of the chief causes of the Protestant Reformation, the storm clouds of which were forming on the horizon in Pico's own lifetime. But Pico was not a Luther, or even a Savonarola, and tradition held him in its grip. Three years before he published his 900 Theses there was born in the sleepy little German village of Eisleben one who would prepare 95 Theses that would shake the world and bring the towers of tradition crumbling down. By then, however, Pico would lie shrouded in the monk's habit in which Savonarola invested his remains, waiting on the Last Trump when all mysteries shall be revealed.

The emphasis upon non-literal interpretation of the Bible, which had developed during the Middle Ages, was an invitation to scholars like Pico to accept the techniques of gematria, notarikon, and themurah. It is of more than passing significance that in the *Apologia* Pico attempts to justify Cabalistic interpretation of the Bible by paralleling it with the anagogical method, which, together with the literal, allegorical, and tropological, provided the basis for almost all medieval exposition of Scripture.[57] The Protestant Reformation, but not the scholarship of the 15th century, saw the fallacies in this fourfold interpretative approach, and one of its major aims was a return to the literal interpretation of the Bible. Indeed, Cabalism serves as an almost classic example of the potential evils of non-literal interpretation. Again Pico is seen as a victim of his age.[58]

Moreover, Pico's "period was transitional in the history of thought. A new sense of the past was developing and, concurrently, a new sense of the future. The old order was changing, but had not yet given place to the new. At such a time, any road looks fair and worthy to be explored. Of cabala this might well have seemed true more than of most other roads. For cabala had a Hebrew source, and Hebrew was recognized by scholarship of the time as the oldest of languages, as the language of divine revelation." [59]

Finally, the overwhelming tendency of the Renaissance in general and of Pico in particular towards eclecticism and syncretism caused him to see truth in systems where actually there was little or none. This approach to truth seemed to grip him and become his master, whereas the reverse should have been true. But it is this very love of all things human which has prevented and will always prevent Pico from being forgotten. Pater's statements on this theme provide a fitting epitaph for the greatest of the Christian Cabalists:

It is said that in his eagerness for mysterious learning he once paid a great sum for a collection of cabalistic manuscripts which turned out to be forgeries; and the story might well stand as a parable of all he ever seemed to gain in the way of actual knowledge. He had sought knowledge, and passed from system to system, and hazarded much; but less for the sake of positive knowledge than because he believed there was a spirit of order and beauty in knowledge, which would come down and unite what men's ignorance had divided, and renew what time had made dim. . . . He seems never to have doubted that nothing which has ever interested living men and women can wholly lose its vitality—no language they have spoken, nor oracle by which they have hushed their voices, no dream which has once been entertained by actual human minds, nothing about which they have ever been passionate or expended time and zeal.[60]

4

The Stars and the Hermetic Tradition

Trust not to all astrologers, *I saie whie,*
For that Arte is an secreat as Alkimy.

—Thomas Norton, *The Ordinall of Alchimy*

Among the occult arts, a few have such long and influential histories and such complex and involved techniques that they stand apart. This is true of the Cabala, with whose emanationism and numerical interpretation of the Bible we have just had contact. It is even more true of those twin pillars of all occultism, alchemy and astrology. Cabala is limited primarily to the Jewish, and secondarily to the Christian, tradition; astrology and alchemy are ubiquitous: they are to be found virtually everywhere occultism is to be found. Thus an examination of the beliefs of the alchemists and astrologers will help us greatly to understand the mentality of the occult, and it will also afford us the opportunity to observe the character of the occult secret society, since the Rosicrucian Order—that prototype of all occult fraternities—arose out of the age-old alchemical quest for the Philosopher's Stone.

ALCHEMY: GOLD FROM DROSS [1]

Most everyone knows at least one thing about alchemy—that alchemists tried "to turn lead into gold."

The vain and bizarre efforts in this direction became part of our literary heritage through Chaucer's "Canon's Yeoman's Tale" and Ben Jonson's play, *The Alchemist*. Often as a result, the labors of the alchemists have been sold short. Even when engaged in apparently ridiculous experimentation, the "sons of Hermes" often contributed mightily to the growth of modern chemistry. It was the boiling of toads in urine that brought about the discovery of ammonia! The great German chemist Justus von Liebig rightly observed in his *Familiar Letters in Chemistry* that "in order to know that the Philosopher's Stone did not really exist, it was indispensable that every substance accessible . . . should be observed and examined."

Moreover, there is the real possibility that some of the endeavors to transmute baser elements into silver or gold actually succeeded—by chemical means kept secret and now lost to us or by occult techniques. The number of carefully recorded cases of alchemical transmutation is remarkably high and we today—living in an age of open, relativistic, Einsteinian possibility in which atomic fission has brought about genuine transmutations by physical means[2]—are in a poor position to assert dogmatically that no alchemical successes were ever achieved. The reproduction of one of these antique accounts here should be of more than routine interest; its author was the distinguished Dutch physician J. F. Helvetius, who published it at The Hague in 1667:

> On the 27th December 1666, in the afternoon, a stranger,
> in a plain, rustic dress, came to my house at the Hague.
> His manner of address was honest, grave, and authoritative;
> his stature was low, with a long face and hair black, his
> chin smooth. He seemed like a native of the north of
> Scotland, and I guessed he was about forty-four years old.
> After saluting me, he requested me most respectfully to
> pardon his rude intrusion, but that his love of the
> pyrotechnic art made him visit me. Having read some of
> my small treatises, particularly that against the sympathetic
> powder of Sir Kenelm Digby, and observed therein my doubt
> of the Hermetic mystery, it caused him to request this
> interview. . . . As soon as his relation was finished, I asked
> my visitor to show me the effect of transmutation. . . .
> When I perceived that all this was in vain, I earnestly

Figure 5. "The Discovery of Phosphorus," by Wright

requested a small crumb of his powder, sufficient to
transmute a few grains of lead to gold; and at last, out
of his philosophical commiseration, he gave me as much
as a turnip seed in size, saying, "Receive this small parcel
of the greatest treasure of the world, which truly few kings
or princes have ever seen or known." "But," I said, "this
perhaps will not transmute four grains of lead," whereupon
he bid me deliver it back to him, which, in hopes of a
greater parcel, I did; but he, cutting half off with his nail,
flung it into the fire, and gave me the rest wrapped neatly
up in blue paper, saying, "It is yet sufficient for
thee" . . . . I commanded a fire to be made, saying to myself,
"I fear, I fear indeed, this man hath deluded me." My
wife wrapped the said matter in wax, and I cut half an
ounce of lead, and put it into a crucible in the fire. Being
melted, my wife put in the medicine, made into a small
pill with the wax, which presently made a hissing noise,
and in a quarter of an hour the mass of lead was totally
transmuted into the best and finest gold, which amazed
us exceedingly. We could not sufficiently gaze upon this
admirable and miraculous work of nature, for the melted
lead, after projection, showed on the fire the rarest and
most beautiful colours imaginable, settling in green, and
when poured forth into an ingot, it had the lively fresh
colour of blood. When cold it shined as the purest and most
splendid gold. Truly all those who were standing about me
were exceedingly startled, and I ran with this aurified lead,
being yet hot, to the goldsmith, who wondered at the
fineness, and after a short trial by the test, said it was
the most excellent gold in the world.

The next day a rumour of this prodigy went about
the Hague and spread abroad, so that many illustrious
and learned persons gave me their friendly visits for
its sake. Amongst the rest, the general Assay-master,
examiner of coins of this province of Holland, Mr.
Porelius, who with others earnestly besought me to pass
some part of the gold through all their customary trials,
which I did, to gratify my own curiosity. We went to
Mr. Brectel, a silversmith, who first mixed four parts of
silver with one part of the gold, then he filed it, put
aquafortis to it, dissolved the silver, and let the gold
precipitate to the bottom; the solution being poured off
and the calx of gold washed with water, then reduced
and melted, it appeared excellent gold, and instead of a
loss in weight, we found the gold was increased, and had
transmuted a scruple of the silver into gold by its
abounding tincture.

Figure 6. Alchemical Gold and Silver as King and Queen (From a MS—ca. 1600—of the *Splendor Solis*, in the German National Museum, Nuremberg)

> Doubting whether the silver was not sufficiently
> separated from the gold, we mingled it with seven parts
> of antimony, which we melted and poured out into a cone,
> and blew off the regulus on a test, where we missed
> eight grains of our gold; but after we blew away the
> red of the antimony, or superfluous *scoria*, we found
> nine grains of gold for our eight grains missing, yet it
> was pale and silverlike, but recovered its full colour
> afterwards, so that in the best proof of fire we lost
> nothing at all of this gold, but gained, as aforesaid.
> These tests I repeated four times and found it still alike,
> and the silver remaining out of the *aquafortis* was of the
> very best flexible silver that could be, so that in the
> total the said medicine or elixir had transmuted six
> drams and two scruples of the lead and silver into most
> pure gold.[3]

Whether or not all such accounts represent reality, alchemy had another, and considerably more important side: *spiritual* transmutation, the search for a means by which the dross of one's base nature could be transformed into the gold of spiritual purity. Exceedingly important studies of this largely neglected aspect of the alchemical tradition have been made by religious phenomenologist Mircea Eliade and by analytical psychologist Carl Gustav Jung. They have observed that the laboratory operations of the alchemist served as a "physical liturgy"—a ritual whereby the adept searched for the means to overcome the disjunction in himself (expressed as the opposing principles of "Sulphur" and "Mercury"). The discovery of the Stone of the Philosophers (often significantly termed the Elixir of Life or the Universal Medicine) would arise on the basis of the "conjunction of opposites" in the personality (symbolized by the alchemical marriage of Sulphur and Mercury). Thus would the alchemist achieve what Jung called "individuation": personal wholeness, salvation. Physical or metallic transmutation interlocked with this because of the fundamental hermetic belief that a "cosmic unity" embraced both the Macrocosm (nature) and the Microcosm (man). The Philosopher's Stone would therefore not only accelerate the organic and natural transformation of base metals into more "noble" elements but would also serve as the means to personal salvation and eternal life.

The redemptive side of alchemy was capable—as is anything related to human salvation—of two approaches, characterized in Christian theology as "works-righteousness" and "salvation by grace through faith." Works-righteousness refers to any and all activities on the part of fallen man to save himself through self-effort; such attempts are doomed to failure because sin, like water, cannot rise above its own level, and the very activity of trying to save oneself is evidence that the sinner refuses to admit the extent of his self-centeredness. Salvation by God's grace, appropriated by faith, is the only way to life, for to rely on God is to see the true extent of one's own sinful incapacity and to go to the one pure source of lifegiving medicine. Alchemy outside the Christian tradition, and the Gnostic, "nature-philosophy" hermeticism of Renaissance Paracelsians and modern esoteric alchemists, is most definitely a variation on the theme of works-righteousness. By self-motivated religio-chemical technique, the adept harmonized the contraries within him, produced the Philosopher's Stone, and transmuted his own existence to a higher, more spiritual plane. Goethe's Faust is a characteristic example of the esoteric alchemist who by trying to save his own life ends up in a genuine devil's pact.

There were also, however, many Christian alchemists, who, losing their lives for Christ's sake saved them. Particularly in the epoch of the Protestant Reformation (the 16th and 17th centuries were the high point of alchemical activity in western history), alchemists imbued with Luther's central conviction that the just shall live by faith employed alchemical operations as a liturgy of biblical salvation. The Philosopher's Stone became "the Stone that the builders rejected": Christ Himself, who alone could achieve the conjunction of opposites in the individual soul and in the cosmos (the "chemical marriage" of Sulphur and Mercury displayed the Marriage Supper of the Lamb). Reformation alchemists produced outstanding works interrelating hermetic symbolism and Scriptural truth (e.g., Heinrich Khunrath's *Amphitheatrum sapientiae aeternae* of 1609, and the many writings of Michael Maier), and some of them, such as Libavius, contributed mightily to the development of today's chemistry.

Did "spiritual transmutations" work? The common rationalistic approach to the question is first of all to demythologize physical alchemy (metallic transmutations were merely "symbolic" of inner, existential transformation) and then to dispense with the spiritual claims of alchemists as subjective will-to-believe. This line of interpretation directly parallels the negatively critical approach to the Bible which first demythologizes the texts by eliminating their historical claims and then subjectivizes their message. But not all cases even of physical transmutation can be easily dismissed, as we have already noted. Where spiritual alchemy is concerned, Carl Gustav Jung made the striking discovery that the fundamental symbols and motifs employed by the old alchemists also appear in the dream life of the modern businessman! These common—indeed, universal—"symbols of transformation" represent what Jung calls archetypes of the collective unconscious: symbolic patterns describing every man's need to have his broken soul mended.

Thus the alchemists were engaged in a real—not a mythical or individual-subjective—quest. Did they find an answer? We know that the Christian alchemists did, for Christ was their Philosopher's Stone, and His historical resurrection from the dead establishes the veracity of His promise that "because I live, you shall live also" (Jn. 14:19). As for the esoteric alchemists who sought (and continue to seek, for many still exist, especially in France) a salvation that can be drawn from within themselves or achieved by technique, they too "have their reward" (Mt. 6:2, 5, 16). It would be fruitless to deny their claims to special spiritual experience. But salvation can be counterfeited, for the Evil One is "a liar and the father of lies" (Jn. 8:44). The quest of the true Philosopher's Stone is dangerous: "whosoever shall fall upon that stone shall be broken; but on whom-soever it shall fall, it will grind him to powder" (Lk. 20:18). A broken and contrite heart will not be despised, and the path to salvation goes in that direction; while the arrogance and false security of self-salvation have no other end than the crushing weight of a millstone.

THE SECRET SOCIETY:
FELLOWSHIP FROM MYSTERY

Secret societies have existed, as one writer puts it, in "all ages and countries." [4] So multifarious have they been that book-length specialized treatments have been devoted just to "secret societies of women" and "erotic secret societies." [5] But in the western tradition, the modern concept of the secret society arises from late 16th-early 17th century Rosicrucianism, whose links with esoteric, Gnostic alchemy are very strong. From Rosicrucianism it is but a step to Freemasonry, whose Scottish and French rites both feature a degree of the Rose-Cross.

The earliest Rosicrucian documents are the *Fama fraternitatis* and the *Confession* of the Order, two brief manifestos published anonymously in 1614-15. These set forth the etiological myth of "Christian Rosencreutz" (Christian Rose-Cross), the alleged founder of the Order. On a pilgrimage to the Near East, he learned many secrets—medical, magical, and Cabalistic—and was taught how to communicate with Elementary Spirits. When he returned to Europe and attempted to show men their errors and the true path, he was scorned, and so he founded his secret fraternity. Its members could transmute metals, and they communicated by a secret writing. They met at appointed times in the house specially built for the purpose. After his death, Rosen-creutz was buried in the house of the Order: now the tomb had been rediscovered with his body "whole and unconsumed," and writings such as Paracelsus' were found interred with him. The time was now right for a General Reformation. In the *Confession*, there is added a strong note of astrological millennialism: the end is nigh and God's earthly kingdom is about to be ushered in.

Who was responsible for these views? Herculean efforts have been made to discover the true origins of Rosicrucianism, and most interpreters have made the Württemberg Lutheran pastor Johann Valentin Andreae the father of the Rose-Cross, owing to his anonymous alchemical allegory of 1616, the *Chymical Wedding of Christian Rosencreutz*. I have, however, restudied this whole question for the first time on the basis of the full range of manuscript and other primary sources, and the result has been the vindication of Andreae, who in fact wrote his book to bring Rosicrucians and those inclined in that direction back to orthodox Christianity.[6] By analyzing the two-thousand page mystical "Naometria" of one Simon Studion, which deeply influenced university life at Tübingen in the years when the Rosicrucian manifestos appeared, and which remains today, still in manuscript, in the Landesbibliothek in Stuttgart, I found that Rosicrucian ideology was already on the scene before Andreae wrote his book. Esoteric mystics such as Studion, Gutmann, and Sperber, whose beliefs related closely to Paracelsus' *Naturphilosophie*, appear to have brought the Order into existence in the 16th century.

Rosicrucianism was (and is, in its current American variety, AMORC) a corporate technique for self-salvation which differs little from the individualistic works-righteousness carried out by Paracelsian and other esoteric alchemists. The same is certainly the case with Freemasonry, whose etiological legend of Hiram Abiff is "in rigorous analogy"[7] with the Christian Rosencreutz myth. The extent to which such myth-making can be carried in the interests of self-realization is illustrated by the Anthroposophical esoterism of Rudolf Steiner, who informs us that Christian Rosencreutz sent his closest disciple, Buddha, to Mars to purify it through his deed of sacrifice, and that in consequence "the Mars-forces, now radiating peace, work into the souls of men between death and a new birth."[8]

Masonry does not rise to such metaphysical levels, but its secret rites convey a religion of works-righteousness in which its members, without benefit of faith in the atoning death of the Christ who declared Himself to be the only Way, look forward to fellowship with the Supreme Architect of the Universe as "the just reward of a pious and virtuous life." In the words of one of Masonry's classic defenders:

> Freemasonry . . . transcends the bounds of Christian and Western civilization; it includes the Moslem, the Hindoo, the Buddhist, and the Jew. Without waiting for their respective faiths to come together in a visible federation or unity, they can all meet together in their own and in each other's Lodges throughout the world and pray and worship together to the same one-and-only indivisible God whom all religious acknowledge and venerate.[9]

Such pitiful and unrealistic syncretisms arise in part because of longings for deeper wisdom, more numinous worship patterns, and truer fellowship than so many churches seem to offer. The Masonic heresy, like heresy in general, points up deficiencies in the orthodox church. Here the deficiency is not just that of a bland and colorless liberalism, but also the superficiality of an evangelical worship that is often indistinguishable from an informal funfest or supper club, and in which the people never receive more than the milk of Christian teaching and platitudes about a fellowship existing in theory but not in practice. To a very real extent, fraternal organizations of the Masonic variety are vultures feeding on the carrion of dead churches—and churches do not die (the Word of God never returns void); they are killed by those within them who preach, in word or in deed, "another gospel which is no gospel at all."

Does it therefore follow that all secret organizations are to be condemned from the standpoint of Christian faith? Certainly secrecy is a dangerous thing. We emphasized early in this book the open and public nature of Christian proclamation. The church has insisted that its marriages take place publicly, before witnesses, not in secret, to prevent immoral reneging on commitments.

When Jesus said that "there is nothing hid that shall not be made known" on the Last Day (Lk. 12:2-3), He was suggesting that concealment is very often a cloak for evil. In the case of secret societies, the opportunity is provided—even when all is innocent—for paranoic interpretation; thus the literature on secret societies abounds in works that purport to find the "creeping Yellow hoard," the "Jewish-Marxist combine," or the "international Socialist conspiracy" sneaking about in the ritualistic garb of one organization or another.[10]

But all of this does not justify a wholesale condemnation of secrecy *per se.* The early church often met in secret even though its clandestine communions of the true Body and Blood of Christ (I Cor. 11:27-30) gave rise to rumors of cannibalism.[11] Secrecy, in other words, can have positive objectives. It can cloak evil and engender self-righteousness, yes, but it can also fight evils in such a way that self-promotion becomes impossible. Benevolent organizations have on more than one occasion remained secret in order to carry out their work in perfect anonymity. Here the motive is to reduce self-seeking, not enlarge it as is the case in Masonic religiosity. Significantly, the Lutheran pastor and littérateur who did most to counteract the early influence of Rosicrucianism, Johann Valentin Andreae, founded an orthodox and secret *Societas Christiana* ("Christian Society") which did much good in its day and had indirect influence on the establishment of the Royal Society in England.[12] In our own century, Charles Williams, Christian poet, novelist of the supernatural, and intimate friend of C. S. Lewis and J. R. R. Tolkien, was a member of A. E. Waite's version of the secret Order of the Golden Dawn.[13] Let us not throw out baby with bath water (a characteristic practice when confronting the occult). Secrecy—like the other defining characteristics of occultism (the paranormal and the supernatural)—is not wrong in itself; we must always determine the *direction* (Christic or Antichristic?) and *use* (good or evil?) before passing moral judgment.

ASTROLOGY: ANSWERS FROM THE STARS

Intimately connected with both alchemy and primitive Rosicrucianism was astrology: the alchemists often formulated the "steps" of the "Work" of transmutation in terms of the twelve signs of the Zodiac or the seven "planetary metals," and the early Rosicrucians developed their apocalyptic millennialism on an astrological base. But astrology has by no means been limited to these connections; it is probably the oldest and most widely influential "sophisticated" variety of occultism, with roots pushing back to man's first fascination with the stars[14] and forward to the horoscopes in today's newspapers. The current interest in the subject is obvious enough from the fact that in 1961, even before the onset of the present "occult revolution," there were some 30,000 astrologers operating in the United States, and in France —the country of civilized rationalism—a single astrological magazine had a circulation of more than 100,000 copies.[15]

What exactly is astrology?[16] In brief, it is the art of divining fate or the future from the juxtaposition of the sun, moon, and planets. So-called "natural astrology" (the influence of the heavens on changes in the weather and on the inanimate world, for example, the moon's influence on the tides) has largely been absorbed into scientific disciplines such as astronomy and meteorology—though astrologers invariably use these phenomena to argue for the soundness of their theory. "Judicial astrology" is the genuinely occult aspect of the subject, for here attempts are made to understand the true character and predict the future of men and nations.

The essence of astrological activity is the casting and interpreting of horoscopes—maps showing the positions of the heavenly bodies relative to a given geographical and temporal moment. The moment can be that of one's birth (yielding the fundamental character portrait), of a historical event (permitting the true interpretation of it), of the present moment as related to one's day of birth (to allow prediction of the future and daily guidance), etc. Horoscopes can be cast of individuals or of corporate persons (such as nations). Horoscopes are set up in geocentric fashion—from the standpoint of the earth —and the planets and "luminaries" (the sun and moon) are appropriately positioned for the time and place in question. Their positions are plotted relative to the "Zodiac": an imaginary belt in the heavens (about 18 degrees wide) which has the ecliptic as its central line; this belt is divided into twelve equal segments (each extending 30 degrees of longitude), designated by constellations (in astrological terminology, "signs"). Each of the planets, luminaries, and Zodiac signs represents certain qualities, depending on a host of traditional associations; thus Mars and Venus associate with war and love, the Sun (gold) and the Moon (silver) can be tied into alchemical symbolism, and character traits can be developed from the animals, etc., which represent the Zodiac (Taurus the bull, Scorpio the scorpion, Leo the lion).

Since the combination of planets, luminaries, and Zodiac signs allow for only 432 possible variations, and since human life appears a bit more complex than this (!), further specificity is necessary. Here two factors are introduced: the twelve celestial "houses." (these result from the slicing of the heavenly sphere like an orange by drawing great circles through the north and south points of the horizon as meridians pass through the poles), and the "aspects" (the positions of the planets and luminaries relative to each other, e.g., "conjunction"—where two planets are side by side in the Zodiac—or "opposition" —where a distance of 180° separates them). The houses and the aspects allow for "individual differences" beyond the general conclusions arrived at from the interpretation of the planets, luminaries, and Zodiac signs alone. Thus the aspect of opposition is "unfavorable," while conjunction involving a luminary (sun or moon) is "favorable," and the most powerful planet in a conjunction imposes its influence on the situation. By a hierarchial ranging and synthesis of these five factors (planets, luminaries, signs of the Zodiac, houses, aspects), the astrologer produces his interpretations and sets forth his predictions.[17]

As one observes the astrological expert work with Ephemerides, Tables of Houses, Proportional Logarithms, etc., one is impressed by the complexity of the operation and hopeful that here occult science is in possession of a neglected technique which can serve mankind by revealing human character more clearly and outlining "the shape of things to come." Are the astrologers possibly like the psychoanalysts in employing a less-than-scientifically-orthodox technique which nonetheless accurately comprehends man on a depth level? As in the case of alchemy, so in astrology Carl Gustav Jung has found the archetypical patterns of the collective unconscious and the search for individuation.[18] Moreover, just as alchemical labor was one of the powerful contributing factors to the rise of chemistry, so the work of astrologers—particularly those in the Reformation tradition, such as Brahe and Kepler—aided mightily the development of modern astronomy.[19] These Lutheran scientists were convinced that astrology was not incompatible with divine revelation; and in more recent times, efforts have been made specifically to justify astrological motifs in biblical terms.[20] Remarkably accurate astrological predictions have been recorded; an influential historical example is Brahe's prophecy based on his study of the "new star" in Cassiopeia (1572), which seemed to portend the life and death of Gustavus Adolphus in the next century. Writes Brahe's authoritative modern biographer:

> It is more curious still that some of his other predictions seem to be fulfilled in the person of Gustavus Adolphus, the greatest champion of Protestantism in the seventeenth century. He was born in 1594 (only two years after the influence of the star should begin to be felt), and his glory was greatest in the year in which he fell, 1632, the very year mentioned by Tycho. He certainly was not born in Finland (for it is Finland and not the adjoining part of Russia which is indicated by 16° east of Uraniborg and 62° Latitude), but in Stockholm; but Finland was still a province of Sweden, and the yellow Finnish regiments were conspicuous for their bravery on many a blood-stained battlefield in Germany. No wonder that many contemporaries of Gustavus Adolphus were startled by these coincidences, and that the concluding part of Tycho's book was translated into several languages.[21]

Yet for all the weight given to such considerations, the validity of astrology is hardly established. True, some standard arguments against it are easily met. When reminded of the continuing geocentric, Ptolomaic focus of their art in spite of the heliocentric, Copernican revolution in astronomy, astrologers properly note (as do orthodox Christians dealing with the problem of Joshua's long day) that it is always legitimate to consider cosmological problems from a phenomenal standpoint. When taunted with the discovery of Uranus and Neptune long after the establishment of astrological theory in terms of seven planets (including the sun and moon as luminaries), the astrologer points out that since these planets are so far from the earth, their effect on horoscopes is minimal and so does not vitiate the astrological labors of the past. All good and well! But what about the issue of the statistical non-validity of astrological judgments?

Since the publication in 1955 of Michel Gauquelin's *L'Influence des astres,*[22] a veritable uproar has occurred inside and outside astrological circles over the statistical question. Gauquelin, at present a staff member of the Centre National de Recherche Scientifique attached to the Psychophysiological Laboratory at the University of Strasbourg, set out to disprove astrology once and for all by examining the rising and setting of certain planets relative to the birthdates of eminent Frenchmen. To his great surprise, he found significant correlations in certain instances (particularly Mars and Saturn aspected the ascendants and descendants of scientists and doctors). Jean Porte of the French National Institute of Statistics did a detailed refutation of Gauquelin's study, pointing out statistical difficulties in it, but especially stressing its limitation to France.[23] Gauquelin defended his work[24] and proceeded to enlarge its scope to other European countries. The results were published in a second book, *Les Hommes et les astres,*[25] and they largely confirmed the conclusions of the study of Frenchmen, though national differences were observed in some cases (Mars aspected the angles of Italian soldiers more than in the case of German soldiers, etc.). The fundamental question is, of course, what does this prove? Statistical correlation is not equivalent to cause-and-effect relationship, and the history of statistics is littered with odd and facetious cases of correlation (the rise of the tides in Baja California and the productivity of the coconut crop in Madagascar . . .). There is also the sad tale of the statistician who drowned wading across a river with an average depth of three feet! Statistical results, in other words, must be *interpreted*.

Now two points loom large in the analysis of Gauquelin's results. First, the correlations he discovered are not necessarily consistent with classical astrological theory. For example, the birth charts of his painters and musicians did not display the presence of Mercury and Venus as they should have done by all proper astrological method. Thus, as even advocates of astrology must admit, Gauquelin's work "does not prove that astrologers know what they are doing. It does not prove that an astrologer can tell a client what is in store for him." [26] Secondly, Gauquelin himself has asserted again and again in his books that "not one point of rapport exists on the purely scientific plane between astrology on the one hand and the structure of my results, on the other—much less between astrology and the spirit of my statistical investigation." [27] Gauquelin's interpretation of his results is somewhat analogous to Jung's "synchronicity, an acausal connecting principle." [28] He does not know why planetary positions correlate somewhat with man's vocational alignments, but he thinks that the answer may lie in the mysterious gene fabric of heredity.[29] Perhaps there is some kind of chromosomal-cosmic interconnection to account for the statistics —but, in any case, it is not what traditional astrology has been talking about. Freiburg University parapsychologist Hans Bender, whom we met in Chapter One and who wrote the preface to Gauquelin's *Les Hommes et les astres*, concurs with the judgment of the Planète editors who published his *L'Astrologie devant la science* that instead of confirming astrology, Gauquelin is in process of "demystifying horoscopes" and perhaps "bringing a new science to birth." [30]

As for strict, traditional astrological theory, where does it stand statistically? A critical Swiss astrobiologist and astrologer of the last generation, Robur, set out to validate astrology by studying the horoscopes of 2,817 musicians. Since musical aptitude depends especially on the Sun's position in the Zodiac on the day of birth, Robur concentrated on this factor as a test case. He thought he had found a correlation, but a recent re-examination of the data by Paul Couderc, titulary astronomer at the Paris Observatory, has shown exactly the opposite. Here are the diagrammatic results:

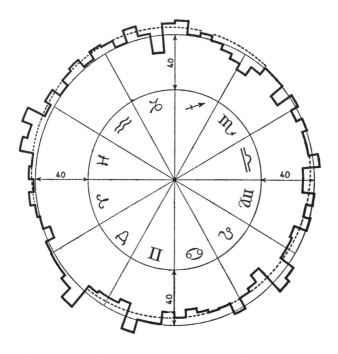

Births of 2,817 Musicians Grouped by 5° of the Zodiac (The deviations have no systematic character whatever. Pure chance is thus responsible for these fluctuations, in line with a Gaussian or normal curve.)

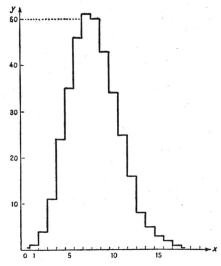

Chance Distribution of the Birthdates of 2,817 Musicians throughout the Year (The abscissa, x, represents the number of musicians born the same day. The ordinate, y, represents the number of times x musicians will be born on the same day. Thus 51 times there will be 7 births; 50 times there will be 8 births; etc. This theoretical distribution follows from the application of Poisson's law. Robur's results fit the distribution remarkably well; therefore, chance alone and not the signs of the Zodiac determine the musicians' births.)

Couderc comments mercilessly: "The position of the Sun has absolutely no musical significance. The musicians are born throughout the entire year on a chance basis. No sign of the Zodiac or fraction of a sign favors or does not favor them. We conclude: the assets of scientific astrology are equal to zero, as is the case with commercialized astrology. This is perhaps unfortunate, but it is a fact." [31]

Where commercialized or popular astrology is operative, the lack of scientific worth is even more obvious. One writer has presented, in tabular form, the predictions for Aries relative to business, home, love, and health, as they appeared in four French magazines for the same week. As might be expected, these predictions are wildly at variance with each other.[32] Yet the magazines are quality periodicals (*Elle, Jours de France*), not trash, and presumably their astrological writers are a cut above average.

I myself obtained—for the fun of it and at a fairly steep price—the "Aquarius 2000" astrology set, which permits one to set up a most detailed personal horoscope. After frightening my mother half to death by calling her long distance to determine my exact time of birth (merely October 18, 1931 is not enough; 5 A.M. was an essential item of knowledge), I carried out the process in depth. Readers who are already acquainted with my difficult, perfectionistic, combattive nature as reflected in numerous public debates on the truth of Christianity and private bickerings over trifles, will be appalled to learn, on the basis of the most important item in my horoscope (Sun in Libra), that I "have a sympathetic, pleasant, and courteous nature," am "unusually sensitive to the feelings of others," "make an excellent peacemaker"; my "chief interests are justice, peace, and harmony," and I have "natural tact."

But astrology has a ready answer for a horoscope interpretation that seems to have no relation to the person involved.

What about "mistakes"? Did your Personality Portrait tell you, perhaps, that you were "unsympathetic" or "tended to be unfeeling toward others," while you know yourself to be a thoughtful and considerate person? You may very well be right.

Your Personality Portrait, after all, describes your personality as forecast at the moment of birth.

In reading your Portrait, it is important to recognize that you have already done a lot of living, and the very process of living affects and changes everyone.

Your environment—your parents and family—your problems and the way you deal with them—the "lessons" that experience has taught you: all these affect your personality and character and behavior.

If your Personality Portrait seemed to unfairly charge you with a lack of sympathy, it is very likely that experience has shown you that there is little profit or happiness in ignoring the feelings of others. In fact, with a little exercise of memory and reflection into your past, you can probably recall some occasions in life when you resolved to make a conscious effort to show—or more important, develop—a concern for others. By now, this has become an established habit and second nature with you. It is now an essential part of your personality—and you can take credit for developing it yourself!

On the other side of the coin, it sometimes (but rarely) happens that an extremely sluggish and unhappy person comes up with a Personality Portrait that makes him sound like a dynamo of energy and a bundle of joy. That person has obviously been defeated by life—so far, at least. His home life may have been too limiting, his parents too strict or too indifferent, or his early years afflicted by illness or just plain bad luck. There is still a lot of energy and spirit lying dormant in that person, and a determined effort on his part, together with encouragement from others, could get him back on the highly promising track that was forecast in the heavens at his birth.

Just as life can go wrong for a person with the most favorable forecast, there is nothing to prevent a person with an unfortunate-sounding forecast from leading a very happy, positive, and productive life. In fact, a "negative" forecast sometimes turns out more beneficial as an aid in living, because it doesn't permit a person to rest on his laurels, as a more favorable forecast might do. One's weaknesses, limitations, or "bad" tendencies should be seen as active challenges rather than irreversible defeats, and meeting those challenges can lead to strength of character and genuine achievement.[33]

Note the conclusion of this line of reasoning: it becomes impossible in principle to determine the validity of a given horoscope portrait. No matter how apparently "off" the portrait, this can be explained away as natal potential which has since been modified by environment or experience. Analytical philosophers rightly emphasize, as we noted in Chapter One, that assertions compatible with any state of affairs whatever say nothing. To say something meaningful, one must at least indicate what could count against it; if no contradiction at all makes a difference to one's claims, then the claims really do not impart any information at all. This seems to be the exact situation with most astrological judgments. They are like the heavily weighted children's toys which, no matter how you throw them, always manage to stand upright (in astrology, the "weighting" in the *derrière* of the system is its ambiguity). Or, to vary the analogy, one thinks of the 19th century British chauvinist who proclaims, "The English have *never* lost a battle"; when someone reminds him of any given English defeat, he replies, "Surely you don't consider *that* a battle."

To be fascinated by the technical expertise of the astrologer in casting a horoscope and to overlook the problem of ambiguity of interpretation is to make the mistake so endemic in liberal theological circles: the blind acceptance of negatively critical judgments on the teachings of Scripture simply because the critic manifests impressive philological skills. Philology is no guarantee of sound judgment, and neither is skill at mathematical interpolation an assurance that the caster of the horoscope can offer meaningful interpretations based on it.

In most disputed areas—biblical criticism and astrology are only two examples—the basic problem generally does not lie on the technical level but on the level of fundamental assumptions. Radical biblical criticism is crippled from the outset, regardless of the philological skills exemplified by its practitioners, because of its fundamental rationalistic, anti-supernatural bias. Similarly, no matter how skilled the astrologer, he is working with what is at root so ambiguous a body of theory that his conclusions are never compelling. This was painfully illustrated to me on February 26, 1972, when I attended a lecture on "Modern Astrology" at Chicago's Palmer House. The "three minutes of quiet meditation" which the lecturer, Mr. Henry Weingarten, insisted upon set the vacuous tone of the evening; ambiguity was so rife that the famous seven devils of the parable would have had no difficulty in finding a habitation. Most unsettling was the question period, when a discussion of "medical astrology" began. A Mr. Calvin Hanes of Chicago, whose card reads "Uranian Astrology Teacher," asserted that he could infallibly predict cancer (the disease, not the Zodiac sign!) by the formula "Saturn plus

Neptune minus Hades." Hades is not what the reader is thinking! It is one of several "hypothetical bodies" appealed to by some modern astrologers to bring the horoscope to "greater precision." I immediately asked the lecturer if, in his opinion, such a formula was valid. He answered that he himself did not place as much emphasis on hypothetical planets. I then (belying my astrological character as a tactful, harmonious, courteous peacemaker) told the two gentlemen publicly that they ought to be locked up, since it was grossly immoral to go about giving irresponsible medical judgments on the basis of theories so vague that even the astrologers can't agree on them—to say nothing of misleading poor, troubled, and sick people with interpretations stemming from hypothetical heavenly bodies! [34]

The very elasticity of astrological interpretation is its most dangerous characteristic. Where people desperately desire a shortcut to self-knowledge and solutions to their problems, and where the answers are ambiguous, they inevitably choose according to self-interest. Thus the floodgates are opened to the reinforcement of evil tendencies rather than the eradicating of these tendencies by the spiritual surgery of the Gospel. In light of such considerations, it should not be regarded as strange that astrology has so frequently been used to guide evil farther along the path it has already taken. The employment of astrology by Hitler and his associates is one of the clearest documented examples of this phenomenon.[35]

Why, though, do some astrological analyses come so close to the mark? To attribute all such instances to "demon influence" seems singularly shortsighted; where the interpretation relates directly to the promotion of evil, perhaps such an approach would be appropriate, but where the work of Christian astrologers like Brahe is concerned, one must be careful not to bear false witness against the neighbor. Moreover, what about the correlations between planetary positions and vocations, as discovered by Gauquelin? These do not support traditional astrological theory, but they are genuine correlations nonetheless.

Let me suggest a possibility. The underlying assumption of astrology is the same as that of alchemy, namely, the unity of the cosmos. For the alchemist, the inorganic and the organic—the impersonal and the personal—operate by the same fundamental laws. For the astrologer, this correlation is focused on the relation between planetary positions and human life. In both cases, the Macrocosm (the universe extrinsic to man) and the Microcosm (man himself) are united in a single harmonic relationship. Now such a description would well apply to the *unfallen* cosmos—the Garden in which Adam lived in perfect harmony with nature and walked with the Lord God in the cool of the day. But as a result of man's self-centered fall, modeled on Lucifer's own passion to "exalt his throne above the stars of God" (Is. 14: 12-15), the perfect relation between man and the cosmos was fractured: man had to leave the Garden, and now "the whole creation groans and travails in pain, waiting for redemption" (Rom. 8:22-23). This does not mean that every trace of the Macrocosmic-Microcosmic harmony has disappeared, but it does mean that, if you will, the monkey wrench of sin has been thrown into the cosmic machinery, so that the original harmony is disrupted on a very wide scale.

Could not Gauquelin's correlations and the successful predictions of astrologers of integrity represent vestiges of the primitive cosmic unity? The maddening aspect of such successes is their unpredictability: they seem to apply to some professions and not others, to some predictions and not others, with no criteria for distinguishing areas of success from areas of failure. But this very irrationality would follow from the disruption of cosmic unity by sin, for sin is at root irrational and arbitrary. The consequences of arbitrary success ought to be fully comprehended: because success over against failure cannot be assured for these techniques, they are relied upon only at one's peril. To assume necessary success in astrological prediction would, if my explanation is correct, really amount to assuming that we still remain in Eden; it would be to disregard the reality of a fallen world where the relation between man and cosmos has suffered deeply from man's own waywardness, and where the only hope to genuine self-understanding is the Christ who alone knows all men and what is in them (Jn. 2:24-25). In a saving relationship with Him we receive the gift of His Spirit who leads us to trustworthy (because divinely given) self-knowledge and provides us with an "earnest" of the restoration of Macrocosmic-Microcosmic harmony at the Marriage Supper of the Lamb.

Since Christ is the Second Adam, and His coming into the world was like the reintroduction of a bit of Eden into the fallen creation, we might expect to see at His birth a particularly clear illustration of the underlying unity of man and the cosmos. Is this perhaps why the stars infallibly led the Magi, those Persian astrologers, to Him? [36] In a fallen world, there is no assurance that the stars will infallibly lead anywhere else, and those who trust in them may themselves become "wandering stars, to whom is reserved the blackness of darkness for ever" (Jude 13). But those who are wise, as the Wise Men were, will follow the star until it stands over the place where the Child is. There they will find the One named both Emmanuel—God with us—and Jesus, "for He shall save His people from their sins."

5

The Land of Mordor

. . .In the land of Mordor where the Shadows lie.

—J. R. R. Tolkien, *The Lord of the Rings*

The map accompanying C. S. Lewis' *Pilgrim's Regress: An Allegorical Apology for Christianity, Reason and Romanticism* places the shire of "Occultica" deep in the southern regions. Lewis' Pilgrim does not visit this shire, but the lay of the land is described in the author's preface: "The delicious tang of the forbidden and the unknown draws them [the inhabitants] on with fatal attraction: the smudging of all frontiers, the relaxation of all resistances, dream, opium, darkness, death, and the return to the womb. Every feeling is justified by the mere fact that it is felt." [1] In his spiritual autobiography, *Surprised by Joy*, Lewis calls this desire for the preternatural "a disease"—which he himself admits to having—and says of it: "It is a spiritual lust; and like the lust of the body it has the fatal power of making everything else in the world seem uninteresting while it lasts. It is probably this passion, more even than the desire for power, which makes magicians." [2] We are now to visit this land of magicians and necromancers, on a road that carries us first through the domains of prophecy, the Tarot, and Faerie.

THE FUTURE BECKONS

In our survey of the history of the occult, we observed

121

the antiquity of methods of divination. Seemingly no technique has been considered too bizarre or too complex for divinatory purposes—from consulting the entrails of chickens to the plotting of national horoscopes.[3] What of prophecy? Can the future indeed be known?

The answer, in principle, must be yes. First, the validity of biblical prophecy cannot be gainsaid. Admittedly, the Old Testament prophets were primarily "forth-tellers" (speaking judgment and grace to their own day), but they also engaged in remarkable foretellings of the future. They prophesied in a most specific manner future events related to the history of Israel (such is that in the case of the twin cities of Tyre and Sidon, the former would be utterly destroyed with its stones and dust laid in the sea, while the latter would continue), and they gave detailed information on the coming Messiah (he would be sold for thirty pieces of silver, etc.).[4] The astrological success of the Magi, to which we referred at the end of the last chapter, appears to have been directly connected with biblical prophecy. Why were the Wise Men searching the heavens for a special sign at the particular time of Christ's birth? Sir Robert Anderson effectively argued that Daniel's prophecy of the "Seventy Weeks" offers a precise chronological prediction of Jesus' Messianic career;[5] doubtless, with the known circulation of the Old Testament Scriptures throughout the Near East in ancient times, the Magi had come into contact with this prophecy. To deny the factual character of such predictions requires one either to maintain that the prophetic writings were produced after the events (an impossible argument where New Testament events are foreseen in the Old, and almost as difficult for prophecies limited to the Old Testament) or to say that the fulfillments were "doctored" to fit the predictions (a charge that is entirely at variance with the moral character of and express standards of truth held by the biblical writers).

Extra-biblical prophetic success is likewise a fact. Almost everyone has heard of the 16th century French prognosticator Nostradamus; his extensive and intense predictions, in bewildering number, repay careful study.[6] Our own century offers the much less well known but equally striking example of the prophetic insights of Papus and Rasputin in the chilling years immediately before the Russian Revolution. Papus, the French occultist, was called to St. Petersburg early in October, 1905, by Russian dignitaries who believed in his powers. Already the country was in turmoil, and the Emperor and Empress were distraught. Papus carried out a necromantic ritual in the presence of three persons: the sovereigns and Captain Mandryka, a young aide-de-camp, later governor of Tiflis. Papus "succeeded in evoking the ghost of Czar Alexander III; indubitable evidences attested the presence of the invisible specter." The ghost declared: "You must, at all costs, crush the revolution now beginning. But it will recommence one day with a violence proportional to the repression that must be exercised now." Papus told Their Majesties that his magic powers could hold the catastrophe in check, but that "the efficacy of his conjuration would cease the moment he was no longer 'on the physical plane.'" Papus died on October 26, 1916—shortly before the Revolution. Moreover, in one of Papus' letters to the Empress, he expressed his hatred of Rasputin (black magicians regularly fall out with each other, illustrating that the essence of evil is selfish aggrandizement), and asserted that Rasputin's death would bring terrible consequences on the Russian people. When the Empress read the letter to Rasputin, he replied simply: "But I have told you this also many times. When I die, Russia will perish." [7] Rasputin's assassination, brought about by a hideous combination of cyanide, bullets, and drowning, occurred on December 15, 1916.[8]

But must not all such instances of prophetic success— biblical and extra-biblical—*somehow* be explained away, on the ground that the future does not yet exist? Is not the "time line" of past-present-future but a sequential model of a subjective impression, having no concrete objectivity? Is not the prediction of the future as unrealistic as time-travel à la H. G. Wells? To this three things need to be said. First (and here we reiterate what was emphasized in Chapter One), occult or miraculous facts cannot legitimately be rejected because we have difficulty in explaining their mechanism or because they create metaphysical problems for us. Facts is facts! If prophetic successes have occurred to a degree unattributable to "chance" or "coincidence," then we must accept their reality and go from there, no matter how inexplicable or disturbing they may be in relation to our past conceptions. Secondly, even if the future were but a "form of inner sense" (as the philosopher Kant held), successful prophetic activity could be due to the seer's "tuning-in" on a mind powerful enough to know what will happen on the basis of his analysis of all the present factors that go to make up the future events. Such a mind would have to be considerably more powerful than ours, for it would have to integrate and analyze a vast number of factors; thus, the mind of God or the minds of high-level supernatural beings would be involved.

However—in the third place—there is every reason to believe that time is not just a Kantian or Bergsonian expression of subjectivity. Einstein's relativity theory demands that as the speed of objects increases, time literally slows for them; if an object's speed were to approach the velocity of light (186,000 mi./sec., the constant in the $E = mc^2$ formula), time would move toward zero for the object.

> I must emphasize that here time is concrete. . . . The evidence is unassailable: physical processes go slower in objects when they travel at high speed. There was no way of knowing this when Einstein wrote in 1905, yet new discoveries in physics (such as the mesons) have born [it] out. . . . A set of radioactive atoms on the perimeter of the whirling turntable has experienced fewer decays than an identical set of atoms that has remained at rest.[9]

Thus even Wellsian time travel is a theoretical possibility, for within an object travelling close to the speed of light, a person would age minimally, and could therefore climb out of his time capsule into a world of the future, where time had continued at its "normal" rate during his voyage![10] As to travel into the past, this may have actually occurred in "time-warp" situations, such as the famous case of Moberly and Jourdain's passage from 20th to 18th century Versailles.[11] Temporal objectivity eliminates theoretical objections to prophecy, for the seer may not only "tune-in" on a transcendent mind for his predictions, but may also exhibit a kind of "x-ray vision" by which he peers farther into the future than others.

Precognition experiments (referred to in Chapter One) lend additional support to this interpretation. J. W. Dunne's "experiment with time," in which he recorded his precognitive dreams,[12] did not receive sufficient later attestation,[13] but a more carefully controlled series of tests by Tyrrell, with philosopher C. D. Broad among the witnesses, produced the following tabulation:

Precognitive Results.

Trials.
2,255

Successes,
Actual.
$539 = 23.9\%$

Successes,
Chance-Expected.
451

Odds against Result
being Chance.
Many millions to one.[14]

If prediction of the future is indeed possible, what interpretation should be placed on it? Is it divine, demonic, or neither? The answer is that it can be any one of the three, depending upon the pattern (Gestalt) of the particular prophetic situation. The simple precognitive faculty, as represented in ESP experiments, is no more "demonic" (or "angelic"!) than a faculty of lightning calculation or the ability to play the piano by ear. Here we are evidently encountering a mental faculty (analoguous to extraordinary vision) which permits some people to look through the temporal haze separating the future from the present.

But just as a musician who plays by ear can use

his talent in a burlesque theater or a cathedral, so pre-cognitive ability can be employed for weal or woe. Where it is used as a basis for exaggerated claims in behalf of its possessor—where, for example, the precognitive agent turns himself into, or allows others to turn himself into, a "seer" who can pronounce on the nature of life and the meaning of the universe—precognition becomes a most dangerous quality. Moreover, used in this way, it opens the floodgates of the psyche to supernatural influences of the negative sort that would provide precog-nitive gifts beyond even the paranormal. The prophecies of Papus and Rasputin, when viewed alongside their ar-rogant, antichristic lives, seem clearly to bespeak unholy influences.

Is this judgment to be placed on our contemporary prophets, such as Jeane Dixon, Edgar Cayce, *et al.*? [15] With Cayce, there is little doubt that the negative axe should strike at the root of the tree: while alive, he employed his powers to bolster a mishmash of Eastern religiosity (karma and reincarnation) and out-of-context biblical teaching, and now this eclectic theosophizing is being promoted by his "Association for Research and Enlightenment." Here we have a classic case of a "seer" being in reality *blind*: the blind leading the blind.

Jeane Dixon's case is more difficult. She is a devout, believing Roman Catholic who prays God to use her to help mankind. Unhappily, her visions have frequently been tied to such Catholic emphases as Fátima which are in tension with the biblical view of Mary, the saints, etc.; and her conviction that, after a world holocaust in the 1980s, a child whose birth she saw in a vision will unite all religions of the world into one with Rome as the center, so that peace will come in the year 2000, can only be related to biblical prophecy at the point of Antichrist. [16] Mrs. Dixon's vision cannot refer to the Second Coming of Christ, for He will come down from heaven "in the same manner" as He ascended up to heaven (Acts 1:11), not be born a second time on earth; and the only other world religious leader set forth in biblical prophecy is the Antichrist, whose reign does

in fact connect with the seven hills of Rome (Rev. 17 ff.).
Either this prophecy of Mrs. Dixon's is simply erroneous,
or she foresees a remarkable religious occurrence that
Scripture has not seen fit to mention, or she is (unwitting-
ly, no doubt) putting a positive construction on the most
negative future event in all history! In the latter case,
she would surely have to be regarded as a naïve tool
of evil forces.[17]

Prophecy, it would seem, easily lends itself to misuse,
faulty judgment, and demonic misinterpretation. Could
this at least partially explain why our Lord and His
Apostles wish us to focus our attention on the present?
"Sufficient unto the day is the evil thereof" (Mt. 6:34).
"Now is the accepted time; behold, now is the day of
salvation" (II Cor. 6:2).[18] Even the pagan lyric poet
Horace advised his love:

> *What end the gods may have ordained for me,*
> *And what for thee,*
> *Seek not to learn, Leuconöe; we may not know.*
> *Chaldean tables cannot bring us rest.*[19]

Whether contemporary prophecy is demonic or angelic
will depend, in the last analysis, on Scripture itself, which
serves as the one sure means of "distinguishing spirits."
Writes the Apostle John: "Beloved, do not believe every
spirit, but test the spirits to see whether they are of
God—for many false prophets have gone out into the
world. This is how you shall know the Spirit of God:
every spirit who confesses that Jesus Christ is come
in the flesh is of God, and every spirit who confesses
not that Jesus Christ is come in the flesh is not of God.
The latter is that spirit of Antichrist which you heard
would come, and even now it is already in the world"
(I Jn. 4:1-3).

But if prophecy is not self-attesting, do not Christians
then beg the question when they use biblical prophecy
as one of the chief evidences of the truth of the Scriptural
message? Not at all, for the prophecies of the Bible
which support its revelatory character are immensely
more powerful than extra-biblical prognostications. The

biblical prophets, unlike virtually all extra-biblical seers from the prophets of Baal to Jeane Dixon employ no mumbo-jumbo or "technique"; thus there is every reason to believe their consistent theocentric claim that their messages derive not from man's efforts but from God Himself.[20] Moreover, the superior nature of biblical prophecies is manifested in their frequent *double* connection with the miraculous (the prophecy in its own right is beyond even the paranormal, and the event prophesied is of a miraculous nature itself, such as the Virgin Birth of Christ). Scriptural predictions are also more specific and less devoid of other possible interpretations than extra-biblical prophecies (Christ sold for thirty pieces of silver).

> Yahweh is not challenging the false gods to set forth
> a prophecy; this any god can do. Rather, He is challenging
> the religions of the world to set forth before they occur,
> a series of precise, humanly unforeseeable prophecies that
> in time are fully confirmed by history. No other religion
> has met this challenge.[21]

That this is by no means a vain boast is illustrated by a mathematician's analysis of the statistical significance level of a mere twenty-five of the most specific Messianic prophecies of the Old Testament fulfilled in the New.

> Regarding these cases of events foretold for Israel's
> Messiah who was to come, if the chances of success were
> even in the case of each one, that is $p = 1/2$ in every case,
> then the overall probability that all n events would find
> their fulfillment in one Person would be $p^n = 1/(2^n)$.
> Thus there would be but one chance in 2^n (33 million, where
> $n = 25$) of all these foretold events coming true if they
> were mere guesses. Now a glance at these prophecies
> concerning Christ reveals that they do not all have an even
> chance of success, for in some instances it is highly
> improbable that the event could occur at all (as for a child
> to be born without a human father). A very conservative
> compromise would be $p = 1/4$; and the overall probability
> for the n prophecies coming true would be $p^n = 1/(4^n)$,
> or one chance out of a thousand trillion if $n = 25$.
>
> Since there are many more than 25 prophecies of events
> surrounding the birth and life of Christ, and a compromise
> chance of success is undoubtedly less than 1 to 4, then the

chance of success, if these predictions were all mere guesses, would be so infinitesimal that no one could maintain that these prophecies were mere guesses! The alternative must be true—these prophecies were all foreseen events, in which "holy men of God spake as they were moved by the Holy Ghost." The prophecies were given by revelation—divinely inspired.[22]

~TAROCCHINI~

THE TAROT

When playing cards first appeared in Europe about 1320, they were cards of the Italian variety, later known as "Tarocchini" or Tarots.[23] There is no evidence to support the occultists' claims that the word derives from the Egyptian, but the origins of the Tarot pack may indeed go back to remote antiquity. The claim has been made that the cards were invented by the gypsies, as a convenient travelling library or storehouse of emblematic wisdom. For the gypsy, "these cards taught at one and the same time, through their symbols, the highest philosophy known to the wise and the darkest arts known to the black magician. Light and Dark exist side by side in the Tarot pack."[24] Like the symbolism of alchemy and astrology, the imagery of these cards does seem to bubble up from the racial memory itself. In the terms of Jungian analytical psychology, the cards express archetypal images.

The full Tarot deck consists of a "Lesser Arcana" or "Trumps Minor" of four suits (Cups, Wands, Swords, and Pentacles), each including fourteen cards (Ace, numbered cards from 2 through 10, Page, Knight, Queen, and King), and a "Greater Arcana" or "Trumps Major" of twenty-two face cards, numbered 1 through 21 plus an unnumbered card ("The Fool"). The total number of Tarot cards is therefore seventy-eight. It is most interesting to observe the reactions of a sensitive person when he first examines these cards.[25] Instead of the indifference which accompanies contact with ordinary playing cards (not due just to their familiarity, but to their banality), there is generally a deep absorption and hushed interest. The cards seem to "grab" their user.

Numerous attempts have been made to interpret the Tarot deck—from Papus' endeavor to draw the cards

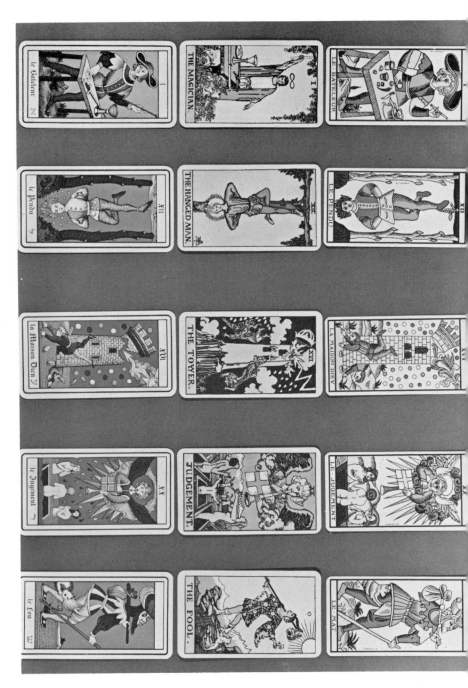

Figure 7. Representative "Greater Arcana" Tarot Cards
(From top to bottom: the Ancien Tarot de Marseille; the Pamela
Coleman Smith Tarot; the Tarot accompanying Oswald Wirth's
Le Tarot)

into his sphere of esoteric Cabalism[26] to A. E. Waite's approach to the cards from the standpoint of a generalized Christian mysticism.[27] Properly viewed, the Tarot cards express the human condition on the deepest archetypal level, and suggest that the only solution for it requires supernatural, outside aid. Thus, for example, in the Greater Arcana (which carries the chief power of the deck), Card XVI shows a Babel-like tower ("The House of God," i.e., man's self-seeking religiosity) being destroyed by divine wrath; Card XX displays the coming forth of mankind from the grave to face Judgment at the sound of the angel's trumpet on the Last Day; Card XII presents a saintly person being hanged upside down from a living tree in the form of a Tau-cross (Atonement in a world whose values are so inverted that it does not comprehend that this seeming martyr is in fact being glorified); Card I ("The Magician") shows a figure with the sign of eternity on his head in possession of the symbols of the four suits (cup, wand, sword, pentacle— all classic representations of both nature and grace), signifying that only a supernatural visitant from eternity can control life and give it meaning; and the unnumbered or floating card, "The Fool," presents one who appears a fool to the blind and fallen world, but who in fact is "a prince of the other world on his travels through this one." [28] High (or deep: they are the same) symbolism of this kind extends through the entire Tarot pack, and explains why great writers such as T. S. Eliot (*The Waste Land*) and Charles Williams (*The Greater Trumps*) have employed its imagery so effectively both in describing the lostness of the human condition and the Christian redemptive solution.[29]

Sad to say, however, the Tarot's history has not generally been on so high a plane. Fortune tellers have put the cards to divinatory use; games have been played with them; and occultists have tried to integrate them into their schemes of esoteric self-realization. Because the cards are so potent symbolically, they are also most dangerous when misused or perverted. Attempts to use them to predict the future are definitely to be discouraged.

Tarot symbolism strikes to the recesses of the unconscious, where the archetypes reside. To try to harness this energy for prognostication and the control of one's destiny is simply to ask for trouble. Contact with this symbolism demands that one remove the shoes from his feet, recognizing that archetypal ground is numinous, and that the self-knowledge there acquired can backlash whenever it does not drive one to the Cross and to the "Fool" who died on it for us.

THE REALM OF FAERIE

In marked contrast with the prognosticators who employ crystal balls or Tarot cards are those possessed with what has been called "second sight." Like biblical prophetic activity, second sight operates without extraneous aids. Without prior warning, those having this faculty "see" a future event, often an accident or death, and can relate the circumstances that will accompany it. Andrew Lang found this strange phenomenon in the folk literature of peoples as widely separated as the Australians and the Incas, but it is particularly associated with the Scottish Highlands. Indeed, so many attested cases have been recorded in that geographical area that the phenomenon is often termed "Highland second sight." [30]

Two characteristics of Highland second sight are particularly striking. First, the possessor invariably regards the power ambivalently: it is a "gift," yet an unfortunate one. A "nerve storm" often accompanies the vision of the future and sometimes complete prostration is the result. The events foreseen are generally tragic and therefore give pain to those who know about them. Secondly, the power relates in some way to the kingdom of Faerie. In earlier times, second sight was directly attributed to the influence of the "wee people" or "good folk"; and some of those having the gift claim even today to be able to see the creatures of fairyland.

Such claims to the real existence of the domain of Faerie strike an ostensively ludicrous note. For the average American a "fairy" is another kind of cat entirely! Anthropologists have made concerted attempts to explain

Figure 8. "The Fairies Are Out," by James Nasmyth

fairy lore on the basis of primitive beliefs as to the survival
of the spirits or wraiths of the dead in or near the bar-
rows where they were interred.[31] These efforts have
been only partially successful; accounts like the following
—and they are representative of hundreds of recorded
cases—cannot very well be reconciled to such an explanation:

> A Protestant minister of Scotland will be our next
> witness. He is a native of Ross-shire, though he draws
> many of his stories from the Western Hebrides, where
> his calling has placed him. Because he speaks from
> personal knowledge of the living Fairy-Faith as it was in
> his boyhood and is now, and chiefly because he has had
> the rare privilege of conscious contact with the fairy
> world, his testimony is of the highest value: . . . "As a
> Christian minister I believe in the possibility and also
> the reality of these spiritual orders, but I wish only
> to know those orders which belong to the realm of grace.
> It is very certain that they exist. I have been in a state
> of ecstasy, and have seen spiritual beings which form
> these orders."
>
> George Gelling, of Ballasalla [Isle of Man], a
> joiner . . . told me: . . . "After tea, my apprentice was late
> returning; he was out by the hedge just over there
> looking at a crowd of *little people* kicking and dancing.
> One of them came up and asked him what he was
> looking at; and this made him run back to the shop."
>
> When I called on the Rev. J. M. Spicer, vicar of
> Malew parish, at his home near Castletown [Isle of
> Man], he [declared]: . . . "Old Mrs. K—, about a year
> ago, told me that on one occasion, when her daughter
> had been in Castletown during the day, she went out
> to the road at nightfall to see if her daughter was
> yet in sight, whereupon a whole crowd of fairies
> suddenly surrounded her, and began taking her off
> toward South Barrule Mountain; and, she added, 'I
> couldn't get away from *them* until I had called my
> son.' "
>
> I am greatly indebted to the Rev. Canon Kewley,
> of Arbory [Isle of Man], for the valuable testimony which
> follows: . . . "A good many things can be explained as
> natural phenomena, but there are some things which I
> think cannot be. For example, my sister and myself
> and our coachman, and apparently the horse, saw the
> same phenomenon at the same moment: one evening

we were driving along an avenue in this parish
when the avenue seemed to be blocked by a great
crowd of people . . . . The throng was about thirty to
forty yards away. When we approached, it melted away,
and no person was anywhere in sight." [32]

If such beings exist, what are they? The best discussion of this question still remains that of Robert Kirk, minister of Aberfoyle, who a year before his death in 1692 wrote *The Secret Commonwealth*; this book remained in manuscript until Sir Walter Scott discovered it in 1815.[33] Perhaps the best testimony to its importance lies in the circumstances of Kirk's death: after completing his book, he fainted while walking on a fairy knoll a short distance from his own door and died immediately; the belief persists even today in his parish that he was carried off by the fairies because he had delved too deeply into their secrets.[34] Kirk argues that the fairy peoples (there is not just one such race—cf. the leprechauns, elves, dwarfs, goblins, etc. of folklore) [35] are an order of being midway between men and angels. They are not without sin, but being more ethereal and less physical than mankind, their sins are more "spiritual and haughty." They will appear at the Judgment Seat of Christ, as we shall, to account for their lives, though their laws and reasons for being are not the same as ours. Unlike the angels (good and evil) they are not now in their final state of salvation or damnation. Sinistrari, the famed 17th century demonologist,[36] applies to them Christ's word in John 10:16: "Other sheep I have which are not of this fold; them also I must bring and they shall hear my voice and there shall be one fold and one shepherd." Like us they are wanderers and pilgrims on the earth, but, being closer to the angelic realms, their contact with man has progressively diminished as the corporate sin of human civilization has become more widespread.

Indeed, "in the earliest mentions of them in literature the fairies are already spoken of as departed or departing. The tradition of them burns up and flickers like a candle that is going out, and then perhaps for a time burns up again, but always the fairies are to be seen only between two twinklings of an eye." [37] Contact with them is thus not to be sought; the second sight—called often "the vision of the two worlds" [38]—is a cross to bear, for we are not fitted yet for more than one world, and, unlike the inhabitants of Faerie, we cannot even yet begin to traverse the sea to the Western Lands.

Like Tarot symbolism, the imagery of Faerie strikes to the archetypal level,[39] thus driving us closer to Christ or leaving us in hatred or despair. Samuel Roberts, a noted Welsh scholar, said that he "believed such things existed and that God allowed them to appear in times of great ignorance to convince people of the existence of an invisible world." [40] It is in this spirit that C. S. Lewis, by way of his seven Narnian Chronicles, and J. R. R. Tolkien, in *The Hobbit, The Lord of the Rings*, and his short stories ("Leap by Niggle," "Farmer Giles of Ham," etc.), have employed the motifs of Faerie to bring sensitive readers to face spiritual reality—archtypally in their own souls and factually in terms of the "existence of an invisible world."

Tolkien has set forth his view of the fairy tale as a *praeparatio evangelica* in a very significant essay where he stresses that the great folklore of the world is fulfilled in the greatest Story of all—the Story of Redemption. Thus the former can prepare the way for the latter, and when one arrives at it one finds that "this story is supreme; and it is true. Art has been verified. God is the Lord, of angels, and of men—and of elves." [41] But to try to use Faerie for one's own occult ends is to court disaster. Those who enter the charmed circle with such an object in mind may never leave it. A consistent tradition reminds us to accept the amazing richness of God's "hierarchy of heaven and earth" [42] but not to try to manipulate it for our own ends. Those who try may find themselves prisoners in the fairy kingdom till the sound of the Last Trump.

VISITATIONS FROM BEYOND

Everyone enjoys a good ghost story. But are ghosts "real"? And if they are, *what* are they and how is their reality to be correlated with established biblical teaching? What is to be said for the spiritualist movement in its endeavor to establish contact with those who have passed to the other side?

Ghosts are most definitely real. At least, *some* ghosts are. Clever manipulative and technical tricks have of course been employed by unethical tricksters—in particular, by professional mediums—to create ghostly phenomena,[43] but after the cases of humbug have been rigorously eliminated, the number of surd ghost experiences relayed by unimpeachable witnesses is most impressive. Here are three accounts, chosen for their representative variety. The first is a classic case from older, but thoroughly documented literature. The second is a modern case of animal haunting. The third is one of over sixty paradigm cases from the files of the British Society for Psychical Research which were analyzed by G. N. M. Tyrrell, one of the most careful investigators in this field in the present century.

> About the year 1667, being with some persons of honour in the house of a nobleman in the west country, which had formerly been a nunnery: I must confess I had often heard the servants, and others that inhabited or lodged there, speak much of the noises, stirs, and apparitions that frequently disturbed the house, but had at that time no apprehensions of it; for the house being full of stranger's, the nobleman's steward, Mr. C. lay with me in a fine wainscoatroom, called my ladies' chamber; we went to our lodging pretty early, and having a good fire in the room, we spent some time in reading, in which he much delighted: then having got into bed, and put out the candles, we observed the room to be very light, by the brightness of the moon, so that a wager was laid between us, that it was possible to read written hand by that light upon the bed where we lay; accordingly I drew out of my pocket a manuscript, which he read distinctly in the place where he lay: we had scarce made an end of discoursing about that affair, when I say (my face being towards the door which was locked) entering into the room, five appearances of very fine and lovely women, they were of excellent stature, and their dresses seemed very fine, but covered all but their faces, with their light veils, whose skirts trailed largely on the floor. They entered in a file one after the other, and in that posture walked round the room, till the

foremost came, and stood by that side of the bed where
I lay (with my left hand over the side of the bed; for
my head rested on that arm, and I determined not to
alter the posture in which I was) she struck me upon
that hand with a blow that felt very soft, but I did
never remember whether it were cold or hot: I demanded
in the name of the blessed Trinity, what business they
had there, but received no answer; then I spoke to Mr.
C. Sir, do you see what fair guests we have come to
visit us? before which they all disappeared: I found him
in some kind of agony and was forced to grasp him on
the breast with my right hand (which was next him
underneath the bed-clothes) before I could obtain speech
of him; then he told me that he had seen the fair guests
I spoke of, and had heard me speak to them; but withal
said, that he was not able to speak sooner unto me, being
extremely affrighted at the sight of a dreadful monster,
which assuming a shape, betwixt that of a lion and a
bear, attempted to come upon the bed's foot. I told him,
I thanked God nothing so frightful had presented itself
to me; but I hoped (through his assistance) not to dread
the ambages of hell. It was a long time before I could
compose him to sleep, and though he had had many
disturbances in his own room, and understood of others
in the house, yet he acknowledged he had never been so
terrified, during many years abode there. The next day
at dinner he shewed to divers persons of principal
quality, the mark that had been occasioned on his breast
by the gripe I was forced to give him, to get him to
speak, and related all the passages very exactly; after
which he protested never to lie more in that room; upon
which I set up a resolution to lodge in it again, not
knowing but something of the reason of those troubles
might by that means be imparted to me. The next night,
therefore, I ordered a Bible, and another book to be laid
in the room, and resolved to spend my time by the fire
in reading and contemplation, till I found myself inclined
to sleep: and accordingly having taken leave of the
family at the usual hour, I addressed to myself to what
I had proposed, not going into bed till past one in the
morning: a little after I was got into bed, I heard
somewhat walk about the room, like a woman in a
tabby gown trailing about the room; it made a mighty
rushelling noise, but I could see nothing, though it was
near as light as the night before: it passed by the foot of
the bed and a little opened the curtains, and thence
went to a closet door on that side, through which it
found admittance, although it was close locked: there

it seemed to groan, and draw a great chair with its foot, in which it seemed to sit, and turn over the leaves of a large folio; which you know make a loud clattering noise; so it continued in that posture, sometimes groaning, sometimes dragging the chair, and clattering the book till it was near day; afterwards I lodged several times in this room, but never met with any molestation.

This I can attest to be a true account of what passed in that room the two described nights; and though Mr. C. be lately dead, who was a very ingenious man, and affirmed the first part unto many, with whom he was conversant; it remains that I appeal to the knowledge of those who have been inhabitants or lodgers in the said house, for what remains, to justify the credibility of the rest.[44]

* * *

In 1950 Mrs. W. E. Dickson wrote to the American Society for Psychical Research describing the haunting "I have had many psychic experiences since childhood, but perhaps the most interesting has to do with our dog 'Butch,' who died exactly one year ago at the age of five years. Butch lived with us in our home and was highly regarded as a member of our family. We loved him dearly and he returned our love.

He died about noon on Tuesday, March 29, 1949. Tuesday night I heard him whining and crying all night long. I wasn't going to tell my husband because I didn't think that he would believe me. However, the next morning he said to me, 'I don't know if you will believe this, but I heard Butch crying all night.' We decided not to say anything about this to anyone, but changed our minds when one of our neighbors (who was with us when Butch was dying) came over and said, 'Don't know whether to tell you this or not, but last night Tuesday I dreamed that I heard Butch crying and went to the door, opened it, and there he was.' The only difference in our experiences was that we were wide awake when we heard Butch, and our friend was dreaming.

For about two months after Butch's death I heard him crying for me, and my husband swears that he heard him bark loudly at the back door to be let in." [45]

* * *

CASE 55. General Sir Arthur Becher, who held a

Staff appointment in India, took a house in Kussowlie for
the hot season. On the first night he awoke suddenly
and saw the figure of a native woman standing near his
bed. He got up and followed the figure, which retreated
into the bathroom and disappeared. The outer door of the
bathroom was locked. A few days later, Lady Becher
saw standing close by her and in the bathroom a native
woman, who disappeared by the same door as before,
which was locked. The same night their youngest son,
aged eight, started up in bed and called out, 'What do
you want, ayah?' evidently seeing a female figure in the
dressingroom. The family lived in the house for months
afterward, but the figure was not seen again. They
learned from other occupants that the figure was a
frequent apparition on the first night or so of the house
being occupied: a Cashmere woman was said to have
been murdered by the door leading into the bathroom.
Here the haunting has reference to the occupants of the
house as well as to the house itself.[46]

Facts are relatively easy; it is the interpretation of
them that is often hard! When faced by such data as
those just presented, many persons simply refuse to
accept them because they think that the interpretations
will destroy their faith (in non-Christian materialism;
in Christian judgment after death; etc.). Some view-
points—such as materialism—are indeed in tension with
spectral evidence; but others—including orthodox Christianity—are certainly not. Consider the following multi-
level explanatory scheme.

1. Ghosts as telepathic hallucinations arising from
the minds of the living. This is the view well expressed
by Podmore, who attributes the ghost phenomenon
to "waking dreams." "Commonsense points to its
source in the dreams of the living whom we know, rather
than in the imagined dreams of the unknown dead." [47]
Podmore's "commonsense" thus leads him to a paranormal explanation; however, it hardly seems to be
able to account for the powerfully objective focus of so
many ghost accounts, particularly when more than one
person sees the ghost at the same time, or independently
at different times.

2. Ghosts as telepathic hallucinations arising from
the minds (brains) of the dead. MacLellan argues:

"We may regard it possible for the minds of deceased individuals to be active and their brain radiations to be generated when both their respiratory and circulatory processes are inactive." Thus, "cremation appears obligatory for the damned if they wish to avoid entering Hell"! MacLellan is convinced that the minds of the deceased can be forced into abnormal spectral activity by "agents skilled in magic or sorcery." Obviously such necromancy must be performed "shortly after the death of the deceased person." [48] MacLellan's theory, by its shift of emphasis from the living to the dead, handles problems not covered in 1., but it fails in those cases where the spector represents a person whose brain *has* been cremated (death by fire) or totally destroyed in some other way.

3. Ghosts as residual human aura. The aura is a radiating luminous envelope or cloud projected from and surrounding the body. It is sometimes referred to as the "subtle body" or "etheric body" or (when separated from its body) the "human double." [49] A tremendous literature exists on this subject, including investigative work attempting, with some success, to render the aura visible by chemical screens.[50] If the aura in fact exists, then it is not unreasonable to suppose that it might remain for a time even after the death of the body, as the glow of an electric bulb can be seen for a few moments after the switch has been turned off. Since the aura is human, not impersonal, it would react as the person had reacted. Most ghostly apparitions involve suicide, passion, violent death, or high emotional tension of some kind; perhaps extraordinary emotion is the trigger that releases the aura to "haunt" for a time the places familiar to the deceased person—and especially those places connected with the emotional trauma. Ghosts generally represent recently—or fairly recently—deceased persons. Since the aura gradually fades away after death, this would serve to explain why few ghosts of Roman soldiers are reported these days! If the more violent the death-trauma or emotional level of the decedent, the longer the "life" of his aura, then

castle ghosts could be accounted for, since the stories associated with them almost always involve hideous events of one kind or another. Note that the aura is *not* the person; thus this explanation says nothing whatever against the immediate arrival of the deceased person at his appropriate eternal habitation, even while his aura continues for a time to walk the earth. Likewise, as in the case of animal ghosts, it does not even require the immortality of the soul for its functioning.[51]

4. Ghosts as the dead themselves, on their way to the reward determined once for all by their relationship or lack of relationship to Christ on earth, but not yet entered fully into that reward. Wrote the great Jung-Stilling: "Those souls, which are not yet dead to the world, and whose imagination is still occupied with the favourite ideas of their former life, seek to realize these ideas. . . . Hence the notorious haunting of old buildings." [52] It should be emphasized that this is not the Roman Catholic purgatorial concept (there is no hint of expiating one's own sins in a works-righteous fashion), nor is any necessary violation done to Heb. 9:27 ("it is appointed unto men once to die, but after this the judgment"), since no postponement or possible reversal of the judgment at death is suggested. Only the time-lag between death and heaven, or death and hell, is extended to account for ghostly phenomena that show more self-direction than the "human aura" would allow for, and yet do not engage either in angelic or in demonic missions to the living.

5. Ghosts as the damned sent back to haunt the living or as Satanic counterfeits of the dead. Where a person whose earthly relationship to Christ has been so negative that his salvation appears very dubious returns from the dead to do harm to the living, he returns by Satanic influence. If saved persons seem to return from the dead denying the faith or attempting to harm the living, we can conclude that demonic counterfeits are the explanation. If Satan can transform himself into an angel of light (II Cor. 11:14), he can certainly disguise himself as a dead saint.[53]

6. Ghosts as the saved sent back to earth by God for a special mission. Elijah and Moses on the Mount of Transfiguration seem to be clear instances of this phenomenon (cf. particularly Mt. 17:3, 8). As a modern example, C. S. Lewis' appearance to J. B. Phillips, cited in Chapter One.

These six explanatory levels offer the tools for dealing with most attested spectral phenomena. Sometimes one interpretation will best fit the data, sometimes another. An important conclusion follows from this multi-level approach, and it cannot be too strongly emphasized: no apparition offers apodictic proof of survival after death. Why? because one can theoretically appeal to telepathy or the human aura as an explanation. This accounts for the seeming paradox that in spite of the impressive collections of spectral and mediumistic "survival" evidence,[54] some of the most distinguished psychical researchers doubt that man survives death. Though he holds that in light of mediumistic messages involving specialized classical allusions, the most satisfying hypothesis is that "we are in indirect touch with some part of the surviving personality of a scholar—and that scholar F. W. H. Myers," Gardner Murphy says of himself: "Now in my sixties, I do not actually anticipate finding myself in existence after physical death."[55] C. D. Broad concluded his Cambridge University Perrott lectures on psychical research with the words: "For my part I should be slightly more annoyed than surprised if I should find myself in some sense persisting immediately after the death of my present body. One can only wait and see, or alternately (which is no less likely) wait and not see."[56]

This is precisely the sad result when one depends on ESP or ghost hunting to solve the problem of survival after death. And the question is too crucial to "wait and see"—particularly if the Bible is right in setting forth two possible eternal destinies. The solution? Check out the evidence for the one validated instance of the total self-conquest of death (physically and spiritually, not just "spectrally"): the resurrection of Jesus Christ. Over five hundred eye witnesses to the fact were still alive when in A.D. 56 Paul could write without fear of refutation: "O grave, where is thy victory? Thanks be to God, who gives us the victory through our Lord Jesus Christ" (I Cor. 15).

By the same token, even less can be said for reliance upon mediumistic spiritualism. If the Tarot cards and the Wee Folk are not to be fooled with, surely the dead should be left alone! The closer one approaches to the throne of the Almighty or to the pit of the Inferno, the more careful one must be. By not recognizing this, spiritualists have fallen into the grossest religious errors. Spiritualism has become quite literally a church (or better, an anti-church), with a creed that eliminates any serious view of sin, Christ's atoning death, and eternal punishment, and that promises "endless progression" on the basis of moral self-betterment.[57]

It was Bishop Arthur A. Ford of the Spiritualist Church —a man who felt at home preaching in Universalist circles and whose career in his own religious body was checkered with notoriety and suspicion of scandal[58]—who assisted the late Resigned Bishop James Pike to communicate with his deceased son in September, 1967. The message from James Jr., who had committed suicide, came to Pike through Ford in the following terms: "He wants you to definitely understand that neither you nor any other member of the family has any right to feel any sense of guilt or have any feelings that you failed him in any way."[59] A few months later, on November 17-19, 1967, Pike and I were featured speakers at the McMaster University Teach-In in Hamilton, Ontario.[60] The Bishop's condition was almost too pitiful to describe. He was as egocentrically nervous as a film star—breaking off dinner conversation abruptly again and again to rush to the door to clap any dignitary on the back who came in; totally unprepared in his formal presentations; irrational (relying on the all-too-obvious self-interested "evidence" of his son's existence while depreciating all the powerful proof of the supernatural in Scripture and history); and desirous—above all—of public acclaim (introducing the U.S.'s "immoral" Vietnam policy into discussions on totally different subjects, thereby receiving ovations from radical Canadian students who should have been reminded of their own government's restrictive immigration practices!).

The late messrs. Ford and Pike at séance

If there were ever a good argument against dabbling in spiritualism, Pike was it. He had, in his own words, "jettisoned the Trinity, the Virgin Birth and the Incarnation," [61] and having thereby lost all criteria for testing the spirits, he became their unwitting tool. Incredible as it is (but a clear reminder of the theological state of contemporary Roman Catholicism), an avant garde Dominican writer on the occult has just provided the following eulogy of the Bishop:

> James A. Pike was for many a living symbol of the contemporary Christian's pilgrimage towards an ever deeper understanding of the ultimate mystery of life. Yet he was able to remain faithful to his Church while wandering the labyrinth of occult theories, claims, and experiences. His example may prevent others from plunging over the edge of the unknown in their quest.[62]

Perhaps Pike's example *will* prevent others from going

over the edge, but, if so, it will be because his tragic
denial of Christian verities and involvement in the miasma
of mediumship will serve as an appalling warning. Let
us conclude our treatment of this dark subject with the
informed judgment of an Anglican who has *in fact* remained "faithful to his Church": "Spiritualism is being
used by the great enemy of souls in his ceaseless warfare
against Christ and his Church." [63]

LUST FOR THE DEMONIC

The last stop on our journey into the shadow-land will
be mercifully brief. No area of occultism is now receiving
such sensationalistic coverage as today's witchcraft
craze, yet the subject poses the fewest complexities of
interpretation. The reason is simply that here one reaches
the "black" end of the occult spectrum; grayness dis-
appears and all becomes clear—hideously clear.

The problem involved in determining whether demon
possession occurs and whether witchcraft works is absurd-
ly simple. The documentation is overwhelming.[64] Even
if ninety-nine percent of all witchcraft cases are thrown
out (and that would be very difficult to do) the remainder
would easily establish the reality of the phenomenon.
The excesses of the medieval and 16th-17th century witchcraft trials were tragic, particularly since they arose
in large part as a theological error—from obliviousness
to the fact that Ex. 22:18 ("thou shalt not suffer a witch
to live") was limited to the social legislation Israel received to keep pure the Messianic stream, and therefore
had no more legitimate application once Messiah's reign
of love began in New Testament times than did punish-
ments connected with Israelite-Canaanite mixed marriages. But the horrors of witch trials must not blind
us to the horrors of witchcraft. C. S. Lewis' well-known
advice is worth repeating: "There are two equal and
opposite errors into which our race can fall about the
devils. One is to disbelieve in their existence. The other
is to believe, and to feel an excessive and unhealthy
interest in them. They themselves are equally pleased

by both errors and hail a materialist or a magician with the same delight." [65] Let us try to keep our balance.

Can't witchcraft be "fun"? Must it be regarded in such a stuffy, moralistic way? Counter-question to the questioner: How about rape, sodomy, child molesting, suicide, murder? Can't *these* be "fun"? Must *they* be regarded in such a stuffy, moralistic way? This parallel is no exaggeration. Aleister Crowley (d. 1947), the self-styled "Great Beast," drank the cup of black magic to its dregs. One of his many mistresses, Edith Y—, was branded with his mark; the sexual and drug practices of his group are too dispicable to recount; a young Oxford undergraduate who came to Crowley's infamous Abbey of Thelema in Sicily died from drugs, combined with "failure to maintain the purity of the magic circle":

> Frater Aud [the undergraduate] was already over-wrought by the intensity of the ceremony, by the drugs he had taken, the incense, the dancing. The light of the candles swam before his eyes—but he slashed at Mischette's throat.
>
> The Ape of Thoth, clad in a scarlet abbai, a long sword hanging from the sash round her waist, left her stool and held up her Golden Cup of Abominations to catch the blood, not a drop of which must be lost.
>
> His blow was too light. The cat, its throat only half cut, squirmed with a scream from his trembling hands, sprang off the altar and darted out of the magic circle, breaking the spell and letting in the massed demons that the Banishing Ritual of the Pentagram had cast out. [66]

After the youth's death shortly thereafter, Crowley declared: "The moment his Work was done, he went out like a match having lighted my cigar." [67] Does this sound like fun? The close parallels with the esoteric-satanic California murder cult of Charles Manson are most instructive. [68] Evidently the devil has a favorite life-style (which is of course a death-style).

Perhaps the answer is some kind of "white magic"—nothing as messy as the examples just given, but something sufficiently exciting to offer the "kicks" we all crave? "Persons wishing to consort with either good or evil spirits for a beneficent or innocent purpose, invoke

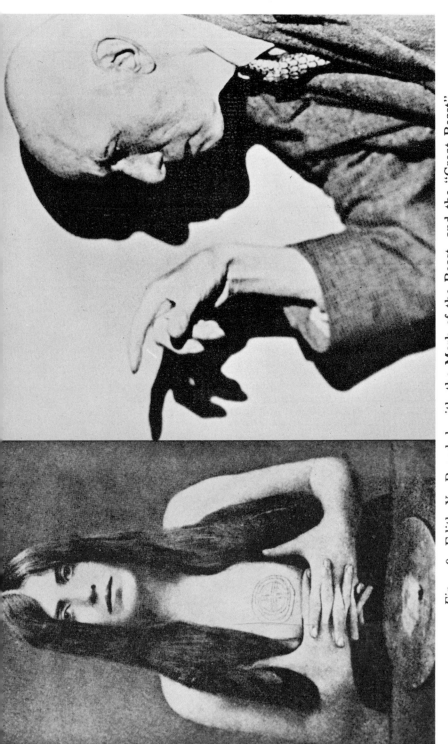

Figure 9. Edith Y—Branded with the Mark of the Beast, and the "Great Beast" himself, Aleister Crowley, six years before his death.

them by ceremonial, or white magic; but as consorting with demons is not by any means healthy for the soul, ceremonial magic might be stigmatized as 'black as a tar-barrel.' " [69] To use evil or improper means to achieve a good end is always wrong (the situation ethicists notwithstanding, but they do not notice this because they are engaged in a bit of legerdemain themselves—creating morality *ex nihilo*!).[70]

The tragedy of most sorcery, invocation of demons, and related practices is that those who carry on these activities refuse to face the fact that they *always* turn out for the *worst*. What is received through the Faustian past never satisfies, and one pays with one's soul in the end anyway. The foolish and greedy man in W. W. Jacobs' classic tale, "The Monkey's Paw," attempted to obtain three wishes from a demonic fetish: first he wished for money, and he received the exact sum—as insurance compensation for the sudden and violent death of his son. Then he wished for his son back, and the son came back—rotting from the grave. His third wish was that his son return to the place whence he had come. This is a parable, and it is hoped that its moral will not be lost on the reader.[71]

There is a definite correlation between negative occult activity and madness. European psychiatrist L. Szondi has shown a high correlation between involvement in spiritualism and occultism (and the related theosophical blind alleys) on the one hand, and schizophrenia on the other.[72] Kurt Koch's detailed case studies have confirmed this judgment, and have brought out the appalling fact that the members of the sorcerer's family can likewise be affected—even if they do not practice the vile activity themselves. Members of subsequent generations in a family where demonic practices have been carried on are prone to mental illness and possession. Being a genuine Christian believer is no guarantee of exemption from the consequences of sorcery and black magic. Just as a Christian can be maimed by a stray bullet from a non-Christian's gun, so he can suffer the spiritual results of others' occult foolishness or perversity.[73]

"Who then can be saved?"—as the amazed disciples once put it. The answer is: anyone and everyone who trusts in Christ and His Word. The great exorcistic liturgies of the historic church have in common the confidence that "greater is He that is in you than he that is in the world" (I Jn. 4:4). The Name of Jesus has, from Apostolic times, been the universal remedy against evil spirits. Not that all beings respond to it (intermediate spirits such as Poltergeists sometimes do not—but their mischievous actions are not on the level of demon possession); not that evil spirits cannot struggle long and hard and use wily tricks to deceive. But the Christ the living Word, represented by the scriptural and sacramental means of grace, will most definitely win the victory. After all, He has already fulfilled the prophecy of the Protoevangelion (Gen. 3:15) and crushed the serpent's head by His atoning death and resurrection. "Fear not, little flock; for it is your Father's good pleasure to give you the kingdom."

God's victory over the evil powers goes even deeper, if possible, than this. But to convey that truth, we shall summon to our aid the muse of literature.

6

God's Devil:
A Ghost Story with a Moral

An aspect of the occult touched only in passing in this book—and almost always neglected in toto in other "serious" writings on the subject—is the sphere of supernatural fiction. Such neglect is a great mistake, for though Bishop Pike was wrong (as usual) in wanting the Creed to be sung but not said, certain truths can be conveyed more effectively in parable or story than in ordinary propositional discourse. Especially is this true of the supernatural realms of Faerie, and even more so of the dark borderlands of occult evil. Indeed someone has suggested that Dante's Inferno is the most effective unit of the Divine Comedy because in describing the nether regions he speaks so fully from his own experience! Whether my tale should be taken as exemplifying that truth is a moot question (though there are genuine autobiographical details imbedded there—I leave to the reader the task of winnowing them). No apologies are in order for the moral quality of the story, for ghost stories are invariably (perhaps inevitably) moralistic: one can hardly bump up against "heaven and its wonders, and hell" without having to face one's own relationship to them and to the spectral haunts of earth. So, with appreciation for the chills I have received from Le Fanu, M. R. James, John

Figure 10. The Demons Astaroth, Eurynome; Baël,
Amduscias; and Belphegor, Asmodeus (From Collin de Plancy's
Dictionnaire infernal, Paris, 1863)

Buchan, and a host of others, most of whom are now themselves shades, here is the tale. *

"So you actually did it. You've become a damned bible-toting clergyman." The smile on Cavender's face was compounded roughly of sixty per cent cynicism and forty per cent genuine interest; knowing from my college days that one could almost never expect a better ratio from him, I realized that no insult was intended. Here, in the hubbub of meaningless small talk which seemed to be moving toward absurdity but never quite reaching it, he wanted a satisfying conversational exchange perhaps as much as I did.

We were standing in front of the large fireplace with the gothic inscription staring out at us as it had so frequently when we were at school together:

AH LIFE! THE MERE LIVING! HOW FIT
TO EMPLOY ALL THE HEART AND THE
SOUL AND THE MIND FOREVER IN JOY!

"How appropriate," I thought to myself. "Since Cavender and I graduated from old Cornell ten years ago, we have both managed to live out Willard Straight's rather banal aphorism—as long as different definitions of 'joy' are permitted."

"Yes," I said laughing, "I've become a clergyman —and I'll even accept the adjective 'damned,' since a cleric doesn't escape being *simul justus et peccator.*"

" 'Saint and sinner at the same time,' eh? Good God, you're not just a cleric, you're a theologian to boot." Cavender's face now registered real surprise and a trace of something vaguely approaching admiration. "Notice that your Latin didn't snow me. Old hell-fire Luther, right? Three cheers for my classical education—it finally seems to be paying off in polite conversation as well as in my authority-conscious profession."

"The law, of course," I replied. "You were moving in that direction in your senior year. And"—I eyed my profane friend to see his reaction—"a caustic wit like

---

* Originally published in *Chiaroscuro*, 4 (1961).

yours would go to waste outside of dramatic courtroom situations.''

"Quite so, quite so," Cavender said, laughing. "And a corporation mouthpiece at that. But why I ended up peeking under Justice's blindfold is the usual drab tale. Whyte's Organization Man, Riesman's Other-directed American, and a wee bit of Oliver Wendell Holmes—put them all together and they don't spell Mother, they spell Ross Cavender. But what I want to know is why you ended up with your intellectual and sartorial collars on backwards. *That* should be worth hearing. I presume that like George Fox you heard the 'call' and now you spend your spare moments walking barefoot and yelling, 'Woe, woe to the bloody city of Lichfield'—or rather— 'New York.' Come on, let's get the hell out of this highball-jiggling madhouse and you can tell me about it."

Without waiting for a reply Cavender started for the door of the Great Hall. His voice trailed off as he elbowed his rather stocky frame through the Amy Vanderbiltish crowd:

"Why in thunder does any sane man come to an alumni reunion? Did all these bastards actually graduate. . .''

I followed as best I could, though not with quite the Cavender aplomb. He headed for the wainscoted browsing-library. Apparently the alumni had not lost the antipathy to scholarly literature which four years of university education manages to create: the library was practically deserted. We sat down in the far corner near the roaring wood fire. Cavender grabbed an ashtray and lit another cigarette from the one he was just finishing. I took out my pipe.

"So," I said, "You want me to tell you how I came to enter the ministry—how I became interested in theology. Actually these are two questions, not one. You remember that in college I was something of a do-gooder —causes, etc. Probably that would have been enough to put me in clerical garb; it certainly landed me in theological seminary. But as to how I got the *intellectual* collar on backwards—that's a different story. That happened *in* seminary, not before."

"Oh, no!" Cavender broke in. "Am I going to hear the fascinating story of how Theology 650 opened your eyes to—what's the Swedenborgian phrase—'heaven and its wonders and hell'? In a sense I suppose I asked for it. But please, don't get too emotional; I have a sympathetic ulcer."

"Relax, Ross," I answered. "It isn't going to be that kind of tale."

"I hope not. And spare the academic minutiae. My LL.B. was no snap, you know. Even today the very thought of the supersedeas writ makes my blood run cold."

"It's odd that you should speak of blood running cold," I said. "That definitely ties in with a certain event in my seminary experience—an event I was about to describe to you. As a result of it, I became—how shall I put it?—theologically inclined. And maybe without it I would never have finished seminary or been ordained. Shall I go on?"

"Sure, sure. As I said, I asked for it. I'll try not to derail your train of thought again."

The fire was burning brightly; the few people who had been in the room when we entered were now gone. The cocktail hour had passed, and the winter evening was already settling down around us. With the realization that I could have told the story only to a skeptic such as Cavender—since his ridicule was predictable —I began.

* * * * *

Theological seminary is an unpleasant period for many who go through it. I think this was doubly so for me. There was the usual feeling of intellectual descent, for, say what you will about a secular university, heat is seldom substituted for light there. But over and above that, I felt definite alienation from the whole program. What did all this doctrine and Biblical study have to do with *life*, and with changing society? In college I had been what C. S. Lewis somewhere calls a "Christianity-and" man — "Christianity-and-pacifism," "Christianity-and-vegetarianism," etc. I wanted to set the world rightside up. Marx turned Hegel's dialectic on its head; I wanted to put corrupt America—or some segment of it—on its feet again. But what good was abstract doctrine? "Justification by grace through faith": I thought it was utterly impractical. "The resurrection": absurd and irrelevant. "The new birth": revolting. "Angelology and demonology": medieval and essentially immoral. It was my middler year in seminary, and I had just about decided to quit the whole business. For the previous week I had been reading and comparing catalogues of schools of social work. No pie-in-the-sky idealism there!

Then I received my preaching assignment to St. Paul's church on the Old Drummer's road.

Perhaps I had better explain the expression "preaching assignment." (*At this point Cavender mumbled that he didn't care much one way or the other—but if it would make me happy . . .*) At the small seminaries of our denomination, the students are expected to lead the services at nearby churches with vacant pulpits. The theory is that the student can't do excessive harm to the congregation, and the congregational experience may conceivably do the student some good psychologically. Morever, at least in my seminary situation, the experience definitely did the congregations and the students good financially, since, on the one hand, the pulpits could be filled at fees so ridiculously low that an ordained man would not even consider them sufficient for carfare, and, on the other, the students were generally so broke that any remuneration was viewed as manna from heaven.

Since I was unquestionably in the latter category (this being, I felt, my only genuine common ground with the other students), I leaped at the chance to take the assignment.

I should mention that our seminary was in one of the older rural sections of the Midwest. Little towns connected by irrationally laid-out roads dotted the whole area in a radius of three hundred miles around the seminary. A file of old church bulletins and maps drawn by previous student pastors was the best way of keeping track of the numerous churches which begged for aid—in the most heart-rending terms—from time to time.

After the assignment came from elderly Dean Rylsford ("bless his heart," I thought, "the seminary would disintegrate without him"), I consulted the file. I went through it three times, looking under "P" for "Paul's," "S" for "Saint," and finally—cursing (but just "damn," for this isn't really "taking the name of the Lord thy God in vain")—under "I" for "Indiana." Nothing. Then I took all the files out of the battered desk drawer, and found, crumpled at the back, an old map telling how to get to St. Paul's. The paper was badly yellowed, and the writing was almost illegible. The map had apparently been held too near a fire on some occasion, for it was plainly scorched. But it gave me the directions I needed, and that was all I cared.

Sunday morning I arose early—but no earlier than absolutely necessary. When faced with a preaching assignment, my regular procedure was to determine the exact distance to the church, divide it by forty miles an hour (the average speed my car could travel without the motor dropping out), add one-half hour for service preliminaries at the church, and then get up not a minute before the required time. Since St. Paul's appeared from the map to be one hundred and twenty-miles away, and the service was scheduled for ten-thirty, I left the seminary at seven.

It was a stormy February day—the first Sunday in Lent, to be exact. Wisps of snow were in the air, and the wind was strong. Fortunately the roads were clear: I would make good time.

The first lap of the journey was along highway 37, a well-paved east-west road crossing the state. I was to go eighty miles due west before turning off onto a county road. I felt relieved that the first part of the trip was to be so unproblematical. I would have an opportunity to run through my sermon again. The speedometer registered exactly forty.

My sermon was on the Gospel lesson for the day, and, if I did say so myself, it was one of my better homiletic creations. A year ago, when I first delivered it on a similar preaching assignment, it had gone over very well. I still remembered the wife of a member of the church council saying at the door after the service: "You have a great future ahead of you, young man." Perhaps she was right, but I was no longer sure that it lay in the ordained ministry. Thank goodness this was a Sunday when I could give one of my really satisfying sermons; I didn't think I could have stomached again, for example, the naïve, supernaturalistic message I had once prepared for the previous Sunday of the church year, when the Gospel lesson reads:

> Then Jesus took unto Him the twelve, and said unto them, Behold, we go up to Jerusalem, and all things that are written by the prophets concerning the Son of man shall be accomplished. For He shall be delivered unto the Gentiles, and shall be mocked, and spitefully entreated, and spitted on: and they shall scourge Him, and put Him to death: and the third day He shall rise again.

I had certainly beat the drum for fulfilled prophecy and a historical resurrection in that sermon! How simpleminded can one be? And I had noticed that the comments at the church door afterwards were not at all as effusive as I would have liked. Some people even had tears in their eyes.

But this Sunday would be different. It is true that on the surface the Gospel lesson seemed typically theological and miraculously-orientated. But it just needed the kind of modern interpretation my sermon provided. You of course remember that Gospel lesson for the first Sunday in Lent. (*"Naturally," Cavender said with a sly smile, "but you might refresh my memory on the details."*)

The lesson is the familiar temptation-in-the-wilderness passage, beginning: "Then was Jesus led up of the Spirit into the wilderness to be tempted of the devil." Old devil presents three temptations: make stones into bread to satisfy hunger, do a miracle to show personal power, and worship evil in order to obtain all the kingdoms of the world. Naturally Jesus refuses. Sounds a bit histrionic and overdone as it stands, eh? That's what I thought, and in my sermon I attempted to bring out the *real* essence of the passage.

First, I pointed out that the modern mind has to give up the primitive idea of a personal evil being ("devil," "Satan," etc.). However, as a symbol the concept still has meaning, for it indicates how far short of evolutionary perfection we still are. (The previous year some of the congregation had appeared puzzled at the phrase "evolutionary perfection," but I determined to retain it, for it's a compliment to a congregation to speak over its head on occasion.) Then I dealt with the temptations themselves. What was the point of them all? Why, to show the evils of selfishness. If Jesus had made the stones into bread for *others*—if he had jumped off the pinnacle of the temple in an attempt to show others that society should learn to control the powers of nature—if he had gained the kingdoms of the world in order to create a model government and social milieu for the benefit of mankind—"then," I had thundered a year before, "then the situation would have been different, far different." This passage, I argued, should warn all of us against the dangers of self-centered lives, and we should follow Jesus, the ideal Master, in rejecting all temptation to do ourselves good when we should be doing good for others.

The sermon sounded even better to me as I reviewed it than it had a year before; and I particularly prided myself that I had exactly countered the advice of my drab homiletics professor: "to present Jesus always as Saviour, never merely as example." But further musing was now impossible, for I had reached the turnoff.

The map told me to go left, that is, south, on county route 6A, and continue on for twenty miles until I reached Sodom Junction. The road was not very well paved, and the wind was definitely increasing in velocity. It was already 9:30; apparently I had let the speed drop below forty miles an hour while I was going over the sermon. Now I had to concentrate entirely on the driving or I would be late. This thought made my stomach turn over, for Dean Rylsford, though a mild man, had one phobia: students must not be late for assigned services. Of course, what difference did it make if I were going to leave seminary anyway? But, I reproached myself, even the philosopher Kant maintained such a regular schedule that the burghers of Königsberg could set their clocks by his walks to and from the university. I pressed harder on the accelerator.

At five minutes before ten I arrived at Sodom Junction—if such a collection of ramshackled old stores and deteriorating houses could be dignified by a name. Why it was called a junction I could not imagine, for there were no train tracks that I could see. But the "Sodom" was certainly appropriate, I said to myself—if one thought of the Biblical Sodom after, and not before, the fire descended from heaven (or rather—I rationally corrected myself—natural volcanic eruption engulfed it).

I was now to turn right on the dirt road which crossed 6A. This was called the Old Drummer's road, according to the map, and St. Paul's church was on a cutoff some twenty miles beyond Sodom Junction. I tried to see a road sign or directional indicator for confirmation, but there was neither. Since it was Sunday morning, the stores were all closed; and even the houses showed no sign of life. "Probably damned superstitious Catholics," I thought, "up for 6 A.M. mass and now back in bed." However, there could be little real doubt about the route, for only one east-west road crossed 6A at the town. I wheeled the car to the right and started off again. Ten o'clock—just a half-hour to go. By my original schedule I should have arrived at the church by now.

I gunned the motor, and in spite of the wretched driving conditions—snow was now coming down steadily and the wind was blowing it directly at the windshield—I managed to maintain an insane speed of fifty-five. Fifteen minutes went by. I was becoming more and more nervous.

The road began to twist and turn. The landscape
(as much as I could see of it) became heavily wooded,
but had a burned-over appearance.

At 10:25, to my great relief, I saw the church, just
off the road to my left.

It was a profoundly depressing sight—more depressing, if possible, than Sodom Junction. The building was
short and squat, and though built in a cruciform pattern,
the transepts were far longer than the nave. Obviously the builders had had only a rough idea of proper
ecclesiastical symbolism. The exterior was of brick, and
was blackened from age or perhaps from a fire which
had given the woods their burned appearance, but which
had been stopped just before it reached the church.

There was no parking area, and no other cars were
visible. I pulled over to the left side of the narrow
road, switched off the motor, yanked the emergency
brake on, and leaped out of the car.

As I did so the wooden double doors of the church
opened (they were a sickly yellow-orange color—perhaps they had originally been an off-shade of red), and
a man of about seventy appeared. He moved stiffly and
slowly down the steps and came toward me. His bent
frame reminded me of a large bug, but that, I said
to myself, was hardly the gracious thought a seminarian
should have toward one of God's old soldiers.

"You must be our young man from N— Seminary,"
he wheezed. "You had us a bit worried, though we seldom
start the services right on time. My name is Oldstone
—Enoch Oldstone—and I am president of the council.
Do come in out of the damp."

I followed him into the church while exchanging the
usual pleasantries. The interior was one of the strangest
I had ever encountered—and I had seen many examples
of midwestern churchmanship.

The strangeness did not come from any bizarre substitutions for the usual appointments, such as in one
little Ohio congregation where I had been appalled to
find colored Christmas tree lights used on the altar
throughout the year. Rather, one received the impression

in St. Paul's that everything was almost correct, but not quite. For one thing, in line with the squat exterior of the building, the horizontal dimension seemed to predominate over the vertical: the pulpit was too low; the altar was too low; the candles on it were too short. And the cross—the altar cross—could its horizontal axis possibly be longer than the vertical? Clearly it was a Greek cross and not a Latin one; there was nothing wrong with that, needless to say, but the vertical axis did look shorter. Perhaps it was an illusion due to the bad lighting, I told myself. The stained glass windows were competently done, but in much too sombre shades. Almost Calvinistic in their severity, I thought. And the scenes! What odd choice had dictated them? Oh, they were Biblical all right, but they depicted such Old Testament episodes as Saul consulting the witch of Endor, and Elisha's bears eating the insolent children; and such New Testament events as Ananias and Sapphira being struck dead, and Simon Magus attempting to buy the Holy Spirit. My eyes travelled to the congregation itself, if it could be called such. There were not more than twenty-five people present in all, though the church could have held ten times that number. They were not seated together, but (I thought with relief) at least they sat near the chancel. Then I saw the reason: an old woodburning stove not far from the pulpit. And yet, it was certainly warm enough in here without sitting that close to the stove. . .

I suddenly realized that Enoch Oldstone had asked me a question. Flustered, I had to have it repeated.

"Would you like to have me go over the peculiarities of our service with you, young man?" he queried in a rasping voice.

"I don't think that will be necessary, thank you," I replied. "I have done a great deal of supply preaching in recent years." (The plural "years" was a bit of an exaggeration, but I liked to set nervous congregational members at ease.) "You might, however, mention any radical differences between your service and the Common Service."

"Well," he began with a hoarse chuckle which I did not entirely like, "we have made a few alterations—but what congregation hasn't, I always say. Every congregation has its favorite portions of the service, and traditions do grow up. Doesn't the Confession put it well when it says, 'It is not necessary that rites and ceremonies everywhere be the same'?"

I nodded painfully, wondering what was coming next. I had never been especially good at introducing liturgical innovations without prior practice.

Apparently sensing my dismay, Oldstone said, "My boy, why not just let me take the opening liturgy? I serve as lay reader here regularly, and"—he gave me an odd look out of the corner of his eye—"we don't get young men of your potential very often. We want to make you feel at home, yes, right at home." (Why did he stress that? I asked myself.) "You just give the sermon. It is on the Gospel lesson, isn't it?"

I nodded.

"Wonderful!" He clasped his thin hands together. "A glorious passage! It's our favorite here at St. Paul's, or as we familiarly call our old church, St. 'Pollyon's. The ending seems a bit inconclusive, but"—he added hastily—"we shouldn't question things deeper than ourselves. As the Good Book says, 'His ways are deeper than our ways.'"

I was sure that the verse read "higher" rather than "deeper," but there was no point in being pedantic. I accepted the offer with great relief.

By then an old lady had begun to play the prelude on the pedal organ. A deep depression was settling over me as we walked slowly up the aisle and took our seats. I was so overwhelmed, either from the exhaustion of driving or from the excessive heat in the chancel, that I fancied the prelude to consist of selections from Wagner's Gotterdammerung. "What absurdity," I thought. I must get a hold on myself before the sermon."

Oldstone carried the liturgy along very effectively, I had to admit. But he mumbled to such an extent that I found it difficult to catch the words. At a few points he seemed to become positively elated, as for example at the Introit and the Gradual when the Psalm reads, "He that dwelleth in the secret place of the Most High." The Gloria Patri and the Gloria in Excelsis did not, as far as I could determine, come into the service at all, but this was probably one of the local variations Oldstone had referred to previously. The Creed plainly had been reworked, and the phrase "principalities and powers" was inserted at several places. But my mind was badly muddled. I could not be certain what was said. The heat was becoming insufferable.

Finally the time for the sermon arrived. I rose and went to the pulpit. Oldstone jumped up ahead of me and removed a worn volume from it to make room for my notes. Did I read the title right as "Malleus maleficarum"?

I looked out at the twenty-five or so men and women in front of me. Their eyes, I realized with suppressed horror, were glowing like so many red coals in the dim light of the church. Some seemed to be licking their lips, as if in anticipation. "For the meat of the Word," I fervently hoped.

I began. My exordium dealing with the primitive foolishness of literal belief in the devil did not seem to go over very well. Some of the congregation were frowning and others were picking at their hymnals in an irritating fashion.

Then I discussed the temptations as such. The congregation clearly appreciated this much more than the preceding. As I argued that Jesus should have made the stones into bread for others, they smiled—or perhaps "grinned" would better describe it. When I noted parenthetically that Jesus, even as the Ideal Man, could hardly have thwarted the laws of gravitation, they began to show real interest. When I came to the possibility of man's gaining the kingdoms of the world for purposes of social reform, they were positively ecstatic. And they didn't seem to have a bit of trouble with "evolutionary perfection."

This positive reaction should have pleased me, I suppose; but, frankly, the effect was just the opposite.

As their eyes grew brighter, and as they licked their lips more obviously, I felt the heat rise until I didn't think I could bear it. And—was it possible?—the congregation seemed, if anything to draw closer to the fire, and bundle themselves up to a greater extent in their heavy coats and scarves. In contrast, I found myself trembling with sweat and fear.

Finally something within me snapped. Instead of using the peroration in my notes, I began to preach *ex tempore* on Jesus as Lord and God—being tempted by the devil to renounce His saving purpose for the human race—but conquering the evil one with those magnificent words, "Get thee hence, Satan: for it is written, Thou shalt worship the Lord thy God, and Him only shalt thou serve."

As I sat down, the congregation showed definite signs of irritation. Their eyes no longer glowed very brightly, and some faces looked ashen. No one was licking his lips. The temperature had dropped appreciably.

Oldstone concluded the service—a bit summarily, I thought, but none too soon for me. At the door he told me that the congregation customarily remained in their pews for Sunday school, but that I needn't stay for that. He emphasized the "needn't." Then he said with an expression of sadness and disappointment: "You were doing wonderfully, my boy, until the last part of the sermon. You ought to change that conclusion; the people didn't like it, I'm sure of that. Too theological for us simple folk. We thought that you'd be able to stay and be, er, a part of our eucharistic service later. From all we heard, you would have fitted beautifully into our little congregation—perhaps on a permanent basis. We haven't had a pastor in many years. . ." He looked wistfully at the communion table, and his pale tongue passed quickly over his thin lips. "But I don't think you're quite ready, my boy. Go back to seminary for a while longer. And THEN COME BACK TO US HERE AT ST. 'POLLYON'S."

These last words were said with almost hypnotic force. I shuddered, but did not reply. He turned and proceeded, bug-like, down the nave. I fled to my car and drove like sixty back to Sodom Junction—to route 6A—to highway 37—to the seminary. That day I became a theologian.

* * * *

"And that's it?" said Cavender with a look combining amazement with authentic concern.

"That's it," I replied. "Except for a little historical background I acquired the following week at the seminary. No one else seemed to know of a St. Paul's church in that locality, so I checked a few old histories of the synod. There had been a church all right, but all the histories agreed that it had burned down in a lightning storm in 1867. One writer said that in the synod at the time some suggested maliciously that the fire had been deserved—that the congregation had been cheating on its benevolence budget for years, and that strange goings-on had been reported there from time to time, especially on All Saints' Eve.

"Oh, yes, and one other thing," I added. "When the Dean heard that I had come back from St. Paul's —or St. Apollyon's as they called it—he said to me: 'Glad to see you, young man. I prayed for you much this weekend. It's been some time since one of the men has been called to supply at St. Paul's. I presume that you will want the advanced seminar in dogmatics next year?' 'Praise God,' I answered, 'that is just what I want.' "

You expect me to roar at the whole thing, don't you? Cavander asked. Well, you get a surprise. Sure, I'm a skeptic, but not a fool. That 'more things in heaven and earth' bit is quite sensible. And wasn't it your Luther who said that the devil is God's devil?

Quite right, Cavender. And that fits very nicely with the Gospel lesson for that first Sunday in Lent: "Then was Jesus led up of the Spirit into the wilderness to be tempted of the devil."

Epilogue

BEFORE YOU CLOSE THE CREAKING DOOR

We wrestle not against flesh and blood, but against principalities, against powers, against the rulers of the darkness of this world, against spiritual wickedness in high places. Wherefore take unto you the whole armor of God.

—Ephesians 6:12-13

A few concluding words are in order both for the evangelical who seeks perspective on the occult and for the general reader whose quest for truth has brought him into contact with "God's devil."

Evangelical believers need a greater measure of maturity when faced with the occult. This judgment may not appear particularly informative, since evangelicals seem to suffer from endemic adolescence (teenage decisions for Christ but few grownup churches, etc.), but where the occult is involved, evangelical immaturity leads to particularly tragic results. Finding it difficult to handle the occult, the evangelical is alternately fascinated and repelled by occult phenomena. It is a known fact that young people at Christian camps have dabbled quite considerably in the occult in recent years. Converts to church-of-Satan groups very often have a history of fundamentalist upbringing.

What accounts for the fundamentalist fascination with the dark world? At least two considerations. First is the characteristic I dubbed, in an *Eternity* article of some years ago, "kookishness." Kookishness refers to "absurd irrationalism associated with a theological position: nuttyness that produces disrespect for the theology proclaimed in conjunction with it." I illustrated with three areas in which evangelicals have shown themselves to be kooks first-class: prophetically establishing the end of the world in all its details; anti-intellectualism and the setting of "the Spirit" over against serious learning and education; and the embracing of right-wing political and social fanaticisms, such as the conviction (à la *Doctor Strangelove*) that "the international communist conspiracy" is poisoning our free society through fluoridation. Connected with such crackpot ideas are, inevitably, occult notions. When evangelicals become convinced that only they know what is "really" going on (only they see the communist menace in its true gravity; only they are aware of the true naturopathic methods of healing, etc.), a gigantic step has been taken on the road to Mordor's Land. For hiddenness is, as we have been at pains to emphasize, one of the chief aspects of the occult, and, indeed, its etymological meaning. The evangelical, in his neurotic defensiveness against a world that so very largely rejects his central convictions, reacts by finding more and more "hidden truths" that the world, in its "spiritual blindness," can only ridicule. Thus the Bible becomes a source of bizarre information on matters that can only puzzle the uninitiated unbeliever—educated though he may be in his own eyes, while lacking the true "wisdom." The bridge to the occult is quite clear in the remarks made in an interview on flying saucers by evangelist Frank E. Stranges, author of *Flying Saucerama*, who told his radio audience (KHOF, Los Angeles) on July 20, 1966:

> What we know about U.F.O.s perhaps is summed up
> in the first chapter of Ezekiel where brother Ezekiel speaks
> of the wheel within a wheel. In the South African series
> in my book *Saucerama*, here is one of the finest examples
> of a wheel in the middle of a wheel. The only moving part
> on this craft, in other words, was the outer rotating rim. . . .
> These are all the same pictures, all the same craft. The
> only moving part was the outer rim. Now Ezekiel goes on
> to say the color of the creature—he calls it a creature. It

might be interesting to note before we even say that, that
he uses the words "eyes were very high and dreadful."
That same Hebrew word "eyes" is the same Hebrew
word used in Ecclesiastes for "windows". . . . And he says
the color of this creature is as the color of beryl, beryl-
lium, the silicate of aluminum. Now the one that crashed
off the Helgeland coast some years ago, which is also in
the book *Saucerama*, they claim was tougher than steel,
and lighter than aluminum!

Here Stranges reveals the true nature of flying saucers,
which unbelievers could not fathom, but which an occult
reading of Scripture makes crystal clear! The distance
to Cabalistic Bible interpretation drops virtually to nil.
Is it any wonder that evangelicals, forgetting that "the
whole armor of God" is all that is needed to stand in
an evil world and therefore defensively seeking the
occult in the Bible, so readily fall victim to dark influences?

Still another and no less consequential reason why
evangelicals are fascinated by the occult is their preoccupation with "spiritual experience." Why do evangelicals prefer revivalistic conversions to conversions of any
other type? Why are "testimony meetings" so important
in evangelical church life? Why is there such a "cult
of personality" surrounding charismatic fundamentalist
leaders? Evangelicalism, with its roots in the open-air
18th century English preaching and the 19th century
American frontier, centers not on Scripture, church, doctrine, or sacraments, but on personal experience. Having
the right kind of conversion, second-blessing, "peace,"
etc. becomes all-important, and without it all else may
be suspect. But since, according to Scripture, experience
itself must be tested from the outside for divine origin
(there being many spirits abroad on the earth), the evangelical who refuses to test the spirits in his own experience
courts disaster. To him the Evil One has only to beckon:
come to me and I will give you an experience such as
you have never had! The urge for special charismatic
gifts and the suspicion toward those without them can
become the other side of the coin to a lusting after strange
gods. Métraux, in his careful study of voodoo in Haiti,

significantly observed: "A Pentecostal preacher describing his feelings when 'the spirit was upon him,' listed to me exactly the same symptoms as those which I had heard from the mouths of people who have been possessed by *loa*." [1] On the positive side, this meant an easy transition from voodoo to Protestantism (so comments Métraux); but negatively it suggests a most perilous experiential focus. If evangelicals were to center their theology and church life on the objective Scriptural verities instead of on the experience which can never be more than a by-product of these verities, they would reach a level of spiritual maturity far more conducive to the proper interpretation of the occult.

But instead of such a balanced approach, the evangelical tendency has been (in this area as in others) to counter one extreme with another. Are our young people fascinated with the occult? Then forbid all contact with it! Here we have an exact parallel with the fundamentalist's general negative reaction to "the world": separate from it. Stay away from the theater, the dance, modern entertainment, secular education, godless books and magazines, etc., etc. Thus treatments of the occult from an evangelical standpoint (even generally responsible treatments) tend to lump all occult phenomena, from scientific ESP experimentation to sorcery, in a single category, which is then labeled "satanic" and the label "Touch Not" affixed to it. The result of such separationism is inevitably to blur the good and the neutral with the bad, and to drive the evangelical who recognizes that not all is bad to reject the entire argument; ironically, therefore, separationism usually produces exactly the evils it tries to counteract! The fundamentalist church in the town in which I grew up, by effectively keeping its young people from all forms of mixed entertainment, succeeded in having the highest illegitimate birth rate of any church in the community!

Moreover, a negative attitude toward all that is occult can blind us to the overwhelmingly important truth (emphasized at various points in this book) that wanderings in the occult labyrinth may be halting attempts to find the way of life. To this possibility we wish to devote a few closing words.

* * * *

If, reader, your interest in the occult has indeed been motivated by a search for the truth, then you and I have taken the right path together. Frankly, I have no interest in doctrinnaire occultists, who, like those men of the last times as described by the Apostle, are "ever learning and never able to come to the knowledge of the truth" (II Tim. 3:7). "Their folly shall be manifest unto all men" says the text, and our study of a diversity of occult philosophies of existence has illustrated that fact without much difficulty.

What is the fundamental failing in the occult perspective? Even before his conversion to Christianity (but on his way toward it), famed Oxford scholar C. S. Lewis recognized the nature of that failing, doubtless in part because he himself had been drawn toward the dark land. Sometime in the 1920s Lewis corresponded on the subject with Owen Barfield, who would later do irreparable harm to his talent by embracing Rudolf Steiner's occult Anthroposophy. One of Lewis' unpublished and undated letters of that period, written at Magdalen College, is headed "The Real Issue between Us." Lewis first describes his own approach by an analogy based upon Plato's myth of the cave: like every man, Lewis is bound to the post of finite personality so that he cannot turn around and observe reality directly; clouds behind him represent that ultimate reality or True Being. His understanding of the meaning of life comes by observing the mirror before him, which displays "as much of the reality (and such disguise of it) as can be seen" from his position. He devotes himself to studying the mirror with his eyes ("explicit cognition") and also reaches backward with his hands "so as to get some touch (implicit "taste" or "faith") of the real. For Barfield the occultist, however, though his position vis-à-vis reality is necessarily the same as Lewis', his reaction to it is far different. Let Lewis' inimitable pen provide the description: [2]

Here we see a gentleman (not identified) engaged on seeing whether a departure from dry academical methods and a newer, freer theory of knowledge may not get some new images out of the mirror. The mirror seems to be playing up well so far. Meanwhile the clouds have ebbed to his ankles. Something like despairing hands stretches to reach from behind but he doesn't notice them. Overhead I detect a curious figuration of cloud that fancy may interpret as a gigantic face in laughter. The hammer and chisel are occult science, yoga, "meditation" (in technical sense) etc.

Text of C. S. Lewis' handwritten caption

Here we see a gentleman (not identified) engaged on
seeing whether a departure from dry academical methods
and a newer, freer theory of knowledge may not get
some new images out of the mirror. The mirror seems
to be playing up well so far. Meanwhile the clouds
have ebbed to his ankles. Something like despairing
hands stretches to reach from behind but he doesn't
notice them. Overhead I detect a curious figuration of
cloud that fancy may interpret as a gigantic face in
laughter. The hammer and chisel are occult science,
yoga, "meditation" (in technical sense) etc.

An orful example. Study of a gentleman
reaching vainly for the inner reality he has
scorned, while he shrinks in horror from the
phantom he has created on the black wall
from which he has succeeding in chipping

off all the looking-glass. (Only those who are not poets cd. get as far as this, of course) On a second mirror invisible to him but visible to his neighbours, ambulance, asylum, cemetery appears successively.

Text of C. S. Lewis' handwritten caption

> An orfal example. Study of a gentleman reaching
> vainly for the inner reality he has scorned, while he
> shrinks in horror from the phantom he has created on the
> black wall from which he had succeeding [sic: succeeded]
> in chipping off *all* the looking-glass. (Only those who are
> not poets c[oul]d get as far as this, of course).
> On a second mirror invisible to him but visible to his
> neighbours, ambulance, asylum, cemetery appears succes-
> sively.

Barfield's occult efforts to find reality not only do not succeed: they destroy the only means of discovering reality, they ignore the "despairing hands" reaching out from eternity to save him from folly and the Lord laughing him to derision, and they open the floodgates to the phantoms of another world which are fully capable of driving him successively to "ambulance, asylum, cemetery." Says Lewis earlier in the letter: "All that your occultism can give us is *not* the Real instead of the phenomenal but simply more phenomena less surely grounded (in the empirical way) than the ones we have already, and less real because they claim to be more. For the highest merit of the phenomenon is to *confess* itself a phenomenon." Though Lewis had not yet focused the eyes of explicit cognition on the empirical facticity of Christ's person and work, and thus had the shackles of the human dilemma loosened for him by the Son who alone "makes free indeed" (Jn. 8:36), he saw clearly that there is no shortcut to reality. Occultists think that by shattering ordinary methods of knowing they will reach hidden truth, but their knowledge must come by empirical means also, and it is therefore subject to the same empirical tests as any other truth-claim. This lucid realization kept Lewis on the track in his search for the true meaning of reality, and made it possible for him later to weigh the vapid claims of the occultists against the solid historical evidence that "God was in Christ, reconciling the world unto Himself."

If we are honest with ourselves, we must all admit the profundity of the occult quest. Who is not moved by these words of Arthur Machen, one of the greatest of the supernatural story writers?

> We shall go on seeking it to the end, so long as there are men on the earth. We shall seek it in all manner of strange ways; some of them wise, and some of them unutterably foolish. But the search will never end.
>
> ' 'It?' ' ' 'It' ' is the secret of things; the real truth that is everywhere hidden under outward appearances; the end of the story, as it were; the few final words that make every doubtful page in the long book plain, that clear up all bewilderments and all perplexities, and show how there was profound meaning and purpose in passages apparently obscure and purposeless. These are the words which, once read, throw their light and radiance back over all the book; as the furnace fires blazing up suddenly at night in my own country in the west, shine far away among woods, and in dark valleys, and discover his path to the wanderer in a wild, dim world.
>
> Doubtless there is a secret, an illuminating secret, hidden beneath all the surfaces of things; and perhaps the old alchemists were thinking of that secret when they spoke of the Powder of Projection, the Philosopher's Stone, that turned all it touched into gold.[3]

Yes, there is a secret: the truth behind the appearances; the end of the story. The occult quest is the search for that Stone of the Philosophers capable of turning all to gold. And the Stone is Christ, as the perceptive alchemists discovered. This is the tried and precious Stone laid prophetically in Zion (Is. 28:16); if any man come in belief to that Christ as to a living Stone, he "shall not be confounded" (I Pet. 2:4-8). Here is the only sure foundation (I Cor. 3:11). All others are chimerical: the castles of occult experience built upon them will turn to mist when the Sun of righteousness shines upon them. Beware of the magic of Midas, who obtained what appeared to be the golden touch, but it destroyed him. Do not be confounded: in Christ alone "are hid all the treasures of wisdom and knowledge. And this I say, lest any man should beguile you with enticing words" (Col. 2:3-4). The promise stands firm for us as for the men of olden time (Is. 45:3, 17):

> I will give thee the treasures of darkness,
> and hidden riches of secret places,
> that thou mayest know that I, the Lord,
> which call thee by thy name,
> am the God of Israel. . . .
> Israel shall be saved in the Lord
> with an everlasting salvation:
> ye shall not be ashamed nor confounded
> world without end.

Appendices

APPENDIX A

THE EARLY CHURCH'S CONCEPT OF DEMONIC ACTIVITY

(from Ethelbert Stauffer, *Die Theologie des Neuen Testaments,*
5. Aufl. [Stuttgart: W. Kohlhammer], trans. John Marsh
[1955], sec. 13)

The primitive church enunciated three fundamental principles for distinguishing demonic activity: the principle of self-glorification, of demonic opposition and of mendacity.

Satan means to become like God (Isa. 14:14; VitAdEv. 15; SEn. 29:4). The glory with which God has adorned his creation has become his temptation. Consequently, the freedom which God gave him works his ruin. The creature means to become something, something without God, something like God—and if need be, in spite of God. So the prime motive of demonic activity is self-glorification.[1] From now on the struggle between one glory and another, between the *gloria dei* and the *gloria mundi* is the dramatic theme of all history, even of the history of the church.[2] The man possessed of a demonic spirit betrays himself in his determination to play the leading part, and in forming some special group to achieve his ends (I Cor. 1:11; II Pet. 2:1ff.; Herm.m. 11:12f). So the NT opposes *superbia* in all its forms, among believers as well as among unbelievers (Luke 6:26; John 5:43; Gal. 5:26; I Tim. 3:6).

The devil is God's adversary, and consequently the enemy of God's creation. His very name betrays that.[3] He is envious of God (Wisd. 2:24; PsPhil. 60:3). All his thoughts and all his desires are set on theomachy.[4] He opposes himself to every-

177

thing that God does, to prove that he is God and to put God's work in the shade, to disturb and destroy it (I Cor. 12:3; I John 4:3; Rev. 12:17). Moses and Aaron performed miracles in God's name. The devil immediately retaliated with miracle-workers of his own sort.[5] In Satan there is a survival of the primordial power of chaos and its hostility to creation (Gen. 15:11; John 8:44). The adversary is the spirit of constant negation —of negation most serious in its consequences for the cosmos and its history. Hence he answers every act of God with some counter-activity, every historical advance with a contrary motion (Gen. 3:15; Matt. 13:19, 25). But the more the adversary gets excited, the more it becomes plain that as he seeks his own glory by his opposition, he is exhausting himself in a negation that in the end can only reveal the profound vanity and unreality of his nature and the sole glory of God!

So the arrogant glory of the adversary can be nothing but illusory, and his theomachy nothing but a fight with illusory weapons (John 8:44; Luke 22:48). His antithesis stands in such servile dependence upon the thesis that it achieves nothing but a demonic aping and perversion of the divine. The adversary affects a piety that misuses the divine name, and works with Bible texts, orthodox ideas and theological pretexts (Matt. 4:6; II Cor. 10:5; I Tim. 4:7; 6:20). He dresses himself up as an angel of light, and his auxiliaries are the hypocrites who wear the garments of piety, the false brethren, false witnesses, false teachers, false apostles, false prophets and false Messiahs (II Cor. 11:13ff.). He boasts of his great achievements (Gen. 11:4; Dan. 7:8; PsPhil. 6:1; Sib. 3:100; Mark 13:22). The satanic powers even undergo something akin to death and resurrection (Rev. 13:3). Yet with all this play acting at piety and miracle the adversary deceives the unwary as to his true nature and intentions (II Cor. 4:4). He bewitches his victims before he destroys them (Gal. 3:1; IgnE. 19:3).[6] The Father of Jesus Christ leads his people through Inferno to Paradise; but the father of lies dangles a heaven in front of his friends—till they fall down into Hell. Moreover, the two great powers of history, eros and mammon, serve him (PsPhokyl. 194; I Cor. 7:5; Rev. 2:24; Luke 16:9ff.). But it is in the ways of his associates that the entire inner deceptiveness of the satanic is revealed in the end (II Cor. 11:15; Acts 13:6ff.; Did. 11:10; 12:5). 'But evil men and imposters shall wax worse and worse, deceiving and being deceived' (II Tim. 3:13). Satan, the misleader of the whole world, becomes at last the misled; he has deceived the whole world with his mendacity, but at last is deceived himself.

In primitive Christianity there is no christology without demonology. But the first word and the last belongs to theology. Satan's fall from heaven is the sign that God retains the upper hand, however powerful and crafty his creatures may be. In the meantime God does not destroy the adversary, or thrust him out of creation into the void beyond, but assigns him to his place in the divine ordering of the world and appoints him to that office which he intended for him in his predestined plan for history. However much the idea of Satan has developed since the time of the Book of Job, the basic thought of Job 1:6ff. remains true: Satan is an authorized minister of God.[7] God has even anticipated the demonic opposition of the adversary and the determined seductiveness of the tempter, and has systematically integrated it into his own world order (Rev. 2:10; 13:5ff.). So really the devil is the power in God's world who always wills evil and yet always effects good. Satan does not escape from God's *ordo*, but remains co-ordinated in it, *ordinatus* as Augustin says in his pregnant Latin. But the Creator is enthroned in awesome glory and lordly majesty over the creature who has become his enemy and who must remain his servant until he has done his work and departed.[8] Great and mysterious in his being God stands supreme even over that *dies ater* on which Satan tempted the first parent of mankind.

Key to Bibliographical Citations of Early Fathers

ApAbr	Apocalypse of Abraham, Ed. G.N. Bonwetsch, 1897
BBar	Book of Baruch
Did	The Didache
GBar	Greek-Slav Baruch Apocalypse, Ed. M.R. James, in *Texts and Studies*, V. I. 1897, p. 84ff.
Herm.m	The Shepherd of Hermas, *Mandates*
IgnE	Ignatius, *Letter to the Ephesians*
PsPhil	*Pseudo-Philo's Liber Antiquitatum Biblicarum*, Ed. Guido Kisch, Notre Dame, Indiana, 1948. (cf. *The biblical antiquities of Philo* . . . tr. by M. R. James, 1917)
PsPhokyl	Pseudo-Phokylides
SEn	*Slavonic Enoch* (The Secrets of Enoch) Ed. G. N. Bonwetsch, 1922
SenEp	L. Annaeus Seneca, *Epistulae morales ad Lucilium*
Sib	The Sibylline Oracles
TestSol	*Testament of Solomon*, Ed. Ch. McCown, 1922
VitAdEv	Vita Adae et Evae

NOTES TO APPENDIX A

1. Self-glorification = *Kenodoxia* (Phil. 2:3) = *Kaukesis* (Rom. 3:27); cf. *Hubris* in the Greek world.

2. BBar. 3:26f.; Matt. 4:9; Rev. 13:12; II Thess. 2:4. Who has issued from the mingling of the sons of God and the daughters of men, according to Gen. 6:4? The *anthropoi onomastoi!*

3. Cf. W. Bauer, Wb, s.v. *diabolos, santanas, kategor, avitikeimenos antidikos, (antichristos).*

4. GBar. 2 (*purgos tes theomachias*); Acts 5:39. There is important comparable material in S. Loesch, *Deitas Christi und antike Apotheose*, 1933.

5. Ex. 2:8ff.; TestSol. 25:3ff. II Tim. 3:8 rests on these interpretations of Ex. 2.

6. He keeps the truth from them, and deceives them about the seriousness of their situation (Jer. 8:10f.; Gal. 6:7; I Cor. 6:9f.; 15:32ff.; I John 1:8). He loves half-truths and superficial talk (Herm.m 11:2f., 13).

7. God holds Satan by the reins (ApAbr. 10), and holds the demonic will in impenetrable limits. Abundant material in W. Böld.

8. I Cor. 2:6ff.: *archotōn . . . katargoumenòn.*

APPENDIX B

A REFORMATION-ERA LETTER
ON DEMON POSSESSION

PART I

The following letter was written to the "Wittenberg Theologians," i.e., Luther, Melanchthon, Jonas, etc., by Dr. Johannes Bugenhagen Pomeranus, saintly pastor of the Wittenberg Town Church, who had officiated at Luther's wedding.

It was not originally intended for publication, but was later felt to be valuable and, together with an account by Melanchthon was brought out as a pamphlet under the title *Zwo wunderbarlich Hystorien, zu bestettigung der lere des Evangelii*. It is also included in two collections of correspondence: First, it is in O. Vogt's *Dr. Johannes Bugenhagens Briefwechsel;*[1] secondly, in E. L. Enders' *Dr. Martin Luthers Briefwechsel*.[2]

Neither Vogt nor Enders includes the original heading. The date is given simply as "the beginning of November, 1530."

Internal evidence indicates that some of the beginning sentences were written on October 31; the rest was presumably finished the next day.

The letter is written in Bugenhagen's dialect, but not Low German. The unique spelling and grammar employed made the translation uncertain in a few places. As far as possible the translation is literal; paragraph divisions, however, have been added editorially.[3]

* * * * *

On the day of the festival of Simon and Judas we arrived safely, by the grace of God, in Lübeck. Once I had gotten there the Devil gave public notice of himself and was recognized in a possessed girl,[4] who, until this time, had been quite well. Before this, his presence in her was doubted, but now he claimed openly to be there and to have entered the young girl through an old woman's curse. The girl had reminded the old woman (the Devil claimed) of a pound which she still owed her, to which the woman responded: "I'll send the Devil into your body."

I was with the girl today, who was well again. Because they feared that the Devil might return, the parents were still concerned. Her parents told me what else the Devil had said: "Aren't there enough preachers here? Why is it that you had to call one from Wittenberg?" He also said: "Bugenhagen has come. I know him well, and have often been with him, etc."[5] When I had heard this from the girl's father, in her presence, I laughed and was reminded of the verse in Acts 19: "Jesus I know well and Paul I know well, etc." It is quite true that he has often tempted me and bothered me with his thousand tricks, trying to disprove my teaching and faith, but because of Christ, who helped me by His grace, he was not able to achieve anything except to provoke me to do battle with him. I have still not forgotten what he tried to do through the Silesian Sacramentalists,[6] etc. In other sins it has seemed as if he was defeating me. But, Christ be thanked, though he was pleased to visit me, he was not pleased to stay. I would remind you again to pray for me in this matter, etc.

But to return to the situation: I asked the girl, who is about eighteen years old and continually bed-ridden, if, after she had come to herself again and was feeling well, she was aware of the way in which she had cursed and mocked. She answered no, that she knew nothing of this. Her parents told me the same thing. They, too, had questioned her when she had regained her senses as to why she had mocked so terribly. She had answered them: "I didn't do it, it was the Devil in me; but I have no idea what I did." They also told me the following: Yesterday, while the Devil was torturing her, the father began to quote to her from the Word of God, and, when that did not help, he took a copy of the German New Testament and held it in front of her. She, however, turned her face away and began biting the pillow that was under her head, etc. I spoke for a while with the girl and she gave proper Christian answers and a good understanding of her baptism.[7] I was especially concerned to convince her not to get the idea that she was forced to belong to the Devil simply because he had tortured her, etc. Finally, I knelt, along with all who were present, laid my hands on her head, and prayed. She thanked me as I was leaving.

While I was writing this letter,[8] however, a messenger came and told me that the Devil had tortured the girl again, had thrown her naked out of bed, and under a table, and then under a chair, and had twisted her neck so badly that she would have died had not her father quickly come to help. The girl's parents pleaded that I should come. So I went, and, as I arrived in front of the house, I heard a loud scream. When I entered and reached the possessed girl I heard with my own ears these words: "Bugenhagen the traitor is coming! Oh the traitor, he wants to torture me and will not allow me to remain! Oh, I must go out!" I stood there dumbfounded, and even though I did not believe the liar, I nevertheless interpreted his words to refer not only to the possessed girl, but to the entire city; that is, that I would not tolerate the Devil's kingdom in it. May the God of all mercy permit and accomplish this through Jesus Christ our Lord, Amen.

All those present claimed that the girl had not formerly known my name, and added that she had mocked horribly before I had entered the house. Now when she screamed, I yelled back and called her by name: "Elizabeth!" The Devil answered: "Elizabeth, Elizabeth." Then I said: "Yes, are you trying to deny it? Why shouldn't I call you Elizabeth? You gave me testimony today that you received that very same name in baptism, by which we are baptized into Christ." He then began to pounce about, screaming so loudly that those present could not hear each other. But I fell to my knees and prayed earnestly with the intensity which the girl's misery and despair wrung out of me, speaking loudly so that all could hear, that the Lord Jesus should free her—for He had said, "In my name they will drive out devils." I think that the others were praying with me since I had turned my back to them.[9] Meanwhile the Devil screamed: "I must go out! Oh I must go out!", and tortured the girl horribly. But her father held her. Immediately after this she lay still, so that her father no longer had to hold her. She lay there, breathing heavily as if she was about to depart. Meanwhile the father told me what the Devil had said to him yesterday before I had arrived:[10] "You doubt that I am present![11] Now look, I have given you a clear sign!" He pointed to a hole in the window which he had broken. "That," said he, "is how I entered, etc."

Though the girl's body was still moving, we were afraid that she was slipping away. While I sat and waited to see what would happen, she opened her eyes just as if she was awakening from sleep. I spoke to her with a quiet voice: "Elizabeth!" She answered: "What?" I continued: "Do you know what you have done and the way in which you mocked?" She answered: "No." So I reminded her in the same way I had earlier in the day. Then I knelt and prayed with my hands on her head that she should be free, etc. Having finished praying, I asked her to say the Amen. This she did willingly.

And so I left; but I have been told that the Devil tortured her again that night, just as we read in the Gospel concerning the swine, etc., and screamed: "I must go out, but where shall be my habitation? There is a horse in Lünenburg; I will enter it, or perhaps the chain-maker." Now the girl's father was of the same profession and was, as we say, an adventurous man, since, to my surprise, he had spoken to me without fear from the start, as soon as he was certain that it was the Devil. Said he: "If it weren't a sin there's a lot I would ask the scoundrel and he would have to answer it all." I, however, forbade him to ask anything secretly of the Tempter or to allow it of anyone else. I did not ask what else had happened.

I am puzzled that Satan can confuse people this way. But no matter what he does or says, he still shows that he is a stupid and condemned spirit. These things happened on the eve of All Saints Day, in the year 1530. May God graciously give us the victory against all of [the Devil's] fiery darts through Jesus Christ our Lord. Amen.

PART II

A. *Historical Background: The Reformation in Lübeck*

Although Bugenhagen has been almost forgotten, he was one of the major figures in the spread of the Reformation, and one of the most beloved of Luther's associates. It was he who was responsible for bringing the Reformation to Pommerania, much of Lower Saxony, and Denmark.

Fifteen-thirty was the year of the Augsburg Confession. Bugenhagen did not attend the discussions but remained behind in Wittenberg.[12] In the fall, he made a short visit to Flensburg[13] and had scarcely returned to Wittenberg when two emissaries, Jacob Crappe and Johann von Achelen, arrived from Lübeck, begging for either Luther or Bugenhagen to bring the Reformation to their city.[14] Since Luther was so fully occupied with other problems, Bugenhagen was selected.

The situation in Lübeck had become quite serious; indeed, the city was on the verge of civil war. The beginnings of the Reformation were felt in early 1530, although two Protestant pastors, Wilhelmi and Wallhof, had already been chased out of the city, probably the previous year. Tensions mounted: there was even a rumor that the Vogt of Möllen had four hundred knights waiting to crush any Protestant move. Bugenhagen himself described Lübeck at this time as "a great and powerful Saxon city, in which the Gospel is preached twice daily and our German hymns are sung before and after the sermon. Pray that a riot may be averted." [15] The city, moving spirit of the Hanseatic league of mercantile ports, had approximately 40,000 inhabitants and was immensely wealthy. The main cathedral alone was served by sixty-six priests.

Bugenhagen left Wittenberg on October 20, arriving in Lübeck eight days later. It was on October 30 that he preached in the Marienkirche for the first time. The events described in the first part of the letter also took place on that day. Bugenhagen's direct encounter with the girl's Devil occurred the following day, the eve of All Saints—on the anniversary, interestingly enough, of Luther's posting of the 95 Theses thirteen years before.

The response to Bugenhagen's preaching came quickly and by November 25 negotiations between the people and the city council over a new *Kirchenordnung* (official ecclesiastical organization and liturgy) began.[16] The consultations dragged on until final approval was secured on February 18, 1531. There is some indication that further crises developed later, and also that Wullenwever, the Protestants' leading spokesman, was eventually hanged.[17] It was only through the help of the King of Denmark, Christian II, that Bugenhagen was allowed to remain in Lübeck during this period.

The *Kirchenordnung* was similar to that of Hamburg and Brunswick. It provided for schools, the conversion of cloisters into houses for the poor, and also the return of Wilhelmi and Wallhof. A special court, consisting of two council members, four citizens, and a secretary was established to handle marital cases.[18]

In February, 1531, Bugenhagen instituted the first superintendent or chief pastor, Hermann Bonus. Two weeks later Lübeck submitted its request to join the Schmalkalden league of Protestant princes and cities.

During his stay at Lübeck Bugenhagen completed the editorial supervision of a translation of the Bible into Low German which was published in 1534. He also preached the Reformation in Rostock before departing.

In May of 1531 Bugenhagen felt free to leave Lübeck. The grateful people of the city arranged for an elaborately decorated wagon for his journey. Offended by all this a young man asked Bugenhagen if the Apostle Peter had ever enjoyed such splendor, to which the Reformer is supposed to have answered:

> My son, let me tell you this. Whenever Saint Peter came to such devout and kindhearted people as your masters in Lübeck, they sent him home again as I am being sent. But when he came to knaves like yourself he had to travel home on foot.[19]

The memory of his visit was immortalized by a Latin inscription in the Egidienkirche:

> D. JOHANNES. BUGENHAGIUS. POMERANUS
> ECCLESIAE. WITTENBERGIENSIS. PASTOR. ET.
> ECCLESIAE. LUBECENSIS. REFORMATOR.
> A. 1530 d. 30. OCTOB. ANNI. HUJUS. PRIMA
> IN. AEDE. S. MARIAE. VERBA. FECIT. AD. POPULUM
> LUBECAE. SUBSTITIT. USQUE. AD. MENSEM.
> MAJUM. 1531.[20]

B. *Theological Considerations on the Occult*

In Bugenhagen's *Von dem christlicher Glauben und rechten guten Werken* ("On the Christian Faith and a Proper Understanding of Good Works"),[21] there is a section on demonology which offers helpful background to his letter. Five points can be extracted:

1. The Devil is a real, personal and present entity.
2. He is the "prince" and "god" of this world.[22]
3. He blinds those who do not believe the Gospel.
4. Only Christ can defeat him:
   > So do not rely on your own strength and works, rather despair completely of your powers, merits and of your self . . . and trust yourself only to Jesus Christ, who is stronger than the Devil.[23]
5. In Christ we can withstand and defeat Satan.

It is quite clear that this attitude is reflected in the event recounted in the letter. Bugenhagen is confident of his adversary's identity and reality. He expresses no surprise at Satan's presence in the girl. We do not know how acquainted Bugenhagen was with demon-possession, but, if Musculus is correct, he may have had contact with a similar incident at Brunswick.[24]

A noteworthy aspect of this case was the fact that the girl was a believer. Bugenhagen does not seem to regard this as abnormal. Indeed, he uses this knowledge in the dialogue with Satan, and it was apparently a factor in successfully freeing the girl.

It is instructive to compare Bugenhagen's method with that of the girl's father. The father, though an honest fellow and wise enough to call on Bugenhagen for help, seemed beyond his depth, incapable of doing much more than using the Bible superstitiously against the Devil, and interested a bit in the opportunist possibilities of questioning Satan. (Was he a bit like the typical evangelical of today?) For Bugenhagen, there was no nonsense of this kind. He confronted Satan boldly and commanded him to leave in Christ's name. Bugenhagen's entire approach was to use the great doctrinal verities of the Word of God against the enemy of souls. His objective stress on Word and Sacrament is sorely needed in the church today in all its confrontations with demonic power.

C. *Reformation References to the Letter*

Bugenhagen's story aroused a good deal of interest among the other Reformers.

Luther refers to it in two letters which were written shortly after the event. In a letter to W. Link, dated December 1, 1530, he comments:

> Pomeranus is working successfully in Lübeck, but Satan is giving him much trouble with a possessed young girl. The clever Demon fabricates wonders.[25]

In a second letter, this time to N. Hausmann (January 21, 1531), Luther states:

> Johannes Pomeranus is laboring bravely, but Satan is resisting him, and has hold of a possessed young girl.[26]

Six years later, at the *Wittenberger Concordienverhandlungen*, Bugenhagen caused a stir by recounting the story.[27] Wolfgang Musculus, in his "Itinerarium," mentions this.[28] Interestingly, Musculus speaks of "the miracle of the liberation of possessed in Lübeck and in Brunswick," implying that Bugenhagen was responsible for more than one exorcism. This would not have been strange; the more one opposes the Devil, the more one seems to come into contact with him.

NOTES TO APPENDIX B

1. (Stettin: Laon Saunier, 1888), p. 101. Vogt's collection was reissued at Hildesheim by Georg Olms in 1966.

2. (Calw: Vereinsbuchhandlung, 1898), VIII, 304.

3. The letter has here been translated for the first time into English, with preliminary editing, by David Beck.

4. "junkfrau", i.e. unmarried girl. This word is used throughout the letter and will simply be translated "girl."

5. Following the practice of his time, Bugenhagen employs "etc." as we would use an ellipsis.

6. "Sacramentalists" were those who decried the real presence of

Christ in the sacraments. Believing themselves "led" directly by "the Spirit," without mediation of Word and Sacrament, they were unable properly to test the spirits and thus often served as vehicles of demonic influence and false doctrine.

7. Bugenhagen stresses the girl's baptism in his exorcistic counselling, since (as he indicates in the next sentence) he wishes to remind the girl above all that she belongs, not to Satan, but to Christ. Baptism incorporated the girl into God's Kingdom; at that time her sponsors, acting in her behalf, "renounced the Devil and all his wicked works and ways."

8. This explains the apparent confusion in Bugenhagen's time references. The letter was not finished until a day or so later.

9. Bugenhagen's meaning is not quite clear. He may mean that the people naturally joined him in prayer when, as a pastor, he turned to face in the same direction they were, as happens in the Lutheran service.

10. I.e. arrived at the house, since the first attack is said to have occurred after Bugenhagen's coming to Lübeck.

11. "ob ich vorhanden were": this would normally mean "existent." However, it seems unlikely that the father would have doubted the *existence* of the demonic as such, though the Devil's presence in his own daughter would have been difficult to accept.

12. Johann Jäncken, *Lebensgeschichte . . . D. Johann Bugenhagens.* (Rostock: Berger & Boedner, 1757), p. 29.

13. H. Meinhof, *Dr. Pommer Bugenhagen und sein Werken* (Halle: Riemeyer, 1890), p. 17.

14. Hermann Hering, "Doktor Pomeranus, Johannes Bugenhagen," *Schriften des Vereins für Reformationsgeschichte,* XX (1888), 82.

15. Vogt, *Briefwechsel,* No. 36, p. 92; trans. in Walter Ruccius, *John Bugenhagen Pomeranus* (Philadelphia: United Lutheran Publication House, n.d.), p. 74.

16. A good discussion of these consultations is to be found in Hering.

17. Meinhof, *loc. cit.*

18. Karl A. T. Vogt, *Johannes Bugenhagen Pomeranus* (Elberfeld: Fridrichs, 1867), pp. 333-336, has an excellent summary of the Kirchenordnung.

19. Ruccius, *op. cit.,* p. 83.

20. Jäncken, *op. cit.,* p. 30.

21. Text in Karl Vogt, *Bugenhagen (op. cit.* in note 18).

22. *Ibid.,* p. 115.

23. *Ibid.,* p. 116.

24. *Analecta Lutherana,* ed. by T. Kolde (Gotha: Perthes, 1883), p. 220.

25. *Dr. Martin Luthers Briefe.* ed. W. de Wette (Berlin: Reimer, 1827), No. 1331.

26. *Ibid.,* No. 1346.

27. O. Vogt, *Briefwechsel (op. cit.* in note 1), p. 105n. His source is the *Analecta Lutherana,* p. 216.

28. *Analecta,* p. 220.

APPENDIX C

THE GOSPEL ACCORDING TO LSD*

Karl Marx religiously believed that religion is the opiate of the people. Now the conviction is growing in avant-garde circles that an opiate can become the religion of the people.

The drug in question is D-lysergic acid diethylamide (LSD-25), one of a group of "psychedelic" (consciousness-expanding) agents that includes peyote, mescaline, psilocin, and psilocybin. In the last two decades, interest in these drugs has greatly increased. During the winter of 1962-63, President Pusey of Harvard removed from his psychology staff Drs. Timothy Leary and Richard Alpert for unscientific and dangerous experimentation with psychedelics. "You may be making Buddhas out of everyone," the university told them, "but that's not what *we're* trying to do."

Exiled from academia, Leary and Alpert devoted their energies to their "International Federation for Internal Freedom," in which continued experimentation with the drug experience could be promoted. Last December, Leary was arrested in Texas for illegally transporting and failing to pay taxes on marijuana and was given the maximum sentence (thirty years plus $40,000 in fines).

Cases of psychotic behavior as a result of LSD "trips" have been making the press of late, and Dr. Donald Louria of the New York County Medical Society reports that during the last year seventy-five persons were admitted to Bellevue as a result of LSD reactions. The serious medical literature on LSD has continued to multiply (see the exhaustive "Annotated Bibliography" published by Sandoz Pharmaceuticals, the only legal manufacturer of the drug—which recently stopped all deliveries of LSD).

Our interest here is not in the chemical or psychological aspects of the psychedelics (for a discussion of their value in controlled psychotherapy and treatment of alcoholism, consult the October, 1965, issue of *Pastoral Psychology*). We wish to focus attention on the repeated claim that LSD offers a prime avenue to ultimate religious reality.

In the course of Leary's Harvard experiments, sixty-nine religious professionals (about half of Christian or Jewish persuasion and the rest adherents of Eastern religions) took psychedelic drugs; over 75 per cent reported intense mystico-religious experiences, and more than half asserted that they had had the deepest spiritual experience of their life (*Psychedelic Review*, I [1964], 325). Pahnke's 1963 Harvard doctoral dissertation

---

* First published in *Christianity Today*, July 8, 1966.

supports these claims by reporting a statistically significant, controlled experiment in which drugs were administered to ten theology students and professors in the setting of a Good Friday service, while ten others received only placebos; "those subjects who received psilocybin experienced phenomena which were indistinguishable from, if not identical with . . . the categories . . . of mysticism." Professor Walter Clark of Andover Newton states that his psychedelic vision was "like Moses' experience of the burning bush."

What interpretation should be placed upon such claims? Roman Catholic scholar R. C. Zaehner, in his book, *Mysticism, Sacred and Profane*, argues that the drug experience, as exemplified by Aldous Huxley in his *Doors of Perception*, is at best a blend of monistic and nature mysticism but does not reach the level of genuinely theistic, Christian mysticism. The Native American Church of the North American Indians, however, claims that Jesus gave the peyote plant to them in their time of need, and, according to Slotkin, they "see visions, which may be of Christ Himself" (cf. Huston Smith, "Do Drugs Have Religious Import?," in *LSD*, ed. Solomon [1964], pp. 152-67). In these latter cases, the drug is evidently viewed as a means of grace, not as an *opus operatum* or magical device.

Yet Zaehner makes an important point: the psychedelic experience has generally been understood in terms of monistic mysticism, particularly its Eastern forms. Alan Watts relates it to Zen. Leary and Alpert have published a manual for LSD "trips" based on the Tibetan Book of the Dead. The vast majority of selections included in Ebin's anthology, *The Drug Experience* (1961; 1965), are written from non-Christian standpoints.

Why is this so? William James suggested the answer as long ago as 1902 when he described his experience with nitrous oxide: "The keynote of it is invariably a reconcilation. It is as if the opposites of the world, whose contradictoriness and conflict make all our difficulties and troubles, were melted into unity" (*The Varieties of Religious Experience*, lectures 16 and 17).

The drug experience, though it may be integrated into a Christian context, never requires such integration, and in fact leads the unwary to believe that the reconciliation of the fallen world can be achieved simply by consciousness (or unconsciousness) expansion. Scripture, however, makes clear beyond all shadow of doubt that true reconciliation occurs solely when a man faces up to his sin and accepts the atoning work of the historic Christ in his behalf. LSD offers the deceptive possibility of bypassing the Cross while achieving harmony within and without. Like Altizer's chimerical endeavor to gain the "conjunction of opposites" through the substitution of a mystical, fully kenotic "Christ" for the historical Jesus, psychedelic mysticism tries to reconcile all things apart from the only Reconciler.

The tragedy of the LSD gospel (which is not a gospel) is nowhere more evident than in its use with dying patients. Dr. Sidney Cohen reports the last days of "Irene," terminally ill with cancer. She had "no religion, no hope," and was given LSD. Then she faced death calmly: "Once you see the pattern of the vortex, it all fits," she said (*Harper's*, September, 1965). Did she see the world aright? Was her consciousness truly expanded? French psychedelic specialist Roger Heim noted that under the influence of the drug his handwriting, in reality black, appeared red; and a cat, given the drug, recoils in fear from a mouse. Reality? No. The only religious "trip" that avoids irrational fear, sees the blackness of the world for what it is, and transmutes death into life, is offered freely, without need of capsule or syringe, by Christ the Way.

APPENDIX D
SUGGESTED READINGS

Because of the extensive documentation provided through notes to the text of this book, it seems unnecessary to offer reading suggestions in the ordinary sense. But the very wealth of literature cited may so intimidate that the reader now does not know where to start!

Therefore, the following five authors are listed for their paramount importance and interest. Their writings are accessible: they are in print and in English. We do not agree with all they say, but—after all—that is true of everything written, save the Bible.

Charles Williams
Montague Summers
A. E. Waite
C. G. Jung
Kurt Koch

The most serious and reliable publisher of occult works in English is University Books, New Hyde Park, New York. This firm has brought back into print, through photolithography, a wealth of valuable occult classics of earlier times. Membership in their Mystic Arts Book Society can provide a substantial saving on their publications and those of related interest.

Notes

NOTES TO THE PROLOGUE

1. Patrice Boussel, *Paris ensorcelé: Guide des voyantes des 20 arrondissements* (Paris & Geneva: La Palatine, 1963).
2. Cf. Rupert T. Gould, *The Loch Ness Monster* (new ed.; New Hyde Park, N.Y.: University Books, 1969).
3. H. J. St. J. Clarke, *Thirty Centuries in South-East Antrim* (Belfast: Quota Press, 1938), pp. 209-210.

NOTES TO CHAPTER ONE

1. Cf. Alan W. Watts, *The Way of Zen* (London, 1957) and Arthur Koestler, *The Lotus and the Robot* (New York: Macmillan, 1961).
2. For a development of this argument, see Montgomery, *Where Is History Going?* (Grand Rapids, Mich.: Zondervan, 1969), chaps. 1-3, and *History & Christianity* (Downers Grove, Ill.: Inter-Varsity Press, 1965), *passim*.
3. Illustrated in detail in my *Suicide of Christian Theology* (Minneapolis: Bethany, 1970).
4. On the relation of interpretations to facts in scientific and theological research, see my essay, "The Theologian's Craft," *ibid.*, pp. 267-313.
5. Some delightful examples are given in Dorothy L. Sayers' Lord Peter Wimsey detective novel, *Strong Poison*. See also Trevor H. Hall's *New Light on Old Ghosts* (London: Gerald Duckworth, 1965), and the exploding of Harry Price's occult interpretation of the famous Borley rectory hauntings (*The End of Borley Rectory* [London: Harrap, 1946]) by Eric J. Dingwall, Kathleen M. Goldney, and Trevor H. Hall in their *Haunting of Borley Rectory* (London: Gerald Duckworth for the Society for Psychical Research, 1956). Attention should probably also be drawn to Paul Tabori's *Natural Science of Stupidity* (Philadelphia: Chilton, 1959)!
6. See J. B. Rhine, *The Reach of the Mind* (New York: William Sloane, 1947); J. B. Rhine and J. G. Pratt, *Parapsychology, Frontier Science of the Mind* (Oxford: Blackwell Scientific Publications, 1957).
7. These writings have been collected and edited by Gardner Murphy and Robert O. Ballou under the title, *William James on Psychical Research* (New York: Viking, 1960).
8. Carl Murchison (ed.), *The Case for and against Psychical Belief* (Worcester, Mass.: Clark University, 1927).
9. Cf. Sherman Yellen, "Sir Arthur Conan Doyle: Sherlock Holmes in Spiritland," *International Journal of Parapsychology*, VII/1 (Winter, 1965), 33-63.

10. Walter Franklin Prince, *Noted Witnesses for Psychic Occurrences* (New Hyde Park, N.Y.: University Books, 1963). This reprint edition contains a new introduction by Gardner Murphy.

11. Gardner Murphy, *Challenge of Psychical Research* ("World Perspectives"; New York: Harper, 1961). Murphy is perhaps best known for his standard *Historical Introduction to Modern Psychology.*

12. The narrative is given in a letter of April 12, 1911 from W. R. Moody to philosopher and psychical researcher Dr. James H. Hyslop; Prince culled it from the April, 1918, issue of the *Journal of the American Society for Psychical Research.*

13. Murphy, *Challenge of Psychical Research*, p. 172.

14. C. D. Broad, *Lectures on Psychical Research* ("International Library of Philosophy and Scientific Method"; London: Routledge & Kegan Paul, 1962). Cf. J. Fraser Nicol's review, "C. D. Broad on Psychical Research," *International Journal of Parapsychology*, VI/3 (Summer, 1964), 261-88.

15. Noteworthy in the same connection is the detailed article on "ESP Phenomena, Philosophical Implications of" by C. W. K. Mundle in Paul Edwards (ed.), *The Encyclopedia of Philosophy* (8 vols.; New York: Macmillan & Free Press, 1967), III, 49-58 (with excellent bibliography).

16. J. H. Pollack, *Croiset the Clairvoyant* (London: W. H. Allen, 1965).

17. Jule Eisenbud, *The World of Ted Scrois* (New York: William Morrow, 1967).

18. Zdenek Rejdak, "Die psychokinetischen Phänomene von Nina Kulagina," *Zeitschrift für Parapsychologie und Grenzgebiete der Psychologie*, XII/2, pp. 106-110.

19. Sheila Ostrander and Lynn Schroeder, *Psychic Discoveries behind the Iron Curtain* (Englewood Cliffs, N.J.: Prentice-Hall, 1970).

20. See Helena Pralnikova and Victor Popovkin, "Le Congrès de Moscou sur la télépathie," Planète [Paris], No. 41 (July-August, 1968), pp. 50-67 (especially pp. 57-58).

21. Gardner Murphy, Introduction to *William James on Psychical Research* (*op. cit.*), p. 18.

22. Cf. Sacheverell Sitwell, *Poltergeists: An Introduction and Examination followed by Chosen Instances* (New Hyde Park, N.Y.: University Books, 1959).

23. *L'Antidemon de Mascon . . . en la maison du Sieur F. Perreaud* (Geneva, 1653). A modern edition was brought out by Philibert Le Duc (Bourg en Bresse, 1853).

24. See the translation by Peter du Moulin: *The Devill of Mascon . . . now made English by one that hath a particular knowledge of the truth of this story* (Oxford, 1658).

25. Herbert Thurston, *Ghosts and Poltergeists*, ed. J. H. Crehan (Chicago: Henry Regnery, 1954), p. 202.

26. See, e.g., Summers' *History of Witchcraft* (2d ed.; New Hyde Park, N.Y.: University Books, 1956) and *Geography of Witchcraft* (reprint ed.; New Hyde Park, N.Y.: University Books, 1958). Cf. Timothy

d'Arch Smith, *A Bibliography of the Works of Montague Summers*
(New Hyde Park, N.Y.: University Books, 1964).

27. George Barton Cutten, *The Psychological Phenomena of
Christianity* (New York: Scribner, 1908), p. 117.

28. Firmin Van den Bosch, *Impressions de littérature contemporaine*
(Brussels, 1905), p. 16.

29. Joris-Karl Huysmans, *Oeuvres complètes* (23 vols.; Paris,
1928-1934), XIII, 255.

30. Cf. Robert Baldick, *The Life of J.-K. Huysmans* (Oxford:
Clarendon Press, 1955), especially pp. 137-84; Baldick's Introduction
to the Keene Wallis translation of *Là-Bas: Down There: A Study
in Satanism* (New Hyde Park, N.Y.: University Books, 1958); *Les
Cahiers de La Tour Saint-Jacques*, Vol. VIII: J.-K. Huysmans (Paris:
H. Roudil, 1963); Pie Duployé, *Huysmans* ("Les Ecrivains devant
Dieu"; Bruges, Belg.: Desclée De Brouwer, 1968).

31. This letter is printed in my *History & Christianity* and *Where
Is History Going?* (cited above, note 2).

32. J. B. Phillips, *Ring of Truth: A Translator's Testimony* (New
York: Macmillan, 1967), pp. 118-19. (Used by permission.)

33. Letter of November 25, 1971 from Professor Omar Gjerness,
Fergus Falls, Minn.

34. David Hume, *Enquiry concerning Human Understanding*, sec.
X ("Of Miracles"). The text of the *Enquiry* is readily accessible in
E. A. Burtt's *English Philosophers from Bacon to Mill*.

35. William T. Blackstone, *The Problem of Religious Knowledge:
The Impact of Philosophical Analysis on the Question of Religious
Knowledge* (Englewood Cliffs, N.J.: Prentice-Hall Spectrum Books,
1963), pp. 157-60.

36. C. S. Lewis, *Miracles* (New York: Macmillan, 1947), especially
chap. 13, pp. 121-24.

37. See a more detailed critique of Hume's position in my *Shape
of the Past* (Ann Arbor, Mich.: Edwards Brothers, 1963), pp. 288-93.

38. Antony Flew, *God & Philosophy* (New York: Delta Books, 1969),
chap. 7, pp. 140-58.

39. Montgomery, "The Theologian's Craft" (cited in note 4 above).

40. I have set forth the evidence for the historical factuity of Christ's
resurrection and for the consequent truth of His claims in the
publications previously cited in note 2.

41. The care demanded is no less than, but also no greater than,
that required for events in general. To require "greater proof" of
supernatural events is to introduce the Humean fallacy under another
guise: common experience of the non-supernatural is supposed to reduce
the probability of the supernatural to such a point that tremendously
greater (infinite?) evidence would be needed to establish an allegedly
supernormal event. But this reasoning assumes what is not in evidence
(and what cannot be in evidence), namely, an already-known uniform
structure of interlocking experience that allows the sum total of
non-supernatural events to reduce the probability of supernatural events.

This naturalistic bias is exactly what is in question! Not knowing the universe as a whole, we have no way of calculating the probabilities for or against particular events, so each event must be investigated *ad hoc*, without initial prejudice. How much evidence do you need to determine if Jesus was killed and rose again? The same amount you need to determine if John the Baptist was killed and if Peter was alive on resurrection morning. How much evidence do you need to determine if poltergeistic crockery flies across a room and smashes? The same amount you need to determine if a wife throws crockery across a room at her husband and it smashes.

42. B. B. Warfield, *Miracles: Yesterday and Today* (reprint ed.; Grand Rapids, Mich.: Eerdmans, 1965).

43. A position especially characteristic of Marburg "demythologizer" Rudolf Bultmann and his post-Bultmannism followers, but by no means limited to them; virtually all of non-evangelical biblical scholarship is riddled with anti-miraculous bias. For critique, see the essays in Montgomery, *Crisis in Lutheran Theology* (2 vols.; revised ed.; Minneapolis, Minn.: Bethany Fellowship, 1973).

44. Cf. R. E. D. Clark, *Scientific Rationalism and Christian Faith, with Particular Reference to the Writings of Prof. J. B. S. Haldane & Dr. J. S. Huxley* (London: Inter-Varsity Fellowship, 1945); Anthony Standen, *Science Is a Sacred Cow* (New York: Dutton, 1950); Alfred de Grazia (ed.), *The Velikovsky Affair: The Warfare of Science and Scientism* (New Hyde Park, N.Y.: University Books, 1966). (The citation of this latter work is not to be taken as an imprimatur on Velikovsky's theories; the book is important wholly apart from the question of Velikovsky's cosmological ideas because it shows so clearly how unorthodox scientific conceptions can be repressed by an ostensibly open-minded but in fact bigoted scientistic establishment.)

45. Murphy, *Challenge of Psychical Research* (*op. cit.* in note 11 above), p. 251.

46. "I shall not say that it is possible; I say only that it is true."

NOTES TO CHAPTER TWO

1. Some of the most useful general histories in the Romance languages and English are: René Kopp, *Introduction générale à l'étude des sciences occultes* (Paris: Paul Leymarie, 1930); Jacques Marcireau, *Une histoire de l'occultisme* (Poitiers: Société E.L.J.M., 1949); Julien Tondriau, *L'occultisme* ("Marabout Université"; Verviers, Belg.: Gérard, 1964); René Alleau, *Histoire des sciences occultes* (Geneva: Editions Rencontre, 1965); François Ribadeau Dumas, *Histoire de la magie* (Paris: Productions de Paris, n.d.); two volumes in the excellent "Que sais-je?" series: Jérôme-Antoine Rony, *La Magie*

(3d ed.; Paris: Presses Universitaires de France, 1959) and Luc Benoist, *L'Esotérisme* (Paris: Presses Universitaires de France, 1963); Nigro Licò, *Occultismo* (2d ed.; Milan: Ulrico Hoepli, 1922; Paul Christian, *The History and Practise of Magic*, trans. Kirkup and Shaw, ed. Ross Nichols (New York: Citadel Press, 1963); Hans Liebstoeckl, *The Secret Sciences*, trans. H. E. Kennedy (London: Rider, 1939); Maurice Bouisson, *Magic: Its History and Principal Rites*, trans. G. Almayrac (New York: Dutton, 1961); Kurt Seligmann, *The History of Magic* (New York: Pantheon Books, 1948); C. A. Burland, *The Magical Arts: A Short History* (London: Arthur Barker, 1966). A very recent work of more than routine interest is *The Occult: A History* (New York: Random House, 1971) by novelist Colin Wilson, author of *The Outsider*. Histories of witchcraft will be mentioned in a later chapter, but attention should be drawn here to *Witchcraft* (New York: Meridian Books, 1959) by Christian littérateur Charles Williams; it treats most areas of the occult and benefits from its author's sensitivity both to the secret and tradition and to the verities of the Faith.

2. Cf. G. L. Tichelman (Royal Tropical Institute, Amsterdam), "*Pohung* and *Matakau*: Scaring Charms in the Bataklands and the Moluccas," *Man*, No. 288 (December, 1954).

3. See, for example, Eliade's *Rites and Symbols of Initiation*, trans. W. R. Trask (New York: Harper Torchbooks, 1965). On the nature of Eliade's phenomenology of religion and my personal contact with him, see Montgomery, *The Suicide of Christian Theology* (Minneapolis: Bethany Fellowship, 1970), pp. 83, 126.

4. A valuable compilation has been published under the title, *Demon Experiences in Many Lands* (Chicago: Moody Press, 1960). See also Paul Verdun, *Le Diable dans les missions* (2 vols.; Paris: Delhomme & Briguet, n.d.).

5. Frederick Kaigh, *Witchcraft and Magic of Africa* (London: Richard Lesley, 1947), p. 32.

6. See above, Chapter One, the text at note 26.

7. I have myself verified Summers' judgment in my copies of most of these key works: Kramer and Sprenger's *Malleus maleficarum*, trans. and ed. Summers (London: Pushkin Press, 1948); Weyer's *De praestigiis* (3d ed.; Basel: Oporinus, 1566), translated into French and published in 2 vols. under the title, *Histoires . . . des diables* (Paris: Delahaye & Lecrosnier, 1885); Bodin's *De la démonomanie* (Lyon, 1593); Le Loyer's *Discours des spectres* (2d ed.; Paris: Nicolas Buon, 1608); Delrio's *Disquisitionum magicarum libri sex* (2d ed.; Lyons, 1604); Sinistrari's *Demoniality . . . Now First Translated into English with the Latin Text* (Paris, Liseux, 1879).

8. We shall discuss astrology and alchemy in Chapter Four.

9. Richard Wilhelm; see the *I Ching*, trans into German by Richard Wilhelm and rendered into English by C. F. Baynes, with Foreword by C. G. Jung ("Bollingen Series," 19; 3d ed.; Princeton, N.J.: Princeton University Press, 1967), pp. xlvii, liv-lviii.

10. The *I Ching*, trans. James Legge (2d ed.; New York: Dover,

1963), p. 40. Cf. Sayed Idries Shah, *Oriental Magic* (New York: Philosophical Library, 1957), chap. 17 ("The Occult Art in China"), pp. 149-72.

11. *The I Ching*, trans. Wilhelm (*op. cit.*), pp. xxxiii, xxxviii.

12. The yang and the yin (whose exact significance relative to the *I Ching* is disputed) represent the fundamental opposition inherent in all of reality (positive-negative, good-evil, active-passive, male-female). This concept in Chinese thought separates it at the most fundamental level from Christianity, which insists that evil is not a complement to good, or the other side of the coin to goodness, but a moral cancer in the universe which shall one day be rendered powerless.

13. J. B. Handelsman, "I Thing," *The New Yorker*, January 8, 1972, pp. 72-73.

14. *The Tibetan Book of the Dead*, ed. W. Y. Evans-Wentz (3d ed.; New York: Oxford University Press Galaxy Books, 1960), pp. 235-37.

15. Louis Jacolliot, *Occult Science in India and among the Ancients*, trans. W. L. Felt, (New Hyde Park, N.Y.: University Books, 1971), pp. 230-32. See also the many examples given by Alexandra David-Neel in her *Magic and Mystery in Tibet* (New Hyde Park, N.Y.: University Books, 1958), and by John Keel in his *Jadoo: Mysteries of the Orient* (New York: Tower Publications, 1957).

16. Jacolliot, *op. cit.*, p. 274.

17. Cf. Ruhi Muhsen Afnan, *Zoroaster's Influence on Anaxagoras, the Greek Tragedians, and Socrates* (New York: Philosophical Library, 1969).

18. See Robert Ernest Hume, *The World's Living Religions* (rev. ed.; New York: Scribner, 1955), pp. 201-205; and Martin Haug, *Essays on the Sacred Language, Writings, and Religion of the Parsis*, ed. E. W. West (London: Kegan Paul [1878]), especially pp. 300 ff. Even if Haug's interpretation is correct that the spirits of Good and Evil are eternally inherent in Ahura Mazda's own nature (i.e., Zoroastrianism is ultimately a monism and not a dualism), the fact remains that Evil is elevated in Parsi thought to a level which invites sorcery and black magic.

19. Quoted from the Sacred Books of the East edition of the *Vendidad* ("Law against the Demons") by Kurt Seligmann (*op. cit.*, in note 1 above), p. 43. See also Seligmann's discussion of the Zoroastrian casting out of the fly demon (pp. 45-47).

20. Chapter Four.

21. Cf. the works of E. A. Wallis Budge: *The Book of the Dead: The Hieroglyphic Transcript of the Papyrus of Ani*; *Osiris: The Egyptian Religion of Resurrection*; etc.

22. *A Miracle in Stone* (1877).

23. Bouisson, *op. cit.* (in note 1 above), p. 303.

24. See the excellent treatments of this subject contained in *Le Monde du sorcier* ("Sources Orientales," 7; Paris: Editions du Seuil, 1966).

25. G. Ernest Wright, *The Old Testament against Its Environment* ("Studies in Biblical Theology," 2; London: SCM Press, 1950), pp. 86-87.

26. See Merrill F. Unger, *Biblical Demonology* (Wheaton, Ill.: Scripture Press, 1952).

27. Whether or not the apparition that appeared to Saul was in fact Samuel the deceased prophet has been the subject of dispute among biblical interpreters; those who hold a priori that the blessed cannot return in such a manner must naturally handle the passage in another way. Thus the learned author of *An Essay on the History and Reality of Apparitions* (London: J. Roberts, 1727) declares (p. 46): "The Appearance of the Thing call'd Samuel, was, in my Opinion, neither more nor less than a Phantasm or Spectre, which (as the Devil is allow'd to do) might personate the old departed Prophet." It will be observed that even an approach such as this (and we will discuss it to greater length in a subsequent chapter) in no way eliminates the occult dimension of the biblical passage.

28. I have pointed up the epistemological significance of this incident for Christian apologetics in my essay, "Inspiration and Infallibility: A New Departure," *The Suicide of Christian Theology* (op. cit., in note 3 above), p. 343.

29. We follow the rendering of C. C. Torrey.

30. For detailed studies of this development, see Bernard J. Bamberger, *Fallen Angels* (Philadelphia: Jewish Publication Society of America, 1952) and Joshua Trachtenberg, *Jewish Magic and Superstition* (New York: Meridian Books, 1961); we shall treat the Cabalistic tradition in the next chapter. The Old Testament Apocrypha (particularly the book of Tobit) already display an angelology and demonology that go beyond the Scriptures themselves and come to influence later Jewish and Christian speculation on the subject (for example, Tobit's view that a disagreeable odor can exorcise a demon). (See the standard Oxford edition of the Apocrypha edited by the great antiquarian and ghost-story writer M. R. James, and Bruce M. Metzger's *Introduction to the Apocrypha* [New York: Oxford University Press, 1957], especially p. 38.) Authoritative general treatments of angelology include such classics as Dutch theologian Jacob Ode's *Commentarius de angelis* (Utrecht: Visch, 1739) and the accessible *Dictionary of Angels, Including the Fallen Angels* by Gustav Davidson (New York: Free Press, 1967).

31. See the standard works of Christian dogmatics under the loci angelology and demonology; cf. also the popular treatments *The Nature of Angels* by Alexander Whyte (London: Hodder and Stoughton, 1930) and *The Mystery and Ministry of Angels* by Herbert Lockyer (Grand Rapids, Mich.: Eerdmans, 1958). The view held by some church fathers (e.g. Augustine) and by the 20th century father of Neo-Orthodoxy, Karl Barth, that evil—and therefore the Satanic host—lacks ontological reality has been effectively refuted by Gustaf Wingren in his *Theology in Conflict: Nygren—Barth—Bultmann*, trans. E. H. Wahlstrom (Philadelphia: Fortress Press, 1958).

32. Cf. the short story "God's Devil," which is found in Chapter Six.

33. The fundamental New Testament motif of Christ's victory over the powers of evil has received particular stress in the work of Swedish

198 / *Principalities and Powers*

theologian Gustaf Aulén. See my "Short Critique of Gustaf Aulén's *Christus Victor*," printed as an appendix in my *Chytraeus on Sacrifice* (St. Louis, Mo.: Concordia Publishing House, 1962). For additional discussion of the attitude of the New Testament and the primitive church toward demonic activity, see below, Appendix A.

34. Montgomery, *The Suicide of Christian Theology* (*op. cit.* in note 3 above), pp. 129, 168-69; *Crisis in Lutheran Theology* (2 vols.; rev. ed., Minneapolis, Minn.: Bethany Fellowship, 1973), I, 91-93.

35. Richard Whately, *A View of the Scripture Revelations Respecting Good and Evil and Evil Angels* (Philadelphia: Lindsay & Blakiston, 1856), p. 75. Whately was author of the superlative apologetic tour de force refuting Hume's argument against miracles, *Historic Doubts Relative to Napoleon Buonaparte*; cf. Montgomery, *The Shape of the Past* (Ann Arbor, Mich.: Edwards Brothers, 1963), p. 172.

36. "With Pythagoreanism begins the transformation of the Greek mode of thought by a foreign element which originated in the Orphic mysticism . . . The spirit, the principles and the practices of the Phythagorean order all have their root in the doctrine of transmigration. This should not be regarded as a subordinate or more or less indifferent appendage" (Edward Zeller, *Outlines of the History of Greek Philosophy*, ed. Wilhelm Nestle, trans. L. R. Palmer [13th ed.; "International Library of Psychology, Philosophy and Scientific Method"; London: Routledge & Kegan Paul, 1931], pp. 31-32).

37. *Timaeus*, 20d-27a; *Critias*, 108c-109a, 113-121.

38. J. V. Luce, *The End of Atlantis: New Light on an Old Legend* (London: Thames & Hudson, 1969).

39. Jean Gattefossé & Claudius Roux's *Bibliographie de l'Atlantide et des questions connexes* (Lyon: Bosc & Riou, 1926) has 1700 entries. See in particular J. Imbelloni & A. Vivante, *Le Livre des Atlantides*, trans. from the Spanish and ed. F. Gidon (Paris: Payot, 1942), and Ignatius Donnelly's newly revised classic, *Atlantis: The Antediluvian World*, ed. Egerton Sykes (New York: Gramercy Publishing Co., 1949).

40. As maintained, for example, by Paul Le Cour, *A la recherche d'un monde perdu: L'Atlantide et ses traditions* (rev. ed.; Paris: Leymarie, 1931).

41. Cf. René Thévenin, *Les Pays légendaires* ("Que sais-je?" 226; 3d ed.; Paris: Presses Universitaires de France, 1961); Bernard Blackstone, *The Lost Travellers* (London: Longmans, 1962); and Sister Sylvia Mary, *Nostalgia for Paradise* (New York and Tournai, Belg.: Desclee, 1965).

42. Unfortunately medieval speculation about Vergil did not stop there; see John Webster Spargo, *Virgil the Necromancer: Studies in Virgilian Legends* ("Harvard Studies in Comparative Literature," 10; Cambridge, Mass.: Harvard University Press, 1934).

43. See the texts collected in Ludwig Fahz, *De poetarum Romanorum doctrina magica* (Giessen: Ricker, 1904), and A. Bouché-Leclercq's *Histoire de la divination dans l'Antiquité* (4 vols.; Paris, 1879) which Wilbur Smith rightly calls "the greatest work on divination in the classi-

cal world that has ever been published" (*Before I Forget* [Chicago: Moody Press, 1971], p. 228).

44. Cf. H. J. Rose, "Metamorphosis," *Oxford Classical Dictionary* (1949), p. 562.

45. *Epistolae*, VII, 27.

46. J. H. Westcott (ed.), *Selected Letters of Pliny* (Boston: Allyn and Bacon, 1950), p. 235.

47. See G. R. S. Mead, *Apollonius of Tyana* (New Hyde Park, N.Y.: University Books, 1966) and Mario Meunier, *Apollonius de Tyane, ou Le Séjour d'un dieu parmi les hommes* (Paris: Bernard Grasset, 1936).

48. *New Schaff-Herzog Encyclopedia of Religious Knowledge* (1949), I, 232. Voltaire is a prominent example of those who "revived this use of Philostratus in the interest of paganism." E. M. Butler, in his *Myth of the Magus* (Cambridge, Eng.: Cambridge University Press, 1948), has related Apollonius to the stream of charismatic mages extending from Zoroaster to Rasputin; the book is a masterly study in the history of ideas.

49. So the New Testament documents were dated by W. F. Albright, perhaps the foremost American biblical archeologist of the 20th century; see Montgomery, *History & Christianity* (Downers Grove, Ill.: Inter-Varsity Press, 1965), p. 35 and *passim*.

50. R. M. Grant, *Gnosticism and Early Christianity* (New York: Columbia University Press, 1959), pp. 9, 13. Grant's expertise as a scholar of Gnosticism has not, however, kept him from erroneous interpretations of the rise of Christianity; see my review of Vol. I of his edition of *The Apostolic Fathers* in my *Suicide of Christian Theology* (*op. cit.* in note 3 above), pp. 237-38. Other valuable treatments of Gnosticism are Jean Doresse's *The Secret Books of the Egyptian Gnostics*, trans. Philip Mairet (New York: Viking Press, 1960) and Edwin M. Yamauchi's *Gnostic Ethics and Mandaean Origins* ("Harvard Theological Studies," 24; Cambridge, Mass.: Harvard University Press, 1970).

51. E.g., G. R. S. Mead, *Fragments of a Faith Forgotten* (New Hyde Park, N. Y.: University Books, 1960).

52. Cf. A. F. Findlay's study of "Gnostic Gospels" in his United Free Church College (Glasgow) Kerr Lectures, published under the title, *Byways in Early Christian Literature* (Edinburgh: T. & T. Clark, 1923), pp. 117-47.

53. One of the most popular collections of these was Sir John Mandeville's *Travels*; see Malcolm Letts, *Sir John Mandeville: The Man and His Book* (London: Batchworth Press, 1949).

54. For examples of this delightful literature, see *Beasts and Saints*, trans. Helen Waddell (London: Constable, 1934); *The Bestiary*, trans. T. H. White (New York: G. P. Putnam, 1954); *A Cloisters Bestiary*, ed. Richard H. Randall, Jr. (New York: Metropolitan Museum of Art, 1960); and Margaret W. Robinson, *Fictitious Beasts: A Bibliography* (London: The Library Association, 1961).

55. Perhaps the best collection of medieval legends remains that

of Sabine Baring-Gould: *Curious Myths of the Middle Ages* (reprint ed.; New Hyde Park, N.Y.: University Books, 1967); the Wandering Jew is treated on pp. 1-31.

56. See Charles Gould, *Mythical Monsters* (London: W. H. Allen, 1886); C. J. S. Thompson, *The Mystery and Lore of Monsters* (New Hyde Park, N.Y.: University Books, 1968); and Rupert T. Gould, *The Loch Ness Monster and Others* (New Hyde Park, N.Y.: University Books, 1969).

57. Albert Farges, *Mystical Phenomena Compared with their Human and Diabolical Counterfeits*, trans. S. P. Jacques (London: Burns, Oates & Washbourne, 1926), p. 537.

58. See above, our discussion at note 15.

59. Quoted in Farges, *op. cit.*, p. 546.

60. See our text at note 16.

61. Edgar Sheffield Brightman, *An Introduction to Philosophy* (New York: Holt, 1925), p. 56.

62. See above, our discussion in Chapter One.

63. Hans Küng and other "New Shape" Roman Catholics of today try (unsuccessfully, we believe) to argue that even Trent did not succeed in solidifying Roman doctrine! See my *Ecumenicity, Evangelicals and Rome* (Grand Rapids, Mich.: Zondervan, 1969).

64. On the Albigensians, consult H. J. Warner, *The Albigensian Heresy* (2 vols.; London: S.P.C.K., 1922-1928); Pierre Belperron, *La Croisade contre les Albigeois* (Paris: Plon, 1942); Fernand Niel, *Albigeois et Cathares* ("Que sais-je?" 689; 4th ed.; Paris: Presses Universitaires de France, 1965); Jean-Laurent Riol, *Dernières connaissances sur des questions cathares* (Albi: Imprimerie Coopérative du Sud-Ouest, 1964).

65. See, along with Huysmans' classic, *Là-Bas* (referred to in Chapter One), Frances Winwar, *The Saint and the Devil: Joan of Arc and Gilles de Rais* (New York: Harper, 1948), and Michel Bataille, *Gilles de Rais* (Paris: Editions Planète, 1966).

66. Johan Huizinga, *The Waning of the Middle Ages* (New York: Doubleday Anchor Books, 1954); cf. Montgomery, *The Shape of the Past* (*op. cit.* in note 35), pp. 92-94.

67. See Edward P. Cheyney, *The Dawn of a New Era, 1250-1453* (New York: Harper, 1936), chap. 4 ("Popular Insurrections"), pp. 110-41.

68. D. P. Walker, *Spiritual and Demonic Magic from Ficino to Campanella* (London: Warburg Institute, 1958); Edgar Wind, *Pagan Mysteries in the Renaissance* (London: Faber & Faber, 1958); Joseph Orsier, *Henri Cornélis Agrippa, sa vie et son oeuvre* (Paris: Chacornac, 1911); Frances A. Yates, *Giordano Bruno and the Hermetic Tradition)* London: Routledge and Kegan Paul, 1964); Désirée Hirst, *Hidden Riches: Traditional Symbolism from the Renaissance to Blake* (New York: Barnes & Noble, 1964).

69. See Paracelsus, *Selected Writings*, ed. Jolande Jacobi, trans. Norbert Guterman ("Bollingen Series," 28; New York: Pantheon Books, 1951); Paracelsus, *Hermetic and Alchemical Writings*, trans. & ed. A. E. Waite (2 vols.; reprint ed.; New Hyde Park, N.Y.: University Books,

1967); the popular treatment by Henry M. Pachter, *Magic into Science: The Story of Paracelsus* (New York: Henry Schuman, 1951); and the superlative scholarly study by Walter Pagel, *Paracelsus: An Introduction to Philosophical Medicine in the Era of the Renaissance* (Basel, Switzerland: S. Karger, 1958).

70. This ideological stream has been treated, albeit without adequate theological perspective, by Will-Erich Peuckert, *Pansophie, ein Versuch zur Geschichte der weissen und schwarzen Magie* (2d ed.; Berlin: Erich Schmidt, 1956), and by Walter Nigg, *Heimliche Weisheit: Mystisches Leben in der evangelischen Christenheit* (Zurich & Stuttgart: Artemis-Verlag, 1959).

71. See Baring-Gould, *op. cit.* (in note 55), pp. 32-54; Elaine Sanceau, *The Land of Prester John* (New York: Knopf, 1944); and Frederic R. White (ed.), *Famous Utopias of the Renaissance* (New York: Hendricks House/Farrar, Straus, 1946).

72. See above, our discussion corresponding to notes 37-42.

73. Pico of Mirandola's opposition to astrology was especially characteristic; see below, Chapter Three (the text at notes 26 and 52-54).

74. Luther, *Tischreden* in the critical *Weimarer Ausgabe* of Luther's works), I, 17.

75. See the essay, "Luther and Science," in my *In Defense of Martin Luther* (Milwaukee: Northwestern Publishing House, 1970), pp. 87-113.

76. The first in-depth study of Andreae's Lutheran hermetics is provided in Montgomery, *Cross and Crucible* (2 vols.; "International Archives of the History of Ideas"; The Hague: Nijhoff, 1973).

77. For a very valuable article on this subject, see H. C. Erik Midelfort, "Witchcraft and Religion," *Archiv fuer Reformationgeschichte*, LXII/2 (1971), 266-78.

78. See Arthur Hertzberg, *The French Enlightenment and the Jews* (New York: Columbia University Press, 1968). Cf. Karl Marx, *A World without Jews*, ed. Dagobert D. Runes (4th ed.; New York: Philosophical Library, 1960).

79. Johannes Von Guenther, "Epilogue" to his *Cagliostro: A Novel*, trans. Huntley Paterson (London: Heinemann, 1928), p. 613.

80. Douglas Knoop and G. P. Jones, *The Genesis of Freemasonry* (Manchester, Eng.: Manchester University Press, 1949); Martin L. Wagner, *Freemasonry: An Interpretation* (Columbus, Ohio: F. J. Heer, 1912).

81. See René Trintzius, *Jacques Cazotte, ou le XVIIIe siècle inconnu* (Paris: Athêna, 1944); Gèrard de Nerval, *Les Illuminés* (Paris: André Delpeuch, 1927), pp. 11-95.

82. Lewis Spence, *An Encyclopaedia of Occultism* (reprint ed.; New Hyde Park, N.Y.: University Books, 1960), p. 346.

83. See A. E. Waite's *The Unknown Philosopher* (reprint ed.; Blauvelt, N.Y.: Rudolf Steiner Publications, 1970) and *Saint-Martin, the French Mystic* (London: Rider, 1922); also, Robert Amadou & Alice Joly, *De l'agent inconnu au philosophe inconnu* (Paris: Denoël, 1962).

84. Spence, *op. cit.*, p. 118.

85. See Marc Haven's *Le Maitre inconnu: Cagliostro* (new ed.;
Lyon: Paul Derain, 1964) and *L'Evangile de Cagliostro* (Paris: Editions
Pythagore, 1932).

86. Spence, *op. cit.*, p. 345; cf. E. M. Butler, *op. cit.* (in note 48
above), pp. 185-214. As an example of absurd occult hagiography, see
Isabel Cooper-Oakley, *The Count of Saint Germain*, ed. Paul M. Allen
(Blauvelt, N.Y.: Rudolf Steiner Publications, 1970).

87. Constantin Bila, *La Croyance à la magie an XVIIIe siècle en
France dans les contes, romans & traités* (Paris: J. Gamber, 1925),
p. 150.

88. A theme carried on by numerous other 19th century writers;
see Claudius Grillet, *Le Diable dans la littérature au XIXe siècle*
(Lyon: Emmanuel Vitte, 1935). Cf. Coleman O. Parsons, *Witchcraft and
Demonology in Scott's Fiction* (Edinburgh: Oliver & Boyd, 1964).

89. The history of that epochal June of 1816 is given by Montague
Summers in his excellent editorial introduction to *The Grimoire and
Other Supernatural Stories* (London: Fortune Press, n.d.); a recent novel-
ization by Derek Marlowe is titled, *A Single Summer with Lord B.*
(New York: Viking Press, 1969).

90. See Nelson Browne, *Sheridan Le Fanu* (New York: Roy Pub-
lishers, 1951); S. M. Ellis, *Wilkie Collins, Le Fanu, and Others* (London:
Constable, 1931), pp. 140-91; and Peter Penzoldt, *The Supernatural in
Fiction* (New York: Humanities Press, 1965), especially pp. 67-91.

91. August Strindberg, *From an Occult Diary*, ed. Torsten Eklund,
trans. Mary Sandbach (London: Secker & Warburg, 1965).

92. See below, Chapter Five.

93. A. P. Sinnett, *The Occult World* (3d ed.; Boston: Houghton, Mif-
flin, 1887); C. Jinarājadāsa (ed.), *The Golden Book of the Theosophical
Society . . . 1875-1925* (Adyar, Madras, India: Theosophical Publishing
House, 1925); Arthur H. Nethercot, *The First Five Lives of Annie Besant*
(Chicago: University of Chicago Press, 1960); Rudolf Steiner, *Occult
Science—An Outline*, trans. Monges and Monges (2d ed.; New York:
Anthroposophic Press, 1950); A. C. Harwood (ed.), *The Faithful Thinker:
Centenary Essays on the Work and Thought of Rudolf Steiner* (London:
Hodder and Stoughton, 1961). Critiques of Theosophy are given in most
standard works on cults and isms (the writings of Walter R. Martin,
J. K. Van Baalen, F. E. Mayer); I myself had occasion to touch on
Anthroposophy in my death-of-God debate with Thomas J. J. Altizer
(*The Suicide of Christian Theology* [*op. cit.* in note 3 above], pp.
138-39).

94. See, *inter alia*, Eliphas Lévi, *Transcendental Magic*, trans. and
ed. A. E. Waite (rev. ed.; London: Rider, 1968); Paul Chacornac, *Eliphas
Lévi, rénovateur de l'occultisme en France* (Paris: Chacornac, 1926);
Jollivet-Castelot (ed.), *Les Sciences maudites* (Paris: "La Maison
d'Art," 1900); Papus, *Traité élémentaire de science occulte* (5th ed.;
Paris: Chamuel, 1898). E. M. Butler, *op. cit.* (in note 48 above), p.
245, emphasizes the influence of Lévi on Theosophy's Madame Blavatsky: "The writings of Bulwer-Lytton and Eliphas Lévi between them

fired the more than combustible imagination of Helena Petrovna Blavatsky."

95. Still another example of this correlation was the intense interest in the occult in Russian imperial circles in the days just preceding the Revolution; Rasputin's central place in this drama is well known. See Maurice Palèologue, *La Russie des Tsars pendant la Grande Guerre* (3 vols.; Paris: Plon, 1921-1922), II, 249-53; III, 93-96, 172-74. In French diplomat Paléologue's correspondence it is revealed that Papus himself had intimate contact, in person and by letter, with the Emperor and Empress, and even necromantically conjured up the ghost of Czar Alexander III for them. More of this in Chapter Five.

96. Cf. as indicators, William Seabrook, *Witchcraft, Its Power in the World Today* (New York: Harcourt, Brace Lancer Books, 1940); the Spring, 1970, number of *Horizon*, devoted to the theme of "Reason and Unreason"; and the March, 1970, *McCall's*, featuring articles on "The Occult Explosion," the Sharon Tate murders, and Madame Blavatsky.

97. Robert N. Bellah, "Civil Religion in America," in *Religion in America*, ed. W. G. McLoughlin and R. N. Bellah (Boston: Houghton Mifflin, 1968), pp. 3-23.

98. Ellic Howe, *Urania's Children: The Strange World of the Astrologers* (London: William Kimber, 1967), *passim*.

99. Martin Luther, "Ein' Feste Burg" (1529).

NOTES TO CHAPTER THREE

1. Several important general works treating the Cabala and its influence on Christianity warrant citation at the very outset: Gershom G. Scholem, *On the Kabbalah and Its Symbolism*, trans. Ralph Manheim (New York: Schocken Books, 1965); Georges Vajda, *Recherches sur la philosophie et la Kabbale dans la penseé juive du moyen âge* (Paris & The Hague: Mouton, 1962); A.-D. Grad, *Le Temps des Kabbalistes* (Neuchâtel: Editions de la Baconnière, 1967); *Adumbratio Kabbale Christianae*, trans. from Latin into French for the first time (Paris: Chacornac, 1899); and especially F. Secret, *Les Kabbalistes chrétiens de la Renaissance* (Paris: Dunod, 1964).

2. S. Karppe, *Etude sur les origines et la nature du Zohar* (Paris: Baillière, 1901), pp. 222-23. See Karppe's full discussion on the origin of the Cabala, pp. 222-27. He calls this meaning of Cabala "le sens ancien" (p. 224).

3. *Ibid.*, pp. 224 ("Le sens intermediaire").

4. *Ibid.*, p. 227.

5. This diagram appears as the frontispiece both in A. E. Waite's *The Secret Doctrine in Israel* (New York: Occult Research Press,

n.d.) and in his *Holy Kabbalah* (New Hyde Park, N.Y.: University Books, 1960).

6. Joseph Leon Blau, *The Christian Interpretation of the Cabala in the Renaissance* (New York: Columbia University Press, 1944), p. 9.

7. See Vol. I, Pt. 2, chap. 1 ("God and the World") of George Foot Moore's classic work, *Judaism* (2 vols.; Cambridge: Harvard University Press, 1927) for a beautiful and sympathetic discussion of the Old Testament view of God's imminent and eminent relationship to His creation.

8. Blau, *op. cit.*, pp. 2-3.

9. Cf. Emil L. Fackenheim, "Can There Be Judaism without Revelation?" *Commentary*, December, 1951.

10. This will remind students of modern Protestant theology of the direct influence of Karl Barth's conception of God as the transcendent Wholly Other on the development of death-of-God thinking. See Montgomery, *The Suicide of Christian Theology* (Minneapolis: Bethany Fellowship, 1970), pp. 76 ff.

11. For Philo's philosophy, see Erwin R. Goodenough, *An Introduction to Philo Judaeus* (New Haven: Yale University Press, 1940).

12. Blau, *op cit.*, pp. 3-4. The elevation of the Old Testament Concept of God from eminence to extreme transcendence at Alexandria, and the attempt to reconcile His imminence and transcendence by the *sephiroth*, is, I believe, one very strong reason why so many Jewish Cabalists became Christians during the Renaissance (see Blau, p. 65). The New Testament conception of God is also one of transcendence, although not *extreme* transcendence (see transcendence series above). God has never been seen by man at any time (I John 4:12), but this does not mean that he *cannot* be seen by man. The extremely transcendent conception of God held by the Jewish Cabalists made it easy for them to accept the view of God presented in the New Testament, which, although only mildly transcendent, still goes beyond the eminent view of God in the Old Testament. The mild transcendence of the New Testament conception of God is further explained by Christ, the *Logos*, who, according to the New Testament, is the Being referred to in the Old Testament passages where man is said to have had direct contact with deity. "No man hath seen God at any time; the only begotten Son, which is in the bosom of the Father, he hath declared him" (Jn. 1:18); on this passage C. I. Scofield comments: "The divine essence, God, in His own triune Person, no human being in the flesh has seen. But God, veiled in angelic form, and especially as incarnate in Jesus Christ, has been seen of men." It was not difficult for the Jewish Cabalists to substitute Christ for the *sephiroth* as a means of explaining God's nature. We shall see that whereas the *sephiroth* did not (and logically could not because of the extremely transcendent view of deity the Cabalists held) have offered an adequate solution to their imminence-transcendence problem, the New Testament view of God's imminence and transcendence, and the place of Christ in it, is capable of hurdling the dilemma.

13. Undoubtedly this was another reason why so many Jewish Cabalists became Christians. Jesus preached terrible judgment upon the Pharisees because of their casuistry, and the basic concept of Pauline theology is that man is justified by grace through faith, apart from the works of the law.

14. Karppe, *op cit.*, pp. 228-29. Karppe backs up these ascertions by innumerable quotations from the *Zohar*, other early Cabalistic writings, and the writings of Talmudists (pp. 229-31).

15. See Gershom G. Scholem (ed.), Zohar: *The Book of Splendor* (New York: Schocken Books, 1949), and S. L. MacGregor Mathers (ed.), *The Kabbalah Unveiled, Containing . . . Books of the Zohar* (London: Routledge & Kegan Paul, 1968).

16. For Cordovero, see Blau, *op. cit.*, p. 10 and Appendix A (p. 115).

17. Friedrich Barth, in his *Die Cabbala des Heinrich Cornelius Agrippa.*

18. *Liber Iezirah qui Abrahamo Patriarchae adscribitur*, ed. John Stephan Rittangelius, (Amsterdam, 1642), 1:1, 2:2, 6:9. The passages given above are the translation of Abba Hillel Silver (*A History of Messianic Speculation in Israel* [New York: Macmillan, 1927], pp. 245-246), with my revisions.

19. This discussion of the three methods of Cabalistic interpretation depends heavily on Joshua Trachtenberg's *Jewish Magic and Superstition* (New York: Meridian Books, 1961), Appendix I (pp. 260 ff.).

20. *Ibid.*, p. 262. Vincent Foster Hopper (*Medieval Number Symbolism* [New York: Columbia University Press, 1938], pp. 60-68) presents evidence for the very great antiquity of this technique.

21. Blau, *op. cit.*, p. 8.

22. Trachtenberg, *op. cit.*, p. 263.

23. Gershom G. Scholem, *Major Trends in Jewish Mysticism* (Jerusalem: Schocken, 1941), p. 14.

24. Blau, *op. cit.*, p. 6. Blau continues: "Only in the later forms of cabalism did an untraditional element, metempsychosis, enter deeply into the cabalistic scheme, not as a substitute for, but as coexistent with the traditional doctrine." Moore, *op. cit.*, Vol. II, Pt. 7 ("The Hereafter"), pp. 279 ff. should also be consulted for information on the redemption doctrine in Judaism.

25. See Silver, *op. cit.*, pp. 244-53, for a discussion of the application of gematria, notarikon, and themurah to the Messianic problem.

26. For a detailed study of Pico's life and conversion, see my essay, "Eros and Agape in Pico of Mirandola," in *The Suicide of Christian Theology* (*op. cit.*, in note 10 above), pp. 404-22.

27. Blau, *op. cit.*, pp. 19-20.

28. *Ibid.*, p. 8.

29. Karppe, *op. cit.*, p. 237. See Karppe's full discussion of the three schools, pp. 237-306.

30. Blau, *op. cit.*, p. 10.

31. *Ibid.*, p. 28.

32. Pearl Kibre, *The Library of Pico della Mirandola* (New York: Columbia University Press, 1936), p. 46.

33. Blau, *op. cit.*, p. 30.

34. *Ibid.*, p. 28.

35. See Pico, *Opera omnia* (2 vols.; Basel, 1572), I, 5-7. (Vol. II of this edition contains the works of G. F. Pico, who wrote the primary-source biography of Giovanni Pico of Mirandola.)

36. *Ibid.*, I, 80-83, 89, 107-13.

37. *Ibid.*, I, 175-81.

38. On the anagogical method—which "led up" to the contemplation of heavenly things (e.g., Jerusalem = the life of dwellers in heaven who see God revealed in Zion)—consult Montgomery, "Sixtus of Siena and Roman Catholic Biblical Scholarship in the Reformation Period," in *Ecumenicity, Evangelicals and Rome* (Grand Rapids, Mich.: Zondervan, 1969), pp. 45-69 (especially p. 66).

39. I have dealt at some length with the problem of the verification of metaphysical assertions in my essay, "The Relevance of Scripture Today," which appears both in Merrill C. Tenney (ed.), *The Bible—The Living Word of Revelation* (Grand Rapids, Mich.: Zondervan, 1968), pp. 199-218, and in my *Suicide of Christian Theology* (*op. cit.*, in note 10 above), pp. 359-79. Reliance is there placed on the conclusions reached by Ludwig Wittgenstein in the final propositions (the section dealing with *das Mystische*) of his *Tractatus Logico-Philosophicus*.

40. On the function of constructs and models in scientific and theological theorizing, see my essay, "The Theologian's Craft," in *The Suicide of Christian Theology* (*op. cit.*, in note 10 above), pp. 267-313.

41. One should note that imminence and mild transcendence are not logical contradictions. It is this which preserves from logical absurdity the New Testament assertion that Christ is the visible manifestation of God.

42. There is of course no linguistic justification either for any one language being more "sacred" or "pure" or even "better" than another. See Robert A. Hall, Jr., *Leave Your Language Alone!*

43. Pico apparently believed that Hebrew was the original sacred language, and probably based the validity of the Cabalistic exegetical techniques on this. See his theses No. 35 (*Opera*, I, 82), and 80 (p. 89).

44. See Genesis 11:1-9 (especially vs. 7, 9).

45. Vincent Foster Hopper, *Medieval Number Symbolism* (New York: Columbia University Press, 1938), p. 69.

46. Trachtenberg, *op. cit.*, (in note 19 above), p. 264.

47. Cf. R.-E. Gérard, *La Mathématique de la révélation* (n.p. [Brussels, Belg.?]: Robert Stoops, 1956), which also includes a long section on the dimensions of the Great Pyramid (see above, Chapter One, our text at notes 22 and 23).

48. Ethelbert W. Bullinger, *Number in Scripture, Its Supernatural Design and Spiritual Significance* (reprint ed.; Grand Rapids, Mich.: Kregel, 1967), p. 26.

49. The great 19th century textual theory, generally held, with some modifications, to the present time; Westcott and Hort's work, however, was in no sense *final*, as the apparatus in the many editions of Nestle's resultant text (*Novum Testamentum Graece*) so plainly demonstrates, with its inclusion of the decisions of such other great modern editors as Tischendorf and Von Soden.

50. Ivan Panin (ed.), *The New Testament from the Greek Text As Established by Bible Numerics* (2d ed.; Toronto: Book Society of Canada, 1935), pp. 592-94.

51. See, for example, Montgomery, "Inspiration and Infallibility: A New Departure" and "Inductive Inerrancy" in *The Suicide of Christian Theology* (*op. cit.*, in note 10 above), pp. 314-58, and *Crisis in Lutheran Theology* (2 vols.; rev. ed. Minneapolis: Bethany Fellowship, 1973), *passim*.

52. Blau, *op. cit.*, (in note 6 above), p. vii.

53. See his *In Astrologiam*, in *Opera*, I, 411-732.

54. W. Parr Greswell, *Memoirs of Politianus, Pico, et al.* (London: Cadwell and Davies, 1805), pp. 345-46.

55. The key passage is II (IV) Esdras 14, which has served as justification for lo! how many occult teachings. A voice calls Esdras from a bush, telling him that it was he who likewise spoke to Moses from a bush and "told him many wondrous things and shewed him the secrets of the times, and the end; and commanded him, saying, These words shalt thou declare, and these shalt thou hide" (vv. 5-6; cf. vv. 45-48). The Jewish Cabalists held that their doctrines were the substance of this secret wisdom which the Lord had given to Moses on the mount and which had been passed on *viva voce* in unbroken succession to them. The parallelism is obvious with the Masonic legend of the commencement of the Order at the building of Solomon's Temple; occult advocates of a "secret tradition" almost invariably employ a motif of this kind to lend dignity and pseudo-revelational significance to their beliefs.

56. Walter Pater, *Studies in the History of the Renaissance* (London: Macmillan, 1873), p. 22.

57. See above, note 38.

58. Cf. Montgomery, "Luther's Hermeneutic Vs. the New Hermeneutic," in *In Defense of Martin Luther* (Milwaukee: Northwestern Publishing House, 1970), pp. 40-85.

59. Blau, *op. cit.*, p. 114.

60. Pater, *op. cit.*, pp. 37-38.

NOTES TO CHAPTER FOUR

1. Minimal documentation is to be found in this section on alchemy, since I have provided a most detailed treatment of the subject, with

a lengthy annotated bibliography, in my *Cross and Crucible* (2 vols.; "International Archives of the History of Ideas"; The Hague: Nijhoff, 1973). The finest recent general survey of the alchemical tradition in English is C. A. Burland's magnificently illustrated volume, *The Arts of the Alchemists* (New York: Macmillan, 1968).

2. Cf. René Marcard, *De la pierre philosophale à l'atome* (Paris: Plon, 1959).

3. A. E. Waite (ed.), *Lives of Alchemystical Philosophers* (London: George Redway, 1888), pp. 201-208.

4. Charles William Heckethorn, *The Secret Societies of All Ages & Countries* (2 vols.; reprint ed.; New Hyde Park, N.Y.: University Books, 1965). Cf. also Serge Hutin, *Histoire mondiale des sociétés secrètes* (Paris: Productions de Paris, n.d.).

5. Marianne Monestier, *Les Sociétés secrètes féminines* (Paris: Productions de Paris, 1963); Gisèle Laurent, *Les Sociétés secrètes érotiques* (Doullens: Sévin, 1961).

6. Montgomery, *Cross and Crucible* (*op. cit.*). The second volume of this work contains the photographically reproduced Foxcroft English translation (1690) of Andreae's *Chymische Hochzeit*, with full editorial annotations.

7. A. E. Waite, *The Brotherhood of the Rosy Cross* (reprint ed.; New Hyde Park, N.Y.: University Books, 1961), p. 123. Cf. Waite's *A New Encyclopaedia of Freemasonry* (2 vols.; reprint ed.; New Hyde Park, N.Y.: University Books, 1970).

8. Rudolf Steiner, *The Mission of Christian Rosencreutz*, trans. Dorothy Osmond (London: Rudolf Steiner Publishing Co., 1950), pp. 81ff. Cf. my *Suicide of Christian Theology* (Minneapolis: Bethany Fellowship, 1970), pp. 138-39.

9. *Light Invisible* by "Vindex" (London: Regency Press, 1952), pp. 137-38. This work, by a modernist Anglican clergyman and Freemason, attempts to defend the Order against the orthodox Christian critique, *Darkness Visible*, by Walton Hannah (London: Augustine Press, 1952). Lutherans, with their characteristic concern for doctrinal purity, have been especially strong opponents of Masonry; see, for example, Martin L. Wagner's *Freemasonry: An Interpretation* (Columbus, Ohio: F. J. Heer, 1912). My own church body will not permit its members to be Masons, and maintains a permanent "Commission on Fraternal Organizations" (KFUO Building, St. Louis, Mo. 63105) which studies the religious aspect of secret societies and publishes a variety of helpful materials on the subject.

10. For a particularly revolting example, see Nesta H. Webster, *Secret Societies and Subversive Movements* (5th ed.; London: Boswell, 1936).

11. See Min. Felix, *Oct.*, XI, 6; Justin, *Dial. Tryph.*, 10, 17, 108; *I Apol.*, 26; *II Apol.*, 12; Tertullian, *Apol.* 2, 4, 7, 8, 39; Eusebius, *Hist. Eccl.*, V, 1. Cf. C. R. Haines, *Heathen Contact with Christianity*

during its First Century and a Half (Cambridge, Eng.: Deighton, Bell, 1923), pp. 49, 56.

12. See my *Cross and Crucible* (*op. cit.*). For the constitution of Andreae's Society, see G. H. Turnbull (ed.), "Johann Valentin Andreaes Societas Christiana: A Modell of a Christian Society," *Zeitschrift fuer Deutsche Philologie*, LXXIV/2 (1955), 151-85. My own scholastic honorary society, Phi Beta Kappa, began as a secret organization (William. T. Hastings, *Phi Beta Kappa As a Secret Society* [Washington, D.C.: United Chapters of Phi Beta Kappa, 1965]).

13. "Perhaps the major achievement of Waite's Temple was to number amongst its members Evelyn Underhill and Charles Williams. While the first named seems to have found Waite lacking in those things for which she was looking—although I suspect that she owes a little more to Waite and a little less to Von Hugel than is generally recognised—Charles Williams' whole outlook and philosophy were permanently affected by Waite's version of the Golden Dawn" (Francis King, *The Rites of Modern Occult Magic* [New York: Macmillan, 1971], p. 112).

14. See, *inter alia*, Rupert Gleadow, *The Origin of the Zodiac* (New York: Castle Books, 1968); L.-F.-Alfred Maury, *La Magie et l'astrologie dans l'antiquité et au moyen âge* (Paris: Didier, 1860); P. Festugière, *La Revelation d'Hermès Trismégiste*, I: *L'Astrologie et les sciences occultes* (3d ed.; Paris: J. Gabalda, 1950); Franz Cumont, *Astrology and Religion among the Greeks and Romans* (reprint ed.; New York: Dover, 1960).

15. Richard Lewinsohn, *Science, Prophecy and Prediction*, trans. A. J. Pomerans (New York: Harper, 1961), p. 113.

16. The finest general work on the subject in English, though it suffers from its author's lack of critical judgment on astrological failings, is Louis MacNeice's lavishly illustrated book, *Astrology* (Garden City, N.Y.: Doubleday, 1964).

17. The preceding discussion of the horoscope has necessarily been kept to a very elementary level. For details concerning the casting and interpreting of horoscopes, see Alan Leo's series of "Astrological Manuals" (London: L. N. Fowler); *The New Manual of Astrology* by "Sepharial" (rev. ed.; Philadelphia: David McKay, n.d.); Max Heindel's *Simplified Scientific Astrology* (6th ed.; Oceanside, Calif.: The Rosicrucian Fellowship, 1928); and the numerous similar publications and aids listed in the Book Catalog of the New York Astrology Center (306 E. 6th St., New York City).

18. Cf. Jung, "The Sign of the Fishes," in *Collected Works*, IX/2: *Aion: Researches into the Phenomenology of the Self*, trans. R. F. C. Hull ("Bollingen Series," 20; New York: Pantheon Books, 1959), 72-94; and *Naturerklärung und Psyche* (Zurich: Rascher Verlag, 1952), *passim*. See also W. E. Peuckert, *L'Astrologie*, trans. Jouan & Jospin (Paris: Payot, 1965).

19. Montgomery, "Luther and Science," *In Defense of Martin Lu-*

ther (Milwaukee: Northwestern Publishing House, 1970), pp. 94-101. Cf. Ingetraut Ludolphy, "Luther üher Astrologie," *Was Gott an uns gewendet hat: Lutherstudien* (East Berlin: Evangelische Verlag-sanstalt, 1965), pp. 46-62, 105-107.

20. For example, Frances Rolleston, *Mazzaroth: or, the Constellations* (London: Rivingtons, 1862); Joseph A. Seiss, *The Gospel in the Stars* (Philadelphia, 1882); Ethelbert W. Bullinger, *The Witness of the Stars* (reprint ed.; Grand Rapids, Mich.: Kregel, 1967); and *Hebrew Astrology, the Key to the Study of Prophecy* by "Sepharial" (Philadelphia: David McKay, n.d.).

21. J. L. E. Dreyer, *Tycho Brahe: A Picture of Scientific Life and Work in the Sixteenth Century* (reprint ed.; New York: Dover, 1963), p. 196.

22. Paris: Editions du Dauphin.

23. Jean Porte, "L'Influence des astres et la statistique," *La Tour Saint Jacques*, No. 4: *L'Astrologie* (May-June, 1956), pp. 86-105.

24. Michel Gauquelin, "La Critique de M. Porte et la réalité expérimentale," *ibid.*, pp. 106-21.

25. Gauquelin, *Les Hommes et les astres* (Paris: Denoël, 1960).

26. John Anthony West and Jan Gerhard Toonder, *The Case for Astrology* (New York: Coward-McCann, 1970), pp. 161-62.

27. Gauquelin, *Les Hommes et les astres*, p. 16.

28. See Jung's work of this title, included in Jung and Pauli's *The Interpretation of Nature and the Psyche* ("Bollingen Series," 51; New York: Pantheon Books, 1955), pp. 1-146. (The remainder of the volume consists of W. Pauli's valuable essay, "The Influence of Archetypal Ideas on the Scientific Theories of Kepler.") Cf. Nandor Fodor, *Freud, Jung, and Occultism* (New Hyde Park, N.Y.: University Books, 1971).

29. Gauquelin, "Existe-t-il une hérédité planétaire?" *Planète*, No. 6 (September-October, 1962), pp. 77-83; "Die planetare Heredität," *Zeitschrift fuer Parapsychologie und Grenzgebiete der Psychologie*, V/2-3 (1962), 168-95.

30 Hans Bender, in Gauquelin, *Les Hommes et les astres*, pp. 11-13; Gauquelin, *L'Astrologie devant la science* (Paris: Editions Planète [1966]), especially pp. 247-50.

31. Paul Couderc, *L'Astrologie* ("Que sais-je?" 508; 3d ed.; Paris: Presses Universitaires de France, 1961), pp. 86-89.

32. Lewinsohn, *op. cit.* (in note 15), p. 112.

33. *Aquarius 2000 Instructional Booklet* (New York, N.Y., Hoi Polloi, Inc.) p. 12 (Quoted by permission.)

34. In earlier history, before the advent of modern medicine, medical astrology was less deserving of criticism; indeed, the medical sections of old astrology texts often strike one as funny rather than perilous. In the *De astrologia* of 17th century English alchemist Robert Fludd, for example, we learn that Saturn governs the melancholic or bilious temperament and brings about leprosy, elephantiasis, diarrhea, etc. (*Traité d'astrologie générale*, trans. Pierre Piobb [Paris:

H. Daragon, 1907], p. 143)! But the levity is quickly abated by examining the over twenty-five titles listed in the medical section of the New York Astrology Center's latest Book Catalog (see above, note 17). Here are a few examples: Max Heindel's *Astrology and the Ductless Glands*; Ada Muir's *Cancer, Its Cause, Prevention and Cure*; William J. Tucker's *Astropharmacology*. The Mystic Arts Book Society's *Book News*, No. 176 (published by University Books, New Hyde Park, N.Y.) features Omar V. Garrison's *Medical Astrology* and advertises it in the following terms: "For the first time, you will find the answers to such vital questions as: When is the safest time for you to have surgery if it is absolutely necessary? Does your horoscope indicate a predisposition to such serious maladies as heart disease, diabetes, arthritis, eye troubles, obesity, and so on?" Though in my judgment the censorship of printed matter ought always to be held to an absolute minimum (freedom of the press is a hard won and easily lost defining mark of a democracy), I am convinced that the public welfare demands legislation restricting the sale of potentially dangerous materials of this kind.

35. See the excellent study by Ellic Howe, *Urania's Children* (London: William Kimber, 1967), especially pp. 104 ff.

36. Cf. "What Was the Star of Bethlehem?" *Christianity Today*, December 18, 1964. This article was extracted from a booklet on the subject prepared by the Adler Planetarium and Astronomical Museum, Chicago.

NOTES TO CHAPTER FIVE

1. C. S. Lewis, *The Pilgrim's Regress* (London: Bles, 1943), p. 12. On "opium" and the psychedelic drugs in general, see below, our Appendix C.

2. C. S. Lewis, *Surprised by Joy: The Shape of My Early Life* (New York: Harcourt, Brace & World, 1955), p. 60.

3. Cf. the magnificently produced and edited *Encyclopédie de la divination* (Paris: Tchou, 1965).

4. On biblical prophecy, see, *inter alia*, such standard works as Alexander Keith's *Evidence of the Truth of the Christian Religion, Derived from the Literal Fulfilment of Prophecy* (16th ed.; Edinburgh: William Whyte, 1837); E. A. Edghill's *An Enquiry into the Evidential Value of Prophecy* (London: Macmillan, 1906); and John Urquhart's *The Wonders of Prophecy* (9th ed.; Harrisburg, Pa.: Christian Publications, n.d.).

5. Sir Robert Anderson, *The Coming Prince* (11th ed.; Glasgow: Pickering & Inglis, n.d.).

6. See in particular Edgar Leoni, *Nostradamus: Life and Literature*,

Including All the Prophecies in French and English (New York:
Nosbooks, 1961); Charles A. Ward, *Oracles of Nostradamus* (New
York: Modern Library, 1940); and Jean-Charles Pichon, *Nostradamus
et le secret des temps* (Paris: Productions de Paris, 1959).

7. These accounts derive from the primary-source correspondence
of Maurice Paléologue (1859-1944), French ambassador to Russia, historian, and member of the French Academy: *La Russie des Tsars
pendant al Grande Guerre* (3 vols.; Paris: Plon, 1921-1922), III, 94-95,
173-74.

8. The account by the killer is included in E. M. Butler, *The Myth
of the Magus* (Cambridge, Eng.: Cambridge University Press, 1948),
pp. 262-63.

9. J. Bronowski, "The Clock Paradox," *Scientific American*, June,
1963, pp. 136, 144. If the mean life before decay of a mu-meson at
rest is 10^{-6} sec., its life-span approximately doubles (2×10^{-6} sec.)
at 160,000 mi./sec.

10. I have discussed the possibility in detail in my *Shape of the
Past* (Ann Arbor, Mich.: Edwards Brothers, 1963), Pt. 1, chap. 2
("History As Time Travel"), pp. 20-33.

11. C. A. E. Moberly and E. F. Jourdain, *An Adventure* (4th ed.;
London: Faber & Faber, 1931). Antony Flew's negative critique of this
experience, in his *A New Approach to Psychical Research* (London:
Watts, 1953), Appendix I, pp. 142-47, is superficial; it reflects his consistent lack of recognition of his rationalist bias (as displayed in his
arguments against the miraculous in his *God and Philosophy*), and
illustrates a critic's judgment that his "book treats the experimental
work cursorily" (C. W. K. Mundle, "ESP Phenomena, Philosophical
Implications of," *The Encyclopedia of Philosophy*, ed. Paul Edwards
[8 vols.; New York: Macmillan, 1967], III, 58).

12. J. W. Dunne, *An Experiment with Time* (London: Faber &
Faber, 1958); *Nothing Dies* (London: Faber & Faber, 1940); *The
Serial Universe* (New York: Macmillan, 1938); Richard Lewinsohn,
Science, Prophecy and Prediction, trans. A. J. Pomerans (New York:
Harper, 1961), pp. 131-41 ("The English Dreamer"); J. B. Priestley,
Man and Time (Garden City, N.Y.: Doubleday, 1964), pp. 242-61 ("Dunne
and Serialism").

13. See G. N. M. Tyrrell, *Science & Psychical Phenomena and Apparitions* (2 vols. in 1; New Hyde Park, N.Y.: University Books,
1961), I, 72-74, 135, 157.

14. *Ibid.*, I, 105. See also, Arthur W. Osborn, *The Future Is Now:
The Significance of Precognition* (New Hyde Park, N.Y.: University
Books, 1961), *passim*.

15. Cf. Martin Ebon, *Prophecy in Our Time* (New York: Signet
Mystic Books, 1968), and Jess Stearn, *The Door to the Future* (New
York: Macfadden-Bartell, 1964).

16. Ruth Montgomery, *A Gift of Prophecy: The Phenomenal Jeane
Dixon* (New York: Bantam Books, 1966), pp. 177-83, 193.

17. James Bjornstad's *Twentieth Century Prophecy* (Minneapolis:

Bethany Fellowship, 1969), though lacking in scholarly precision and comprehensiveness, offers a useful critique of Jeane Dixon and Edgar Cayce from an evangelical viewpoint.

18. These biblical verses apply even to evangelical readers! One of the greatest present-day weaknesses in conservative Christianity is its preoccupation with the details of biblical prophecy (the endemic construction of "charts of the end time," the hassels among pre-, mid-, and post-tribulationists, etc.). Such activity is part of a defensive, separationist mentality that removes itself from modern life culturally (by its blue laws) and temporally (by its prophetic mania). Thus much talk of "witness" goes on without the Great Commission actually being carried out.

19. Horace, *Odes*, I, 11. The translation is that of Eugene and Roswell Martin Field: *Echoes from the Sabine Farm* (New York: Scribner, 1895), p. 69.

20. "No prophecy of the Scripture is of any private interpretation. For the prophecy came not in old time by the will of man, but holy men of God spoke as they were moved by the Holy Spirit" (II Pet. 1:20-21). Contrast the prophets of Baal in their contest with Elijah (I Kings 18:25 ff.). Jeane Dixon has employed, *inter alia*, cards, astrology, the crystal ball, and numerology.

21. W. A. Criswell, "The Bible and Prophecy," in *Prophecy in the Making: Messages Prepared for the Jerusalem Conference on Biblical Prophecy*, ed. Carl F. H. Henry (Carol Stream, Ill.: Creation House, 1971), p. 20.

22. Hawley O. Taylor, "Mathematics and Prophecy," in *Modern Science and Christian Faith* by Members of the American Scientific Affiliation (Wheaton, Ill.: Van Kampen Press, 1948), p. 178. Quoted by permission.)

23. W. Gurney Benham, *Playing Cards* (London: Spring Books, n.d.), pp. 1-9. Cf. Gertrude Monkley, *The Tarot Cards Painted by Bonifacio Bembo* (New York: The New York Public Library, 1966).

24. Basil Ivan Rákóczi, *The Painted Caravan: A Penetration into the Secrets of the Tarot Cards* (The Hague, Netherlands: L. J. C. Boucher, 1954), p. 15. Cf. Charles Godfrey Leland, *Gypsy Sorcery and Fortune Telling* (new ed.; New Hyde Park, N.Y.: University Books, 1962).

25. The finest decks are the Pamela Colman Smith Tarot (New Hyde Park, N.Y.: University Books), the Ancien Tarot de Marseille (Paris: B.-P. Grimaud), and the Greater Arcana bound with Oswald Wirth's *Le Tarot, des imagiers du moyen âge* (Paris: Tchou, 1966).

26. Papus, *The Tarot of the Bohemians: Absolute Key to Occult Science*, trans. A. P. Morton, ed. A. E. Waite (reprint ed.; New York: Arcanum Books, 1958).

27. A. E. Waite, *The Pictorial Key to the Tarot* (new ed.; New Hyde Park, N.Y.: University Books, 1959). This is the best available book on the Tarot; it contains a superlative annotated bibliography and full-color reproductions of Pamela Colman Smith's 78 Tarot designs.

28. *Ibid.*, p. 152.

29. Cf. Gertrude Monkley, "The Waite-Smith Tarot: A Footnote to *The Waste Land*," *Bulletin of the New York Public Library*, LVIII/10 (October, 1954), 471-75; and Mary McDermott Shideler, *The Theology of Romantic Love: A Study in the Writings of Charles Williams* (New York: Harper, 1962), pp. 63, 175-76.

30. One of the best studies is William Morrison's *Highland Second-Sight*, ed. Norman Macrae (Dingwall, Scotland: George Souter [1908]). These testimonies are not touched by John L. Campbell and Trevor H. Hall's *Strange Things: The Story of Fr. Allan McDonald, Ada Goodrich Freer, and the Society for Psychical Research's Enquiry into Highland Second Sight* (London: Routledge & Kegan Paul, 1968).

31. Cf. T. C. Lethbridge, *Gogmagog: The Buried Gods* (London: Routledge & Kegan Paul, 1957).

32. W. Y. Evans-Wentz, *The Fairy-Faith in Celtic Countries* (reprint ed.; New Hyde Park, N.Y.: University Books, 1966), pp. 90-91, 124-26. (This fine collection of testimonies and folklore material is unfortunately marred by the author's attempt to correlate the realm of Faerie with his own Eastern mystical-religious belief in reincarnation.) See also Lady Gregory, *Visions and Beliefs in the West of Ireland, with Two Essays and Notes by W. B. Yeats* (2d ed.; Gerrards Cross, Bucks, Gt. Brit.: Colin Smythe, 1970); W. B. Yeats, *Irish Fairy and Folk Tales* (New York: Modern Library, n.d.); and cf. H. R. Bachchan, *W. B. Yeats and Occultism* (Delhi, India: Motilal Banarsidass, 1965).

33. Robert Kirk, *The Secret Commonwealth of Elves, Fauns, & Fairies: From the Manuscript* ("Rare Text Library of Philosophical Research," 2; Toddington, Eng.: Helios Book Service, 1964).

34. W. B. Yeats, in Gregory, *op. cit.*, p. 337.

35. See the informative and entertaining article "Fairies" by Julian Franklyn, in his *A Survey of the Occult* (London: Arthur Barker, 1935), pp. 95-99.

36. Sinistrari, *Demoniality . . . Now First Translated into English with the Latin Text* (Paris: Isidore Liseux, 1879), para. 96-100 (pp. 191-201); cf. para. 77-85 (pp. 161-73). A very valuable work, though Sinistrari's attempt to locate the incubi and succubi in the kingdom of Faerie rather than in the demonic realm is not particularly convincing.

37. K. M. Briggs, *The Fairies in Tradition and Literature* (London: Routledge & Kegan Paul, 1967), p. 210.

38. James MacDougall, *Folk Tales and Fairy Lore in Gaelic and English, Collected from Oral Tradition*, ed. George Calder (Edinburgh: John Grant, 1910), p. 183.

39. Cf. Carl Gustav Jung, "The Phenomenology of the Spirit in Fairy Tales," in his *Psyche and Symbol*, ed. V. S. de Laszlo (Garden City, N.Y.: Doubleday Anchor Books, 1958), pp. 61-112.

40. Evans-Wentz, *op. cit.*, p. 146.

41. J. R. R. Tolkien, "On Fairy-Stories," *Essays Presented to Charles Williams*, ed. C. S. Lewis (London: Oxford University Press, 1947), p. 84. See also Montgomery, "The Chronicles of Narnia," *Religious Education*, LIV/5 (September-October, 1959), 418-28.

42. Cf. D. E. Harding, *The Hierarchy of Heaven and Earth: A New Diagram of Man in the Universe*, with a Preface by C. S. Lewis (New York: Harper, 1952).

43. Simeon Edmunds, *Spiritualism: A Critical Survey* (London: Aquarian Press, 1966), especially chap. 9 ("Fraud"), pp. 102-24; D. H. Rawcliffe, *The Psychology of the Occult* (London: Derricke Ridgway, 1952), pp. 163-96, 309-32. (Rawcliffe's work, though containing valuable material, is seriously marred by his reductionist behaviorism.)

44. From Richard Bovet's *Pandaemonum* (1684), 8th relation; quoted in John Ferriar, *An Essay towards a Theory of Apparitions* (London: Cadell & Davies, 1813), pp. 87-93. Remarkably, Ferriar attempts to explain this case, and all others he cites, on the basis of such psychological factors as "recollected impressions"!

45. Raymond Bayless, *Animal Ghosts* (Secaucas, N. Jersey: University Books, 1970), pp. 102-103. (Quoted by permission.) The original report was published in the *Journal of the American Society for Psychical Research*, October, 1952.

46. Tyrrell, *op. cit.*, (in note 13 above), II, 146.

47. Frank Podmore, *Telepathic Hallucinations: The New View of Ghosts* (New York: Frederick A. Stokes, n.d.), p. 124.

48. Alastair W. MacLellan, *Extra-sensory Perception, Witchcraft, Spiritualism and Insanity* (Ashingdon, Essex, Eng.: C. W. Daniel, 1958), pp. 5, 33.

49. Cf. G. R. S. Mead, *The Doctrine of the Subtle Body in Western Tradition* (London: J. M. Watkins, 1919); and Ralph Shirley, *The Mystery of the Human Double* (new ed.; New Hyde Park, N.Y.: University Books, 1965). Mead's excursions into theology are unhelpful, owing to his powerful Gnostic bias.

50. The two classic works on the subject are: Oscar Bagnall, *The Origin and Properties of the Human Aura* (rev. ed.; New Hyde Park, N.Y.: University Books, 1970); and Walter J. Kilner, *The Human Aura* (new ed.; New Hyde Park, N.Y.: University Books, 1965). Bagnall has used two sensitizing dyes: *dicyanin* and *pinacyanol*.

51. The concept of the "subtle body" does, however suggest interesting theological possibilities in conjunction with Paul's discussion of the various kinds of "celestial and terrestrial bodies" in I Cor. 15:35 ff. In verse 44, the *sōma psychikon* is contrasted with the *sōma pneumatikon*. Jesus' resurrection body, though definitely physical, had special, celestial characteristics. All of this suggests that the real presence of Christ's Body in the Eucharist (I Cor. 11:27-30) is by no means a wooden or irrational notion.

52. Johann Heinrich Jung-Stilling, *Theory of Pneumatology*, trans. and ed. Samuel Jackson (London: Longman, 1834), p. 381.

53. Whether Samuel really came back, or whether a Satanic personi-

fication of Samuel appeared when Saul consulted the witch of Endor depends on whether Samuel's message on that occasion is regarded as God's judgment on Saul or an instance of platitudinous false prophecy. I take the former view, and am not troubled by the witch's success at necromancy. Most sorcerers get more than they bargain for.

54. E.g., F. W. H. Myers, *Human Personality and Its Survival of Bodily Death*, ed. Susy Smith (rev. ed.; New Hyde Park, N.Y.: University Books, 1961); A. T. Baird (ed.), *One Hundred Cases for Survival after Death* (New York: Bernard Ackerman, 1944).

55. Gardner Murphy, *Challenge of Psychical Research* (New York: Harper, 1961), pp. 251, 273.

56. C. D. Broad, *Lectures on Psychical Research* ("International Library of Philosophy and Scientific Method"; London: Routledge & Kegan Paul, 1962), p. 430.

57 J. Arthur Hill, *Spiritualism: Its History, Phenomena and Doctrine*, with an Introduction by Sir Arthur Conan Doyle (London: Cassell, 1918), Pt. 2, chap. 1 ("Spiritualism As a Religion"), pp. 143 ff.

58. William Seabrook, *Witchcraft: Its Power in the World Today* (New York: Harcourt Lancer Books, 1940), pp. 332-41 ("Bishop Arthur A. Ford of the Spiritualist Church"). In reporting on the televised Pike-Ford séance, *Time* magazine stated that Ford was now a minister in the (liberal branch of the) Disciples of Christ (*Time*, October 6, 1967, p. 55).

59. James A. Pike (with Diane Kennedy), *The Other Side: An Account of My Experiences with Psychic Phenomena* (Garden City, N. Y.: Doubleday, 1968), pp. 246-47. A spirit message on the same occasion from Pike's predecessor as Episcopal Bishop of California, the Rt. Rev. Karl Block, declared: " 'You did a magnificent job, and you have magnificent work yet to do.' He says, 'I think that in the future, maybe the distant future, that book you have in your hands, your book, will be almost as important as the theses that Luther nailed onto the church door' " (p. 257). Apparently "Block" had not been filled in on Pike's sudden death-to-come only two years later; but, then again, neither were the mediums (including Ford) accurate who kept up Diane Kennedy Pike's hopes when the Bishop disappeared in the Judean desert: Ford "called Diane Pike in Jerusalem to tell her he had a vision of her husband, 'alive but sick,' in a cave not far from where she had left him. . . . She was encouraged by messages from other mediums, who reported visions of Pike still alive in a cave. The visions proved to be false. Sunday morning, on a rock two miles from where Diane had last seen her husband seven days earlier, an Israeli border policeman found the body of James Pike" (*Time*, September 12, 1969, p.47). For Ford's own account of his mediumistic activities, including the Pike séance, see his book, *Unknown but Known: My Adventure into the Meditative Dimension* (New York: Signet Mystic Books, 1968), especially pp. 14, 66-69.

60. The university lecture I delivered on that occasion appears as the title essay of my book, *The Suicide of Christian Theology* (Minnea-

polis: Bethany Fellowship, 1970). In it I criticize the Bishop's theology a detached critique of his views will be found in the same volume on pp. 47-61.

61. *Look* magazine, February 22, 1966.

62. Richard Woods, O.P., *The Occult Revolution: A Christian Meditation* (New York: Herder & Herder, 1971), p. 215.

63. Donald Hole, *Spiritualism in Relation to Science and Religion* (London: The Society of SS. Peter and Paul, n.d.), p. 95.

64. The great source collection is Henry Charles Lea's *Materials toward a History of Witchcraft*, ed. A. C. Howland (3 vols.; new ed.; New York: Yoseloff, 1957), based on the Cornell University witchcraft collection. See also the literature cited in Rossell Hope Robbins, *The Encyclopedia of Witchcraft and Demonology* (New York: Crown Publishers, 1959), and our citation of classic demonological works in Chapter One (where Kaigh's lycanthropy case is discussed). Representative modern interpretations of the witchcraft phenomenon include: Margaret Alice Murray, *The Witch-Cult in Western Europe* (reprint ed.; Oxford: Clarendon Press, 1962)—rationalistic; Julio Caro Baroja, *The World of the Witches*, trans. O. N. V. Glendinning (Chicago: University of Chicago Press, 1964)—rationalistic; Montague Summers, *The History of Witchcraft and Demonology* (reprint ed.; New Hyde Park, New York: University Books, 1956), *The Geography of Witchcraft* (reprint ed.; Evanston and New York: University Books, 1958), and *The Vampire: His Kith and Kin* (New Hyde Park, New York: University Books, 1960)—supernaturalistic; Charles Williams, *Witchcraft* (reprint ed.; New York: Meridian Books, 1959)—supernaturalistic. On the witch trials of New England, see especially Cotton Mather, *On Witchcraft: Being the Wonders of the Invisible World* (reprint ed.; Mount Vernon, New York: The Peter Pauper Press, n.d.); and George Lyman Kittredge, *Witchcraft in Old and New England* (revised ed.; New York: Russell and Russell, 1956). Our Appendix B provides the first English translation of an important Reformation account of demon possession.

65. C. S. Lewis, *The Screwtape Letters & Screwtape Proposes a Toast* (new ed.; London: Bles, 1961), p. 19.

66. John Symonds, *The Great Beast: The Life of Aleister Crowley* (New York: Roy Publishers, 1952), pp. 206-207.

67. *Ibid.*, p. 210. On Crowley, see also Francis King, *The Rites of Modern Occult Magic* (New York: Macmillan, 1971), *passim.*

68. Ed Sanders, *The Family* (New York: Avon, 1972).

69. Franklyn, *op. cit.* (in note 35 above), p. 283.

70. See Joseph Fletcher and John Warwick Montgomery, *Debate on Situation Ethics* (Minneapolis: Bethany Fellowship, 1972).

71. "The Monkey's Paw" is included in Dorothy Sayers' *Great Short Stories of Detection, Mystery and Horror*, II (London: Gollancz, 1959), 206-216. For documented cases illustrating the fact that "when Demons first approach their Followers, they bring them Money; but afterwards, when the Glamour has vanished, it is found to be nothing but Dung, Bricks, Leaves or some such Matter," see Nicolas Rémy, *Demonolatry,*

trans. E. A. Ashwin, ed. Montague Summers ("Church & Witchcraft Series," 4; London: John Rodker, 1930), Bk. 1, chap. 4 (pp. 7-8). Cf. Francesco-Maria Guazzo's discussion as to "whether the Devil can Truly Enrich his Subjects," in Guazzo's *Compendium maleficarum (1608)*, trans. E. A. Ashwin, ed. Montague Summers ("Church & Witchcraft Series, 3; London: John Rodker, 1929), Bk. 1, chap. 9 (pp. 25-28).

72. L. Szondi, *Schicksalsanalyse* (2d ed.; Basel, 1948), pp. 305-309.

73. Kurt E. Koch, *Christian Counseling and Occultism*, trans. Andrew Petter (Grand Rapids, Mich.: Kregel, 1965). Cf. also the essay "Schizophrenia and Spiritualism" in Edmunds, *op. cit.* (in note 43 above), pp. 187-94.

NOTES TO EPILOGUE

1. Alfred Métraux, *Voodoo in Haiti*, trans. Hugo Charteris (New York: Oxford University Press, 1959), p. 357.

2. This C. S. Lewis letter is copyrighted by the C. S. Lewis Estate.

3. Arthur Machen, "With the Gods in Spring," bound with his *Strange Roads* (limited ed.; London: Classic Press, 1923), pp. 39-41.

Indices

INDEX OF OCCULT SUBJECTS

INDEX OF SCRIPTURE REFERENCES

INDEX OF NAMES